# Canadian Metropolitics

## Governing Our Cities

# *Canadian Metropolitics*

---

## *Governing Our Cities*

Edited by

James Lightbody

University of Alberta

Copp Clark Ltd.

Toronto

ISBN: 0-7730-5425-1

Executive editor: Jeff Miller
Editor: Curtis Fahey
Cover photo: Steven Evans Photography Inc.
Typesetting: Carol Magee
Printing and binding: Metrolitho

**Canadian Cataloguing in Publication Data**

Main entry under title:
Canadian metropolitics: governing our cities
Includes bibliographical references and index.
ISBN 0-7730-5425-1
1. Municipal government - Canada. I. Lightbody, James, 1945–
JS 1708.C35 1995 320.8'5'0971 C94-932824-3

Copp Clark Ltd.
2775 Matheson Blvd. East
Mississauga, Ontario
L4W 4P7

Printed and bound in Canada

1 2 3 4 5 5425-1 99 98 97 96 95

# Contents

CONTENTS

# *Preface*

I LIKE THE POLITICS of the city. It was through urbanization that ancient peoples built the major civilizations of the modern world. Even today, any great society is best defined by the wealth of the human spirit captured within its largest communities. And, if indeed "all politics is local" as the legendary American congressman Tip O'Neill often declared, then the heart of our democratic process lies on the doorsteps of city hall. This, at least, is what I choose to believe. City politics are too important to be rooted in the indifference of the majority.

*Canadian Metropolitics* is an anthology written for mid-career undergraduates in the social sciences by the instructors who teach them. It explains who and what is important in current Canadian city politics, and why, how, and when. After exploring the basic historical, legal, and political-economy contexts of modern Canadian city government, which is often where other very good textbook treatments end, this book uses several issues as points of departure to demonstrate the special relevance of city politics to students who are also educated and interested democratic citizens. The final chapter pulls together the several separate discussions into something of a survivor's guide.

*Canadian Metropolitics* is interdisciplinary in approach. Its common theme is the contemporary Canadian city; its unifying approach is the public-policy perspective. Specific topics such as city planning, public education, intergovernmental relations, the environment, and the particular significance of gender in municipal politics illustrate divergent facets of the modern Canadian city. While the book acknowledges the importance and relevance of competing theoretical approaches, its emphasis is at heart practical in accumulating knowledge and applying it. Each chapter contains selected data and numerous practical examples which will be familiar to students.

This book is not blinkered by a strictly central Canadian focus. As well, from the point of view of instructors, the book's value lies partly in the fact that its contents closely parallel actual course outlines. *Canadian Metropolitics* is designed to be a core text, not a supplementary anthology (though it may also be used as such). Each author was asked to write specifically for this book, and each chapter presents a discrete topic, approach, or issue. For students, the book affords the opportunity to provide local examples from their personal experiences to illustrate or supplement the main themes being advanced. The book's comprehensive index helps to integrate the discussion of concepts, political actors, and institutions.

I believe that the strengths of *Canadian Metropolitics* are many. For but a few examples, try these. In her chapter, Linda Trimble evaluates how and, more important, why women have forged such successful careers at the city hall level. She expands upon contemporary feminist theory and presents impressive new data to support her argument that traditional role perceptions help only a little in our appreciation of what genuinely is at stake. Peter Smith's critical examination of past Canadian city planning in the metropolis leads him to present a very strong case for an activist, interventionist, planning profession as an antidote to what he implicitly sees as ineffective political leadership. Mary Louise McAllister uses current issues in environmental management to explain what is on the table for each of us as citizen stakeholders in so-called environmental politics. And Tim Thomas explores the institutional and practical political barriers that account for the failure of genuine citizen leadership at city hall, providing examples drawn from cities across Canada's regions and cultures. Other chapters are equally provocative. In short, all these authors are very good at what they do. I thank them, and the many others in the small community that studies Canadian city governance, for their support of this project.

Federal-provincial politics have always struck me as an interminable game of chess with set strategic moves and pieces whose powers are very well known. Let's be honest: constitutional debates are rather boring. In stark contrast to this kind of politics is the never-ending story that unfolds through city hall. The city is potentially the most directly democratic of any of our governing institutions. Still, no city council is without its unbelievable character, no city policy is complete without a wrangle, and no regulation is without its unintended consequence. City politics are like a game of poker, with its bluffs, ruses, and powers of deceit. In this game the poker face counts for much, each player is independent, and there is always room for another chair at the table! City politics are alive; they are still the stuff of coffee-shop talk. It is my hope that students will find as much joy in surviving big city politics as my generation has. I also hope that this book is helpful in that pursuit.

Responsibility for *Canadian Metropolitics* lies principally with my editor at Copp Clark Longman, Jeff Miller, who knows his business, and baseball, very well indeed. His curiosity, energy, and support sustained this project whenever the deepest darkness of Edmonton's winter closed in (as during August 1992). I am also appreciative of the fine work, keen eye, and factual zealotry of our structural and copy editor, Curtis Fahey.

My own students have always asked serious and important questions while my city's councillors and senior administrators have generously provided a constant parade of unintended humour with which to illustrate lectures and essays. Only a city such as 1990s Edmonton, for instance, would drop the motto of "City of Champions" for "Turning up the Heat"—from glory to gas in the shift of a single slogan!

My daughters, Tanya and Teresa, have lived patiently within my real world of politics and have always helped to keep this world, and the many ministers, mayors, and bureaucrats who comprise it, in proper perspective. Finally, special thanks to a special friend, Lisa.

# 1

## *Why Study City Politics?*

James Lightbody

THE POLITICS OF CANADIAN CITIES are important. The purpose of this introductory chapter is to set the stage for understanding the context in which those politics take place and what, in the shape of decisions, develops as a result of those politics. Public policy is the primary dependent variable—that is, the consequence of the political process—which political scientists try to explain. The other writers in this book come to their particular subjects from differing academic perspectives. But, ultimately, we are all concerned with who gets what, when, where, and why.

Not all citizens demand only, or even primarily for that matter, policy options to which a price tag can be easily attached; government is more than a Shoppers' Drug Mart, after all. As will become clear in this text, we may expect such non-monetary decisions to be important, especially at city hall where priority choices about matters such as parking, protection, and privacy are scrolled on the daily policy menu. Indeed, it is in regulating the intensity of closely interdependent city living that modern Canadians and their governments most directly establish the boundaries of, and set the terms for, their daily existence. This is not at all to say that cities do not take important actions affecting people's pocketbooks; frequently, the first and best measure of what a city government is really up to is its budget documents. The point is that Canada is a nation of cities, and the choices made by city councillors directly define our lifestyle.

Although Canadians often like to think of themselves in sylvan terms, there is no denying that Canada is an urban community. The federal government's statistical definition of urbanism is a population centre of 1000 or more people in an area with a population density of 400 per square kilometre. In the 1991 census, 76.6 per cent of Canadians were counted as urban. For statistical purposes, a census metropolitan area is defined as "a main labour market of a continuous built-up area having a population of 100 000 or more" and, by 1991, 61 per cent of the national population lived in such areas. All twenty-five Canadian CMAs increased their population from 1986 to 1992 and substantially over half of us live in the Quebec City through Windsor urban corridor.

*Table I:*
*Population of Canadian cities and census metropolitan areas, 1991*

| *Cities* | | | *Census Metropolitan Areas* | | |
|---|---|---|---|---|---|
| 1. Montreal | 1 017 666 | (1)* | 1. Toronto | 3 893 046 | (1)* |
| 2. Calgary | 710 677 | (3) | 2. Montreal | 3 127 242 | (2) |
| 3. Toronto | 635 395 | (2) | 3. Vancouver | 1 602 502 | (3) |
| 4. Winnipeg | 616 790 | (4) | 4. Ottawa-Hull | 920 857 | (4) |
| 5. Edmonton | 616 741 | (6) | 5. Edmonton | 839 924 | (5) |
| 6. North York | 562 564 | (5) | 6. Calgary | 754 033 | (6) |
| 7. Scarborough | 524 598 | (7) | 7. Winnipeg | 652 354 | (7) |
| 8. Vancouver | 471 844 | (8) | 8. Quebec City | 645 550 | (8) |
| 9. Mississauga | 463 388 | (9) | 9. Hamilton | 599 760 | (9) |
| 10. Hamilton | 318 499 | (10) | 10. London | 381 522 | (12) |
| 11. Laval | 314 398 | (13) | 11. St Cath Niag. | 364 552 | (10) |
| 12. Ottawa | 313 987 | (12) | 12. Kitchener-Wat. | 356 421 | (11) |
| 13. Etobicoke | 309 993 | (11) | 13. Halifax | 320 501 | (13) |

* Indicates 1981 Rank
Source: Statistics Canada, *Census Metropolitan Areas and Census Agglomerations,* Catalogue 92-303 (Ottawa: Statistics Canada, 1992).

What constitutes a "city" is quite another matter. Demographers, and other social scientists, have many fascinating differences among themselves as to the definition of a distinct city (especially within intensively built urban corridors), often using commuter-sheds to the main place of work as a key variable. Fine, but most citizens hold to their own personal sense of identity and location, depending on the situation. For example, there may be important psychological villages without government form even within the boundaries of our largest cities, places such as the Beaches in Toronto, Gastown in Vancouver, and Old Strathcona in Edmonton. At the same time, however, few persons vacationing at Disney World, for instance, would go to the bother of volunteering that they are from "Etobicoke" rather than simply saying "Toronto."

Yet, once a year, when property taxes are due, people come to the poignant recollection that they reside in Dartmouth, say, and not Halifax. Cities in Canada are institutions, legally incorporated under provincial statutes, and their boundaries are seldom the same as their metropolitan environments. For particular reasons, Calgary and Winnipeg are the main exemptions to this rule. Most metropolitan areas in Canada are governed by a number of local municipalities. For example, the largest city within the Victoria metropolitan area is Saanich. There are over 5000 incorporated units of local government among the provinces; Canada has about 120 cities as such. And the defining characteristic of Canadian metropolitics is that, even where an area-wide second tier of government exists, the local town or city commands a powerful allegiance based on the political orientations of citizens.

The practical consequence of this is that any attempt to reduce the large number of local level municipalities through some form of consolidation is virtually predestined to fail. The strength of this community attachment to local cities, often underestimated by metropolitan reform advocates, is hard to understate: in 1980, to take one example, the school children of St Albert (a small suburb of Edmonton then under threat of amalgamation) were all urged to send Valentine's cards to Premier Peter Lougheed deploring the initiative, with the wording, "We love our city, let us keep it." Prior to this, in a publicity-stunt variation on a mediaeval ceremony, their parents had physically beaten the length of the community's borders with birch fronds to ward off evil spirits (presumably residing in the core city to which most of them commuted to work). For whatever reasons, St Albert exists today as an autonomous municipality.

One theme that has lingered over practical discussions of Canadian city politics is the persistent sense of nostalgia for our roots in some fictitious, but glorious, rural past. This belief partly derives from a strong cultural heritage in which the city itself was thought to be evil; a decision to move into such a place was somehow inherently immoral and a desertion of civilized values. Why else indeed would otherwise sensible citizens cast rodents as city mascots? Even today, as a nation, a large chunk of our shared cultural mythology is defined by the romance of the farm, the frontier, and the wilderness. How little of our currency, for instance, bears other than rustic symbols! To move from the sublime to the ridiculous, what images do big city telephone books present of their communities? In 1986 Quebec City's book portrayed a shed in a maple sugar bush, while Montreal's showed pink foxtails in the Laurentian mountains; Calgary produced a montage of elk, a kodiak bear, a person in a kayak; Victoria unveiled a farmer's field at the steps of a mountain, and, as John Sewell has noted, Halifax's book had a drawing on the front cover of lush foliage viewed from a cabin window while the back cover boasted "a stretched out dead chipmunk and other collector's specimens."[1] Only Edmonton and Vancouver, among the major cities, had urban vistas.

The more serious side of this honest misrepresentation is reflected in patterns of political representation. All of Canada's provincial legislatures through the present have endured a rural imbalance in representation greater than that permitted federally. For instance, in Alberta, for the provincial election in 1993, fifteen of the province's eighty-three ridings were 25 per cent larger (urban) or smaller (rural) than the size of the average provincial constituency. Edmonton's constituencies were 11.3 per cent, and Calgary's 15.4, larger in population than the provincial average. At the extreme, Calgary-Egmont's 27 858 voters had the same legislative power as Cardston's 8675. What this means in practical terms is that the urban Calgary elector had about one-third the value to a government seeking re-election as a rural Cardstonite. The recent stance of the Supreme Court of Canada has not given much support to appeals under the Charter of Rights and Freedoms for representational parity between urban and rural voters.[2]

This legislative imbalance has clear consequences for the types of policy questions raised in cabinet, caucus, and commons. In Alberta, no municipal affairs minister represented an urban riding for the entire span of Social Credit (1935–71), and no such Manitoba minister represented a Winnipeg area riding until 1969 despite the fact that by shortly after the Second World War more than half of the province's population lived there and nineteen of the twenty-four major municipal governments in the province lay within the metropolitan zone. Departments of municipal affairs, symbolically and practically, became service agencies for rural and small town Canada.

So cities have had to fend for themselves, and often they have done this quite well as the skill of the respective political leadership has permitted. In the province of Quebec, the mayor of Montreal ran rough-shod over the provincial department of municipal affairs to impose his form of metropolitan government on Montreal island in the aftermath of the 1969 police strike. For a further example, to obtain a better share of revenues locally generated, the city-owned telephone system in Edmonton reprogrammed its computers on Valentine's Day, 1984, to prevent the provincial telephone company from recording the origins of long distance calls.

More fundamentally, in law and in character, our general local government framework still displays its nineteenth-century origins. As we will observe throughout this text, despite numerous reform initiatives the heart and soul of Canadian city form and structure, its ideas and applications, has remained Ontario's Municipal Corporations (Baldwin) Act of 1849. This fact has placed serious restrictions upon what even the most intelligent and progressive city councillor may accomplish when in office. Seven generations later, the style of governance promoted by the Baldwin Act—a style that took root and flourished at a time when government as a whole was intended to accomplish very little and popular democracy as we understand the concept today was still widely mistrusted—continues to cramp severely the interventionist ambitions of city governments.

## *City Politics Matter*

Canadian cities make important policy choices that have a direct impact upon our personal lives. In its varied forms, the policy that emanates from city hall codifies important social values, regulates personal privacy, and generates and restricts economic activity over and above the protective, social, and recreational services we most directly notice. Cities such as Edmonton, Calgary, and North York are each four times the size of the province of Prince Edward Island. As corporations, they are themselves very big businesses. Measured by its purchases of goods and services from small business, for instance, Edmonton is annually among the twenty largest Canadian corporations. Metropolitan Toronto and Montreal would be, by population alone, the third and fourth largest Canadian provinces. Cities own telephone companies, railway lines, airports, parking garages, and billion-dollar utilities such as Edmonton Power and its Genessee power plant. Cities also license businesses, bicycles, massage parlours, taxis, and dogs.

Taken together, Canadian municipalities are major actors in the national economy. If we were to look at total government expenditures as a percentage of gross domestic product (GDP) in 1989, the federal government accounted for 18.62, the ten provinces for 14.68, and the combined local authorities for 8.02 per cent. Further, the data in Table 2 demonstrates rather vividly the scale of combined municipal operations in the area of government employment. It is twice that of the national government and equivalent to that of the provinces. Of course, significant questions of accountability arise when the self-professed amateur politicians in cities raise and spend such large sums in a non-partisan system with neither governmental nor any comprehensive extra-governmental opposition.

All that said, the fiscal position of local governments in the intergovernmental arrangement, as shown in Table 3, is difficult at best, and it must be remembered as well that most local authorities, by law, are not allowed to enter into debt on current (or operating) budgets. When one looks at the pattern of revenues and expenditures overall, we see that for the calendar year 1990 Canadian municipalities stood deeply in debt. But this is *before* transfer payments from other levels of government. The subordinate financial position of even our greatest cities stems from unchanged and by now outdated revenue sources: local government direct revenues, as a percentage of GDP (4.28 per cent), are almost exactly as they were in 1926. Even the most casual observer of the system would recognize that demands for city expenditures have changed significantly in number and nature from that earlier time. The disparity between the cities' limited funding

*Table 2:*
*Public-sector employment,* 1992

| | *Employees (hundred thousands)* | *% change from 1991* | *% of total paid workers* |
|---|---|---|---|
| *Public sector* | 2685 | 0.0% | 23.0% |
| Federal | 562 | -1.5 | 3.8 |
| Provincial/terr. | 1111 | -0.5 | 10.0 |
| Local | 1012 | +1.4 | 9.2 |
| *Government (excludes business enterprises)* | 2335 | +0.3 | 19.9 |
| Federal | 413 | –1.3 | 2.5 |
| Provincial/terr. | 964 | –0.2 | 8.7 |
| Local | 959 | +1.5 | 8.7 |

Source: Statistics Canada data as reported in the *Globe and Mail,* 2 November 1993.

sources and their ever-growing responsibilities accounts for much of the rancour underpinning intergovernmental relations in Canada. Nor is this all. If, as is currently suggested, the 1990s will be the decade of the deficit for all levels of authority, then the broader levels of government can be expected to try to restrict their expenditures. In the past it has often been possible, after the usual alternatives of privatizing, user-pay, and slashbacks have been explored, to "off-load" programs onto Canada's cities. Whether the resource of the property tax base has become exhausted for this purpose will increasingly become the object of intense debate.

Still, there is a perception that cities do not deal with the grand issues of "high politics" and so their politics usually possess a low level of salience for most citizens. Issues of war and peace, economic and fiscal policy, employment and health standards, and the never-ending constitutional debates (which hold direct relevance for very few Canadians) are debated and occasionally resolved at the national level. Provincial governments in the 1990s play major roles in devising standards for the implementation of important federal programs

*Table 3:*
*Expenditures/Revenues in the national system before transfers (in $ millions), calendar year 1990*

| | *Federal* | *Provincial* | *Local* |
|---|---|---|---|
| Revenues | $126 313 | 114 541 | 28 762 |
| Expenditures | 125 081 | 98 575 | 53 886 |
| Surplus/Deficit | +1 232 | +15 966 | −25 124 |

Source: Statistics Canada data as presented by the Canadian Tax Foundation, *Provincial and Municipal Finances, 1991* (Toronto: 1992), 3:2.

(social assistance, medicare, hospitalization, post-secondary education) and directly involve themselves in the exploitation of natural resources, the development of transportation arteries, and the provision of schooling.

Set against these concerns, how can the local issues of planning, potholes, and police protection compete? None of this is often the arena of media hype; few civic policies hold the attention of the community cosmopolitans for long, and those which do suggest that the agendas of city elites, and their very focussed lobbies, are not the same as those of local electors. To put this another way, whereas the urban political leadership cadre seems to be drawn from those who are concerned with such concepts as "progress" and "modern government," neighbourhood electors tend to be concrete, parochial, and short-term in their demands of councils. For the former, environmental issues are "writ large" (ozone depletion, global warming); for most of the rest of us, what our neighbours do to, and in, their backyards holds more immediate, sustained environmental consequence.

If cities are theoretically at the heart of generating wealth in our civilization because of their accumulation of a critical mass of abilities, they have turned this phenomenon into a somewhat tawdry affair in the twentieth century. The infatuation with unrestrained growth, often expressed in brazenly sophomoric terms, has become synonymous with the Canadian metropolis. It is a coveted form of recognition for Canadian cities to be singled out in a survey by a major national publication as one of "Canada's best cities for business." Winnipeg, Moncton, Vancouver, Edmonton, and Montreal were so chosen in 1993 by the *Globe's Report on Business* as the finest coddlers of business in the country! A U.S. businessman is cited: "We looked at Provo, Utah, and Omaha, Nebraska—but those cities' 'special treatment' and TLC are perfunctory and institutionalized at this point. We were looking for a city that would develop an infrastructure for us as a partner. And in Winnipeg, Manitoba, you're admitted like an adopted son."[3]

Now, for most people, to be chosen ahead of some small town in Utah or Nebraska, even for the better surfing, would be no big deal. But Canadian cities have given away the keys consistently. In this, Winnipeg has had a solidly typical track record; to attract the CPR main line in the 1870s, that city's council not only provided land grants, a $200 000 bonus, and a $300 000 bridge over the Red River but also exempted railway lands "from city taxation forever." These days it seems more fashionable for city promoters to lobby for major league sports franchises but business boons still abound. Even social-democratic municipal partisans have been swept up in unabashed hucksterism as their labour supporters (especially among the building trades) have clamoured for the jobs that come with large-scale developments. This is one reason for the persistently observed shift to the right by leftist city councillors over their time in office.

Boosterism has had direct consequences for the general direction of city politics, in both senses of that word; that is, who should be in charge and what they should be charging towards. In his insightful analysis of Winnipeg's formative period, Alan Artibise wrote of the city's business elite and its role in civic government: "There was never any doubt as to who would control the government . . . a centralized form of government assured Winnipeg's businessmen that their conception of desirable public policy would prevail."[4] The same comment could apply to virtually any other Canadian city. The business concept of public policy meant, very simply, that the expansion of economic enterprise should be the primary focus for local government: all of its energies and concerns ought to be directed towards sustained commercial growth even if such an approach were to mean the neglect of all other objectives. This has been the single most dominant theme in twentieth-century Canadian urban development.

JAMES LIGHTBODY

# *The Apolitical World of City Politics*

One of the most strongly held myths about Canadian metropolitics is that city elections are non-partisan. Few communities have actually gone so far as Vancouver, where the dominant electoral coalition since the depression of the 1930s has actually been called the Civic Non-Partisan Association. But little seems as frowned upon, outside unbridled evidence of graft, as the mere thought that some party-like entity is organizing to take control of the municipal agenda. And, where the local branches of national parties have actually tried to enter the municipal fray (as with the Liberals in Toronto in 1969, and the NDP in Winnipeg in 1971), traditional organizational support was lacking and the voters were markedly unamused.

While there may be many reasons for this outlook, the fundamental salience of Canadian civic non-partisanship can be directly traced back a century to the municipal reform movement in the United States. This movement arose in reaction to the spoils system, which in turn was a product of the boss rule and machine politics of major American cities. The reformers devised a package of institutions intended to de-politicize city government and to model it instead upon the apolitical form of the business corporation. Central to their approach was an abhorrence of party organization, which was seen to lead inexorably to patronage, graft, and all the other splendid kinds of ward-heeling. Canadian municipal reformers took to these bright ideas as readily then as our winter snowbirds now enjoy the seasonal culture of Palm Springs and Miami.

There are probably very few town halls across Canada where the insiders cannot identify accurately the federal or provincial party associations of most sitting councillors. Political attachments are a part of an active social life. Those who may be active at one level of politics are those most likely to be interested in any electoral race, at any level of politics. Although the small scale of the operations in most Canadian cities renders these partisan affiliations of little practical importance in policy making, party-like activity has been a constant in our municipal life. The great success stories, as judged by electoral victories and longevity, have been cadre organizations (small in number, focussed on elections, comprised of local notables with access to wealth) such as the Civic Non-Partisan Association (NPA) in Vancouver, the Independent Citizens' Election Committee (ICEC) in Winnipeg, and, possibly, Jean Drapeau's Civic Party in Montreal. Usually formed to confront a rising challenge from labour, these shadowy coalitions of local Liberals and Conservatives produced little ideological coherence in the form of platform policy except a solid dose of boosterism, civic-government efficiency, and "common sense" (that being theirs, as it turned out). A unifying theme was always that the partisanship evident at senior levels was somehow irrelevant to the municipal scene.

It now seems somewhat ironic, then, that the more obvious the past federal and provincial partisan ties (and experience) of major candidates in Canadian metropolitics, the more their municipal campaigns have emphasized leadership style and personality at the expense of substantial ideological divergence over more serious policy matters. In fact, it may not be going too far to say that past partisanship has now become a most positive advantage in cities, an almost critical element in the success of "non-partisan" mayoralty campaigns in the Canadian metropolis. Party ties mean strategists and workers, donors of funds, name recognition, and, often, credibility with the local press galley. In this way, a past party life is a valuable political resource not available to the innocent newcomer. Even though partisan ties at the federal or provincial level are hardly ever advertized, the gladiators lurk behind the scenes of all municipal election contests, their political affiliations submerged under a flood of rhetoric about "business-like" government and the pursuit of some amorphous common good.

Because of the often issue-specific and hands-on nature of many local government decisions, the question of political ideology is seldom baldly debated at city hall. The corollary is that the ideological underpinnings of most decisions are not immediately recognized. Ideologies have been often muted at the municipal level, especially as policy coalitions emerge, dissolve, and reform, both inside council and out, according to the particular decision at hand. Canadian cities present the true politics of immediacy. For instance, the urban reformers of the 1970s were widely perceived as radicals because of the comprehensiveness of their challenge to local authority; however, the reality may have been that they were genuine conservatives committed to preserving an existing neighbourhood against freeway or developer intrusion.

Finally, it has become somewhat of a standing cliché in Canadian local government texts that it is the provinces which directly dictate what cities may do, may not do, and must do anyway. Specifically, permissive and mandatory powers are outlined for them by provincial government statute. The former is normally established by a general municipal government act, while the mandatory functions are set by specific legislation such as the Public Health Act. Importantly, no city can do anything not expressly permitted by some provincial statute or regulation.

Having said this, within the framework set by the respective province, types of city policy decisions will vary. Policies that require taxation and expenditure may be said to be either allocative or redistributive in nature. Allocative policies produce public goods such as fire protection which apply equally to all citizens. Redistributive schemes such as social services attempt to apply or redirect accumulated wealth selectively to those in need. The policy choices of council ultimately take the form of by-laws either requiring certain actions or prohibiting them (zoning by-laws or parking restrictions, for instance). A city council may also delegate its authority to make decisions in a particular policy arena either to its permanent bureaucracy or to a specialized agency such as a development appeal board, transit authority, or police commission. Other decisions might be purely symbolic, as when folkloric heros or civic pioneers are honoured by the naming of streets, parks, or bridges. Seldom are living politicians so recognized.

Curiously, policy might also be considered to have been made when city councillors choose not to decide. In such an instance they may not be certain as to whether or not there is sufficient support behind a demand for change, or they may not have a clear understanding of the interests of specifically affected groups. So the decision is made not to decide (usually pending further study) and the matter may be referred "back to committee." To the casual eye it may even seem as though councillors are sitting about like Greyfriars' Bobby, waiting for something to pop up. But the important point is that a decision has been made not to decide and this choice usually reinforces the status quo. This would certainly characterize the approach taken by most traditional town councils.

But the newer style of urban councillor is more interventionist, asserting an action agenda which, as it comes into conflict with provincially imposed limitations (statutory and fiscal), establishes the flashpoints for intergovernmental conflict regardless of partisan loyalties. Ontario's NDP government of the 1990s, for example, has not held an easy working relationship with the many city councillors associated with that party, just as jurisdictionally inspired conflict ruffled federal-provincial feathers during the few months in 1979 when Conservative Prime Minister Joe Clark dealt with Alberta's Conservative Premier Lougheed. The lesson here is that cities have become more important, more independent, governmental actors. They have become more partisan as they have become more interventionist. While partisan ties may ease some intergovernmental relations (and cause friction in others), they do not cause basic jurisdictional differences to disappear.

No matter how partisan it has become, the governmentally splintered metropolis produces multiple public goods from a number of jurisdictions. At the heart of the public-choice school of political science is the thought that the sum total of these goods would be smaller if each metropolitan area was subject to unitary government. That is, each of many municipalities might find it desirable to maintain a community swimming complex, resulting in a dozen or more for a metropolitan centre, whereas if the region were governmentally unified it could get by with far fewer. Given the numerous problems that otherwise beset the governmentally polycentric metropolitan region, it is certainly a judgment call, ultimately from the user's perspective, as to which form makes the more effective use of public funds.

## *The Intergovernmental Maze*

Canadian municipalities have passed through three very distinctive reform periods. Each of these periods has culminated in some form of statutory statement, and each has made its own mark upon the politics and policies of Canadian cities . All have had a negative impact upon the ability of municipalities to participate effectively, as governments, in major intergovernmental policy arenas.

Canada's earliest municipal reform initiatives took place during the first part of the nineteenth century, roughly from 1820 to 1849, and were a significant part and parcel of the much larger struggle for responsible government in the colonies. This period culminated in the Municipal Corporations Act of 1849, which provided municipal institutions for what is now the province of Ontario. While these reforms systematized a structure of representative, responsible local government that would be recognizable to us today, they also enshrined the enduring subordinate status of local government units. In an age when the whims of popular democracy were much distrusted (hence, the legacy of the federal Senate), the province was given the responsibility of protecting the credit of the municipalities and the civil and property rights of citizens. These powers have never been surrendered.

A second era of reform emerged towards the end of the nineteenth century, spilling into the twentieth. The changes of this period were introduced by business leaders anxious to protect their control of the municipal enterprise and to maintain the city's role as a willing consort in the expansion of the private sector. Business became especially aware of the reform program's benefits to the city in the wake of the Winnipeg General Strike of 1919. Faced with the threat of growing political awareness among labour, businessmen devised various innovations in the political system. At-large elections, for instance, maximized considerably the impact of their natural political resources of wealth and social prestige. Some form of centralized political executive (such as a board of control) was another idea of business interests that received a sympathetic municipal ear.

These reforms, particularly the whole ethos of non-partisanship, depoliticized the city, reducing in the process any perception that cities *per se* had any key role to play in the intergovernmental game. After all, there is nothing really "political" in taking the garbage out. Especially absent among Canadian reformers' demands was the peculiar American notion of "home rule" which guaranteed cities an independent jurisdictional arena. The key elements of American non-partisanship, combined with the British "weak mayor" format and provincial regulation of municipal government, rendered Canadian cities politically impotent.

The final period of reform thinking to encroach upon Canadian cities emerged in the 1960s almost as an unintended consequence of developments in the United States. President Lyndon Johnson's "War on Poverty" programs embraced the rhetoric of direct citizen participation, and the same ideal was later powerfully reinforced by the struggle in American city streets against the United States' involvement in the Vietnam War. The spillover into Canada was fuelled by American expatriates in universities and quasi-autonomous research enterprises. They focussed upon confronting large-scale core city urban redevelopment and the freeway networks intended to service this enterprise. Even remote urban villages such as Halifax, Ottawa, and Edmonton were considerably affected by these anti-establishment political activists, their guerrilla sympathizers within the civic bureaucracy, and their citizen-group allies at the neighbourhood level.

The legislative culmination of these developments are to be found in the Winnipeg Unicity reforms of 1971.[5] This bold initiative not only merged the dozen municipalities in the greater Winnipeg metropolitan area into one government, thereby accomplishing an administrative centralization, but also tried to decentralize democratic control (somewhat as envisaged by the new reformers) through a system of community committees and residents' advisory groups. From an intergovernmental perspective, however, the decisive event occurred when Premier Edward Schreyer spoke proudly in public of a new partnership with a more autonomous City of Winnipeg and then, in the privacy of caucus, assuaged the fears of rural members that cabinet "was spawning an uncontrollable monster" by promising provincial controls in the traditional manner through the Manitoba Municipal Board. This was hardly the stuff of which real partnerships are forged. And, more broadly, in questioning the fundamental legitimacy of existing civic authorities, these new reformers may well have undermined any potential for more rambunctious posturing by them in the overall tri-level process.

The common thread in all of this has been the reality that Canadian cities have never held a separate identity with autonomous political clout. This is reflected in the status of the municipalities within the Canadian intergovernmental network. In the central-local equation cities hold the short end. For example, the referendum of 26 October 1992 on the Charlottetown Accord concluded another round of constitutional-amending discussions in which Canadian cities never featured prominently except as provincial offspring, somewhat like the television walk-on characters Larry, his brother Darryl, and his other brother Darryl. On television it was explained that the boys' mother had not been imaginative; the boys never speak, they appear scruffy, separate but not distinct, questing for road-kill. The motto of their restaurant, The Road Kill Café, was "You kill it, we grill it"—which is a rather apt metaphor for municipalities' lack of independent revenue-generation capabilities and spending discretion in provincial-local relations. In short, there never has been an autonomous existence for cities in the Canadian federal system.

This subordinate status has been reinforced most vividly at the level of horizontal intergovernmental relationships. Even the ambitious Canadian standard for comprehensive regional-government reform set in Canada's centennial year by the Ontario (Smith) Committee on Taxation, which aimed its plans directly at enhanced municipal autonomy, emphasized that "the Province has a constitutional responsibility for the structure of municipal and school authorities."[6] The committee set twin goals of *service* and *access*, the former to be judged by the criteria of business efficiency, the latter by measures of direct citizen participation. Satisfactory formal structures provided through provincial intervention ultimately proved very elusive as greater efficiency required the economies of scale and the promotion of specialization and "access" became an inverse function of size. Probably because the committee itself began by genuflecting to "Ontario's time-honoured municipal structure," municipalities were never taken seriously as full partners in development. Partnership implies equality, and the "time-honoured" Baldwin traditions had also, it must be remembered, vested the provinces with the prerogative of protecting the credit of local jurisdictions.

Further, in 1954 Ontario pioneered the modern two-tier metropolitan form of urban government among the anglo-democracies with the creation of the Corporation of Metropolitan Toronto. In this case, the new metropolitan government was modelled on the century-old county structure inherited from the Baldwin regime—a structure that was now simply, albeit boldly, applied to an urban area. Metro Winnipeg in 1961 was based upon the Toronto initiative; the Greater Vancouver Regional District (beginning in 1965), although informed by it, was scrupulously not. Regrettably, the continuing problem in such two-tier structures has always related in some way to what political scientist Stefan Dupré has chosen to label "hyper-fractionalized, quasi-subordination." By this he means that the structures of decision making are so divided territorially, and with so many functions delegated to functionally specialized agencies (such as transit commissions), that almost everyone has a say but no one body is ever clearly accountable.

So a Canadian pattern of subordinate city status has resulted from a variety of factors: the provinces' natural inclination to do nothing, in the absence of demonstrated crisis, when it comes to matters of metropolitan reform; the absence of compelling arguments to alter intergovernmental relationships by delegating provincial power to the cities; and, finally, the political benefit to provincial administrations of having a bunch of municipalities literally at their doorsteps (as most provincial capitals are located within the largest metropolitan area) scrapping among themselves. No wonder, then, that contemporary metropolitan governments are no longer seen to have a determining role to play in effective, long-term, urban planning.[7]

## *Participation in City Politics*

In an especially perceptive piece of writing, Harold Kaplan has concluded that, while the Baldwin Act formalized the expectations set forth in the struggle for responsible government in Canada, it did not reconcile three strongly competing images justifying the role for local government in that system.[8] One, rooted in the history of courts of quarter sessions, offered cities a judicial *raison d'être*. Even today, councils hear local grievances and dispense justice on an individual basis. A second image, promoted by some reformers experienced in the British tradition, gave local government a distinctive role as a chartered public corporation whose affairs were to be measured by the usual criteria of business efficiency. A last, more radical strain of thought advocated local democracy as an experiment in direct democracy along the lines of the New England town meeting, a training-ground for instilling democratic practices and developing future political leaders.

These differences were not reconciled in 1849 and each, today, establishes a cultural cornerstone for policy conflict at city hall. What results are two basic rules of thumb. First, no decision is ever final at city hall since it can always be challenged by reference to one of the other competing images for legitimacy. The developers' principle that it is easier to beg forgiveness than to ask permission stands splendidly as a working example of this behaviour. Secondly, even the most aberrant demand can be justified by one of these continuing strands in our civic political culture.

What the three concepts share is the sense that local government is somehow distinct from the more general levels, and so the latters' practices of cabinet government and rigorous caucus discipline are not relevant. These are considered the usages of more distant institutions. But if local government is to be somewhat different, to be "closest to the people," a phrase too often heard, then how are we as individuals to participate in some meaningful fashion in this most important aspect of our democratic citizenship?

There are many limitations upon the creative capacities of councils to facilitate involvement. The most imposing and persistent is the burden of sheer size. As Canadian cities emerged from the reforms of the 1970s, simple largeness became a huge psychological barrier to direct citizen action. There is no longer any physical town hall big enough to accommodate the traditional face-to-face town meeting. Even reforms of upper-tier governments in Ontario over the last few years have neglected to reconcile size with democracy. For example, in 1989 Sarnia, with 58 per cent of the voters in Lambton County, received but 15 of 37 positions on regional council; and, in another case, Mississauga, with 63 per cent of the voters in Peel Region, 10 of 21 councillors.[9] May this be an indication of provincial dismissal of the importance of local representative democracy? Should the serious pattern of electoral misrepresentation not soon be subject to judicial review under the Charter? Ultimately, ought urban voters to accept the legitimacy of such political systems when responsible authorities themselves do not?

A further perennial problem stemming from as far back as the turn-of-the-century is the role of boards and agencies in the city's policy affairs. When these bodies were created, it was felt that specific areas (such as education, policing, and public health) were too specialized and sensitive to be left to the dimwit generalists on councils and ought properly to be handled by panels of "blue ribbon" citizens.

While the existence of such agencies does increase the potential for direct citizen participation in policy making, it also seriously detracts from the general authority of the elected representatives since many of their major responsibilities are spun off to quasi-subordinates. The delicate question of patronage also arises whenever these "objective experts" are to be appointed by council, and campaign workers are often asserted by the councillors to be very good citizens indeed.

Local democratic reformers have generally believed that mass participation in politics has to go beyond all this. Still, our study reveals that few citizens are directly involved in politics. According to a recent analysis in Britian by authors sympathetic to wider citizen involvement, only some 50 000 people in an electorate of 43.5 million can be described as being among the political and administrative elite at the national and local levels. In Canada, the only question much debated is the comparative one of how small and relatively open to recruitment our own elite class is. Yet, while these activists are a distinct minority, they do drive the agendas of city councils. Where, and how, an ordinary informed citizen should best exert influence upon them is surely an appropriate target for study.

Canadian metropolitics have become major league in another fashion as well. It now costs about a quarter of a million dollars for a novice without strong-name recognition to mount a credible mayoralty campaign. It is to be remembered that our mayoralty elections are city-wide, encompassing usually the territory of a half-dozen federal and a dozen or more provincial constituencies, and in these the political resources of wealth and/or a lofty social position become critical. Sadly, our cities' reformers have not seriously considered the focussed accountability which would result from a mayor elected "from and among" the councillors, except at the upper-tier metro-government level. The last real consideration of this alternative occurred during the reform of Winnipeg government in 1971, but the initiative was set aside in favour of a "city-wide" mayor to balance the fissiparous inclinations of fifty ward-based aldermen.

Some citizens have neither the time nor tastes for the largely electoral politics we have been considering but are still intensely interested in municipal policy making. They may, therefore, choose to participate in pressure-group activities intended to influence the choices or strategies of city councillors. These activities are essentially of only two kinds; groups are institutionalized into the process or not. Institutional groups are bodies such as the local Chamber of Commerce, certain professional associations (architects, engineers), government-clientele associations (social-service groups, cultural organizations), and many well-established neighbourhoods (usually upper class). They employ their political resources of social standing, professional knowledge, and corporate wealth in an ongoing policy dialogue with city hall. Normally they deal with the senior administrators, and, should they lose on a particular fight, maintaining this long-term relationship is far more important than the immediate decision.

Newer types of groups over the past generation have directly challenged this established way of doing business. They have been based in certain neighbourhoods (threatened by redevelopment), on single issues (freeway expansion plans), and around specific functional areas of government (social services). The behaviour of these groups has been generically described as noisy, negative, and reactionary. This is often the kindest description they will hear. They are noisy because the whole point is to exploit the media to gain attention to counteract institutionalized power and resources. They are negative by definition because they exist to oppose what they view as offensive initiatives on the part of the city. And they are reactionary because by their nature they have not been built into the consultative process. In the 1990s, the NIMBY (Not in My Backyard) phenomenon is a less creative offshoot of the single-issue group, a spontaneous explosion of dissent over a project or plan (such as a dump location). While NIMBY protest is not at all irrational behaviour in politics, it tends to consider no alternative but the termination of the offensive initiative. The groups that rally under this banner claim, very rightly, that the suggestion of other alternatives is not their responsibility.

Recourse to the basic tools of direct democracy in the form of the initiative (a technique by which, through petition, laws crafted by citizens are put directly to a referendum), the referendum (a decision by all electors defined as "a binding verdict of the people"), and the recall (a process by which an elected official's position is legally declared vacant) has become the legitimate child of 1990s cynicism. Widespread calls for the use of these devices are a symptom that both governing elites and the broader public, each concerned with the manipulations, motives, and apparent fickleness of the other, have become jaded with the established order. These pressures are growing in intensity as the 500-channel super-universe unfolds and politics becomes more immediate, direct, interactive, and accessible for the many outside the old circles. As with any time of serious political change, there will be concomitant stress. What seems most probable is that it will be the city political arena which first tests whether established precedures can be adapted to this new era or not.

In all of this, it is important to understand that what we "know" about metropolitics comes primarily from two sources. There is the first-hand contact we acquire in our daily lives through such obvious and specific things as parking meters, potholes, and police. Our more general knowledge of city affairs derives from the various news media, which provides the descriptive basis on which we evaluate events. In theoretical terms, the role of these media is not only to report the details but also to place events into the context of civic culture. Importantly, they might be considered filters sifting what is important from what is less so. In reality, however, in towns and most cities the city hall press gallery is "in the loop," a part of the system upon which they are reporting. The better reporters trade on insider information, treating favoured councillors and the more accomplished administrators with kid-gloves, often floating policy trial balloons for them. There is an acknowledged tendency among the media to view outsiders such as new groups and non-establishment candidates in the same light as incumbents do, as a threat to the established order of business. As to the critical capacities of local electronic newsreaders, most communities are fortunate if their television and radio stations can reproduce the lead paragraphs from the morning tabloids accurately: in short, these media usually follow the lead of the newspapers on most stories.

It is necessary also to remember that newspapers are businesses. To read the commercial pages and the principal local business-affairs columnist is to view tub-thumpers for the local board of trade who are just as ingenuous as the sports writers who boost the city's major league franchises. Finally, in an age when the significant municipal politics of other major cities tend not to be covered locally at all, this vigorous "villaging" of the mass media means that few citizens can fashion independently objective standards against which to measure the local political agenda and the performance of their city's indigenous political classes. For this, city electors are abandoned to the leadership of the already dominant cosmopolitan city elites, who develop interpretations and make assessments based on their personal and professional sources and travels outside the community.

## *Conclusion*

So why *should* we study Canadian city politics? There are a handful of rather compelling reasons.

*Canada is an urban community, and the city governments in its two dozen or so metropolitan areas are major institutional players.* Our culture may sustain arcadian images as ideals, but we simply do not live in some fantastic Frontierland. While government institutions forged to service the agrarian society may not yet have been adapted well to fit 1990s realities, service demands will continue to necessitate such a realignment. From the time of John Stuart Mill, there have been those who have viewed small-scale community government as the cornerstone of our democratic practices. What we might now appropriately respond to this old saw is, "some corner, some stone!" Associations of municipalities, such as the national Federation of Canadian Municipalities, will have to overcome their collective predilection for seeking lowest common-denominator plans and instead devise, advocate, and implement a realistic political strategy for the nation's cities.

*Three fundamental problems directly confront our metropolitan cities:* historic sources of revenue in no way match the expenditure responsibilities of contemporary cities; the legal boundaries of cities in the metropolis have not for decades been coterminous with the problems to be resolved politically; and, in responding to the cash crisis of deficit and public debt, broader-scale governments have too easily been "down-loading" the servicing of their responsibilities onto cities. It is a sad fact of metropolitics that, as some segments of the urban middle class and certain businesses have relocated to the suburbs (taking their property and business taxes with them), less mobile citizens in the central city—those frequently in need of redistributive policies—must turn to governments whose pockets have been picked.

To put it plainly, the tax base has fled beyond the artificial legal boundaries of the city.

*Urban party-like activities and traditional pressure groups are under stress.* Although much has been written about the necessity of involvement, who still gets elected? By the 1980s, judged by gender, ethnicity, and occupation, those who play the game have made of it—with some prominent exceptions—an essentially white, male, and professional business. At a time when it has become increasingly common to employ professional senior-level organizers in metro-city mayoralty campaigns, the question has become not when but where formal party organization will finally transcend the traditional "party-like" activities. This may yet work to expand the types of persons who can become effective gladiators.

*The political class of Canadian cities is changing.* In Canada there has been insufficient advancement from municipalities to provincial legislatures and national parliaments to justify belief in urban government as a training-ground for democracy. Until the 1990s, for instance, no prime minister and only two premiers (Thomas Patullo of British Columbia and George Drew of Ontario) had served previously as local mayors. As this is written, however, three premiers (in British Columbia, Alberta, and Nova Scotia) have served as metro-city mayors, as have the leaders of the official oppositions in the two former provinces.

Perhaps more important, we may increasingly see new cultural minorities' penetration of the city electoral system, especially where there exist block wards. Two factors will be at play here. Those discriminated against in the social and economic realms turn typically to non-establishment political movements to strike out at the agents of their disbarment. Similarly, local politics, by being more open, may provide a venue for recruitment and political mobility that is simply not available on the provincial and federal levels. The first stages of this revolution have been witnessed within neighbourhood groups already active in our larger cities.

*Cities will be the most susceptible to a new wave of reform.* In social-science terms, the legitimacy of the cities' political system has always been fragile. It has never had to work at binding citizens' loyalties because municipalities can always borrow from the constitutional supremacy of the province in times of stress. In this sense, Canadian cities have perpetually existed with a crisis of legitimacy. Furthermore, Canadian cities are provincial statute creations and as such are easily susceptible to reformist whims. These are not always wise: for instance, for Vancouver's 1993 civic elections, the province removed the deposit requirement for candidature and some 139 candidates (23 alone for mayor) presented themselves for election. The history of conflicting cultural expectations has always been conducive to such alternative reform vogues. Even in failure, the sad history of the Winnipeg reforms of 1971 did not write "paid" to the cultural strand of popular democracy.

*City government is the one most directly relevant to a person's pursuit of a satisfactory life.* Cities can prevent annoyance, or be annoying, but they deliver the local public goods. Canada's new age of fiscal austerity has meant severe cuts to even the provincial standards historically maintained through shared-cost programs. These grants-in-aid have stood in a ratio of about 9:1 over the general municipal grants, which are monies transferred without strings attached. Traditional local opposition to conditional grants was fuelled by concern that the existence of such programs distorted the priorities of local councils. This concern has, in the 1990s, been replaced by paroxysms of anxiety that donor governments will reduce or eliminate programs to leave metro cities essentially "holding the bag" for public expectations. What this may mean is that people on the street, in order to sustain what is essential to them in government, will necessarily have to become conversant with complex questions of state-revenue generation and expenditures which have previously been the exclusive domain of benevolent governing elites. The Charlottetown referendum in 1992, and the subsequent strategic voter protest of 1993, demonstrated that Canadians are prepared to try.

Notwithstanding their important role in determining most Canadians' quality of life, city politics are still very much the "politics of appearance." These are politics in which personality is paramount, a style no longer much possible on the larger stage where processes have become institutionalized and relatively impersonal. The only required investment for involvement is personal energy and a little time. What this effectively means, however, is that city politics are, on balance, short-term and gains-oriented. The sad legacy of apoliticalism in the making of decisions in city politics is that it does emphasize style at the expense of specifics, incrementalism rather than innovation, and symbolism instead of substance.

While the overall picture painted in this introductory chapter may seem demoralizing for those who care deeply about the city and its politics, the acid test of any democratic system remains whether or not it fulfils public expectations more often than not. We make these judgments daily.

## Notes

1. *Globe and Mail*, 10 April 1986.
2. Andrew Sancton, "Canada as a Highly Urbanized Nation: New Implications for Government," *Canadian Public Administration*, vol. 35, no. 3 (autumn 1992), 287.
3. Ann Walmsley, "City Lights: Best Cities for Business," *Globe and Mail, Report on Business* (August 1993), 49.
4. Alan F.J. Artibise, *Winnipeg: A Social History of Urban Growth, 1874–1914* (Montreal: McGill-Queen's University Press, 1975), 58.
5. M. Brownstone and T.J. Plunkett, *Metropolitan Winnipeg: Politics and Reform of Local Government* (Berkeley: University of California Press, 1983).
6. The Ontario Committee on Taxation, *Report* (Toronto: Queen's Printer, 1967), vol. 2, chapter 23: 550.
7. Sancton, "Canada as a Highly Urbanized Nation," 288–91.
8. Harold Kaplan, *Reform, Planning and City Politics: Montreal, Winnipeg, Toronto* (Toronto: University of Toronto Press, 1982), 55–112.
9. Sancton, "Canada as a Highly Urbanized Nation," 287.

## Selected Sources

Bunting, Trudi and Pierre Filion, eds., *Canadian Cities in Transition* (Toronto: Oxford University Press, 1991).

Higgins, Donald J.H., *Local and Urban Politics in Canada* (Toronto: Gage, 1986).

Kaplan, Harold, *Reform, Planning and City Politics: Montreal, Winnipeg, Toronto* (Toronto: University of Toronto Press, 1982).

Loreto, Richard A. and Trevor Price, eds., *Urban Policy Issues* (Toronto: McClelland and Stewart, 1990).

Magnusson, Warren and Andrew Sancton, eds., *City Politics in Canada* (Toronto: University of Toronto Press, 1983).

Tindal, C.R. and S. Nobes Tindal, *Local Government in Canada*, 3rd ed. (Toronto: McGraw-Hill, Ryerson, 1990).

# 2

## *The State in the City: A Political-Economy Perspective on Growth and Decay*[1]

Christopher Leo

SUBURBAN DEVELOPMENT has arguably been the single most powerful influence shaping Canadian society in the second half of the twentieth century. It has certainly been the single most important influence in shaping our cities. The suburbs of Canadian cities bristle with images that dominate the consciousness of most Canadians born after the Second World War: single-family homes situated on twelve- to eighteen-metre widths of private green space, shopping malls, neighbourhood schools, community centres, and, of course, the ubiquitous automobile, which has made it all possible. It was widespread ownership of private automobiles which conferred the mobility that allowed large numbers of us to live in such spacious surroundings. The spaciousness, for its part, made the residents of suburbia radically dependent on automobiles, since they had to travel farther and farther for work, shopping, and entertainment. Countless books and articles have been written about suburbia, the private automobile, and their myriad influences on our imaginations and our lives. A recurring theme of this literature—one that crops up in many forms and is enunciated from many points of view—is the individualizing and privatizing influence suburbia has had on our society.[2]

Such observations are profoundly revealing, but there is more to the story. Suburbs, like cities generally, are collective entities; they are the product, at least in part, of state action; and the costs of their creation have been borne, not only by the individuals who opted for greater privacy and more space, but also by society as a whole. None of these themes has received much attention in the scholarly literature—an omission that this chapter attempts to remedy. Its purpose is to undertake a broad-based investigation of the politics and consequences of suburban development. A broad-based investigation is necessary because the politics of urban growth and decay cannot be understood unless an array of varied influences is taken into consideration, and it also has the advantage of offering a useful perspective on city politics as a whole.[3] This broad base involves two elements: the intergovernmental context of city politics, and urban political economy. The first of these elements is not very well represented in the Canadian literature on urban politics; the second one is, but there is always room for more of a good thing.

Any study of city politics must begin with the recognition that local government is part of a much wider context, a bit player in someone else's drama. Karl Marx, had he taken any interest in such matters, might have said that local government exists in itself but not for itself. What is this wider context? Conventionally, it is defined by saying that local governments are "creations of the provinces," a phrase that goes all the way back to K.G. Crawford,[4] which is a Canadian municipal expert's way of saying "to the dawn of time." Caroline Andrew reinforces and updates our understanding of province-city relations in her chapter of this book, and Frances Frisken has shed important light on the subject.[5] But provincial domination is only one aspect of the picture. Less well developed in the literature—but not completely absent—is the awareness that the federal government also influences city politics. A few Canadian writings have paid serious attention to the day-to-day importance of the federal government in shaping our cities.[6] But they have not had much impact, and there has not been any sustained pursuit of that feature of city politics, even by those who have occasionally addressed the issue.

For example, John Sewell, who in 1977 effectively stressed the importance of the federal government in dictating the terms and conditions for suburban development, lost sight of that point when in

1993 he wrote *The Shape of the City*.[7] As well, textbook treatments of the subject are cursory and probably leave most students with the impression that the federal government has generally had little to do with cities. The conventional account catalogues a period of federal interest in local politics in the 1970s but suggests that this interest came to an end with the dissolution of the federal Ministry of State for Urban Affairs and the failure of attempts to develop a tri-level consultation process involving federal, provincial, and municipal governments. Most students are likely to conclude that, both before and since, the federal government has stayed clear of local politics.[8] In that respect, our urban literature is very different from that of the federation next door. In the United States, the interrelatedness of local and national affairs has been well recognized. In the much-discussed *City Limits*, Paul E. Peterson argues that the inherent weakness of local government dictates a strong federal-government role in cities. As well, the centrality of national affairs to city politics has been a major theme in the writing of John Mollenkopf and is prominently featured in Dennis R. Judd and Todd Swanstrom's important new text.[9] Many more examples could be cited.

This chapter focusses on the importance of provincial and federal, as well as municipal, governments in urban affairs. It argues that city politics is part of a national political system and that the workings of this system are often best understood, not by looking at discrete levels of government, but by treating the state as a unitary phenomenon which has an impact upon cities.

At the same time, the chapter will take account of another element that impinges on the operations of local government: the exercise of influence by a variety of powerful groups in society. This issue is well represented in both the Canadian and the American literature in the form of the oft-repeated observation that local government has been and still is dominated by special interests, which, in a variety of ways, block an open and democratic political process. Different authors have characterized these interests in different ways, but when we examine the characterizations, they turn out to be remarkably similar, despite the fact that they grow out of different national contexts. James Lorimer, writing of Canadian urban politics, referred to these special interests as the property industry: those who stand to gain from land development, including developers themselves, the real-estate business, the construction industry, lawyers and accountants associated with those concerns, large-scale property owners, and so on.[10] John R. Logan and Harvey L. Molotch, addressing American cities, offer a more abstract characterization, referring to those who see property in terms of its exchange value—that is, its ability to produce income or profit—rather than its use value, as a home, a place to meet others, or simply a place to enjoy.[11] Clarence L. Stone and Heywood T. Sanders focus their concerns about the political economy of American cities on corporate interests, whose primary goal is local economic development.[12] By any definition, in either country, these special interests, which wield power at all three levels of government, are very important in determining the course of urban affairs.

Such observations depart from a more conventional approach to city politics, which operates on the explicit or implicit assumption that government is a kind of neutral decision-making and implementation machinery that tabulates public opinion and produces policies responsive to the demands it identifies. A political-economy perspective takes its point of departure from the observation that there is more to decision making for the society as a whole than simply reflecting public opinion, and that there is more to the state than simply the machinery of government. The decisions that govern our lives are not just the mechanical outcome of a head-counting exercise; they are a response to all the various forms of power that exist in society—the power of those who own or control real estate, control production, and draw on the resources of such organizations as boards of trade, chambers of commerce, labour unions, professional associations, and public bureaucracies. These power centres all have interests of their own, are active at all levels of government, and can influence the governance of cities in many ways.

## *Suburban Development and Inner-City Decay*

Canadian cities in the post–Second World War era have been profoundly shaped by interventions from all three levels of government. At the end of the war, the federal government anticipated that the return to civilian life of large numbers of veterans would pose a problem of housing supply, and it decided to meet this problem head-on by stimulating private enterprise. Federal, provincial, and municipal governments all became involved in a massive program of government support for suburban development. Since it was private enterprise that was being stimulated, the interventions of government were not always obvious to the casual observer. For example, an amendment to the federal Insurance Act allowed insurance funds to flow into housing finance, thus freeing a large pool of capital which in turn helped a generation of Canadians to mortgage their way into their private suburban paradises.[13] The Central (now Canada) Mortgage and Housing Corporation (CMHC), a federal crown corporation, provided subsidized home loans, while the conditions on CMHC mortgages helped establish the framework of provincial and municipal planning and zoning regulations. As a result, the federal government, through the CMHC, created the housing programs that made stricter planning necessary. Provincial government legislation and regulations set out what was to be expected of municipalities, while municipalities passed and implemented most of the actual planning legislation. This regulatory regime, in turn, had much to do with dictating the characteristic form of suburban development: single-family homes, situated on large lots, with a large expanse of front yard looking out over a wide street, which often lacked a sidewalk; and a strict separation of this type of residential area from commercial and industrial development, so that residential neighbourhoods were located at a distance from shopping malls and shopping strips while both residential and shopping areas were separated from industrial parks, where many of the jobs were concentrated.[14]

In pursuing these policies, governments at all three levels were not only reinforcing the rapidly growing popular preference for the private automobile over public transportation; they were also giving it free reign, and entrenching it. The money lavished on suburban road-building provided easy access to locations distant from the inner city and made large-lot housing development feasible. The clear separation of residential areas from shopping strips, shopping malls, and industrial parks, which was dictated by the provincial and municipal regime of planning and zoning, assured that residents of the suburbs would become dependent on private cars for everything: trips to work, shopping, and even such small errands as a run to the milk store. Low-density development patterns imposed obstacles on the expansion of public-transit systems, which found it difficult—in many instances impossible—to plan routes capable of drawing enough passengers to make transit widely available without swamping the public purse. Declining transit service, in turn, further reinforced dependence on private transport.

To be sure, this was not a case of the state imposing its will on a reluctant public. The suburbs and cities we have today are the product of a complex mix of corporate initiative, popular preference, and state action. As a perusal of such writers as John Sewell, John C. Bacher, and Humphrey Carver makes clear, the rise of the suburbs is a case study in political economy: the state was responding, not only to popular opinion, but also to the demands of E.P. Taylor and other development magnates, to the professional biases of bureaucrats in the Department of Finance and the CMHC, to the sensitivities of Liberal Party contributors as well as those of the international financial community, and to the interests and concerns of a variety of other parties.[15] In any event, the actions of municipal, provincial, and federal governments were an important ingredient in the mix. And the particular mix found in Canada was not an inevitable product of social and economic forces, as we can see by the examples of the United States, where suburban development has been even more automobile-dominated than in this country, and Europe, where it has been much less so. State action could have taken different directions, and produced different outcomes. The actions of the state had an important impact, and that impact is comprehensible only if we view it from a political-economy perspective.

Throughout the 1950s and into the 1960s, automobile-dominated development was widely seen as an uncomplicated boon, but in time it became clear that there were clouds over suburbia's green, well-tended pastures. A deterioration in the quality of public transportation, even as city-transit systems required growing subsidies, was an early warning, as society's growing dependence on private cars began to take its toll. Another was the gradual decay of inner-city residential neighbourhoods as middle-class residents and the businesses that served them decamped to the suburbs. The results that began to show themselves differed in different types of cities. In such development magnets as Toronto and Vancouver, the threatening prospect was that of an inner city vacant of housing and filled with glass towers, with streets crowded during rush hours but empty and very possibly dangerous at night. In slow-growth centres, such as Winnipeg and Edmonton, where development pressure was not strong enough to fill up the streets being vacated by suburban emigrés, it was empty storefronts and vacant, rubble-strewn lots that loomed. All of these fears have, to a greater or lesser extent, become the current reality of Canadian cities.

The third warning signal of the clouded future bestowed upon us by suburban development is only now being driven home to politicians and the public, in the form of the so-called infrastructure crisis. Conventionally, developers of low-density suburban subdivisions are required to cover the costs of extending basic services—such things as sewerage, water lines, roads, bridges, and parks—to the areas they are opening up. More often than not, a city council, deciding whether to permit the subdivision, is persuaded that it will bring a bonanza of tax revenues from new housing at essentially no cost, since the developer is allegedly paying for the services. In the usual decision-making process, however, a plethora of hidden costs remains uncalculated. Once ensconced in their new homes, and paying taxes, residents will understandably demand that they receive the full range of services available to other city residents. They will want comparable access to community centres, libraries, and recreation facilities. They will expect similar levels of police and fire protection as well as transit service. Also uncalculated, as a general rule, is the fact that, as roads, sewerage, and water lines are extended into low-density districts, the per capita cost of maintaining them rises. Hence the infrastructure crisis: for several years, municipal leaders have been pressuring federal and provincial governments for contributions to a massive infrastructure renewal program to combat deteriorating streets, bridges, sewage systems, and water lines.[16] Rarely if ever is the value of suburban development questioned; indeed, approval of new subdivisons continues apace. But deteriorating transit systems, inner-city decay, and crumbling infrastructure nevertheless stand as mute testimony to the costs of suburban development.

It is important in this area as in others not to let our thinking become trapped in a municipal box. Significantly, in all the materials available for the preparation of this study, there is no mention of any connection between the deterioration of urban postal services and suburban development. Yet suggestive facts are available for anyone old enough to remember them. Until the mid-1960s, the postal service maintained residential delivery in Canadian cities six days a week and most urban residents lived within easy reach of a full-service postal branch. In the 1990s, six-day delivery is something grandpa rants about, many residents of newer subdivisions are forced to accept so-called "superboxes" as a consolation for the absence of any residential delivery, and full-service postal branches are becoming a rarity, even downtown. Obviously, many things have changed since the early 1960s, but any suggestion that the proliferation of low-density development was not at least part of the problem would seem quixotic. The fact that we are not studying the connection between the growth of the suburbs and the deterioration of urban postal services underlines the aridity of compartmentalized thinking about municipal and senior governments, and it may also tell a tale about how hard it is to look critically at the enthusiasms that have dominated our lives. Whatever the reasons for the neglect of this subject, it is clear, on the one hand, that government policy has had a great deal to do with shaping our cities as we know them today, and therefore with producing the urban problems we now face; and, on the other, that we can take the full measure of these government influences only if we abandon compartmentalized thinking and consider the actions of the state at all three levels as a single phenomenon.

## *Combatting Inner-City Decay*

So far, we have seen that the state has helped to bring about a particular style of suburban development which, in turn, has produced a set of knotty problems: transit decline, inner-city decay, and deterioration of infrastructure. We do not know yet how the third of these problems will ultimately be addressed, but the Canadian state has been trying to respond to the first two since about the mid-1970s. It is a hard reality of urban planning that low-residential densities and effective public transportation are quite simply incompatible. Canadian transit providers have done the best they can to evade that reality; for example, in the early 1970s some attempts were made to develop a "dial-a-bus" service for neighbourhoods of low-residential density.[17] In the end, however, it has been accepted in practice—though not always in rhetoric—that there is little to be done beyond spreading an often unsatisfactory level of service as widely as possible and pressing the limits of politically acceptable subsidies. Though these half-measures have met with generally more success in Canada than in the United States, half-measures they remain and more ambitious dreams have long since been shelved.

Over time, serious government attempts to save urban transit lost their identity as a separate venture and the focus shifted to a series of efforts to prevent or reverse the decay of inner cities. City centres that remain viable as both business and residential areas generally offer a sufficiently high concentration of population to provide at least part of the basis for a viable transit system. The idea of rolling the two attempts into one, therefore, was defensible, even if somewhat feeble. Attacks on inner-city deterioration took many different forms, most of them involving complex interactions of at least two levels of government. We can get an idea of the types of programs undertaken by looking at a few examples in two categories: commercial and public facilities and inner-city housing.

## *Commercial and Public Development*

Two types of areas were candidates for renewal through the development of some combination of commercial and public space: areas that had been affected by the exodus of residents and businesses to the suburbs; and areas that had deteriorated as a result of another aspect of suburban flight, namely the relocation of transportation facilities and industries. The latter areas were in need of renewal because factories and warehouses, once restricted to inner-city locations with easy access to harbours and railway terminals, had increasingly moved to outlying locations to take advantages of their good roads. The inner-city decay found in both types of areas was addressed by some combination of preservation of older structures, park development, and construction of new facilities.

Three good examples of programs different enough from each other to indicate the range of variation in these schemes are Toronto's Harbourfront, Vancouver's Granville Island, and Winnipeg's Core Area Initiative (CAI). Harbourfront and Granville Island were both projects designed to rescue waterfront industrial and warehouse areas whose economic importance had declined with the eclipse of water and rail transport and the rise of motor vehicles. They had become dilapidated, seedy districts located in downtown cores characterized less and less by industrial activity and more and more by the expansion of retail trade and the proliferation of office towers.

The two projects had a great deal else in common. Harbourfront was the fulfilment of a Liberal election promise in 1972, while Granville Island was a pet project of Liberal cabinet minister Ron Basford, who represented the riding of Vancouver Centre. Both were restoration-oriented projects that sought to preserve something of the ambiance of a waterfront industrial district while putting it to an entirely different use. Both were focussed on recreation with a mildly bohemian flavour, and both proved to be great popular successes. Harbourfront's public areas include parks, a waterfront walkway, and spaces for the display, rehearsal, and performance of art, music, and drama, with a tilt toward the youthful and avant-garde. The area also offers shopping, restaurants, office space, and housing, some of which is subsidized. Though there has been a great deal of controversy over the commercial development,[18] the public facilities have been and remain popular favourites. Granville Island offers a narrower, but shrewdly targetted range of attractions, including a tourist hotel in a renovated building, restaurants, theatres, a farmers' market, a brewery that serves draught beer, craft shops, and a children's market.

Winnipeg's Core Area Initiative also involved a dominant personality at the federal level, Liberal minister Lloyd Axworthy. In other respects, it was very different. It addressed the needs of the first of the two areas described above, a declining inner city whose viability was threatened by the exodus of residents and businesses to the suburbs. The problems of the area under redevelopment, therefore, went beyond those of decaying buildings and physical infrastructure to include the myriad social ills of an inner-city residential population that is left in the wake of a middle-class exodus to the suburbs. The distasteful reality of most downtown redevelopment schemes is that they ignore such social ills and sometimes aggravate them through the demolition of serviceable low-income housing. To their credit, the architects of the CAI did devote some attention to the core area's social problems, while at the same time substantial resources went to physical upgrading and to creating the conditions for private investment.

The result was a program with many, varied elements. The CAI laid the basis for, and provided some funding for, the Portage Place shopping mall and The Forks, a recreational and commercial complex at the confluence of the Red and Assiniboine rivers near the centre of the city. Through government funds and leveraging of private investment, it also secured or contributed to substantial upgrading and redevelopment of public facilities in such business districts as Chinatown, Little Italy, and the Franco-Manitoban district of St Boniface; the establishment of small businesses; renovation of the previously decayed Logan and Central Park residential districts; a large amount of more widespread home repair and new housing construction downtown; industrial development; job creation and education programs for disadvantaged residents of the core; and a wide array of social programs, ranging from alcoholism counselling through job training and education to day-care centres.[19]

All three of these schemes, and others like them, involved complex interactions among all three levels of government, and the complexity and degree of interaction increased with the passage of time.[20] Toronto's Harbourfront was administered by a corporation, formed in 1976 and owned by the federal government, but its development necessitated co-operation with provincial and local governments over planning issues and the financing of particular parts of the project. The Granville Island Trust, formed two years later, is administered by the CMHC and therefore is structurally similar to Harbourfront. In both cases, the projects are under the control of federal-government corporations, and in both cases implementation requires extensive interactions with the other two levels of government. The growing complexity of such arrangements is suggested by the structuring of the Winnipeg Core Area Initiative and the Portage Place and Forks projects in the same city, all initiated in the 1980s. The CAI, instead of being under the control of only one government, was a tri-level government agency working under a board with equal representation from the governments of Canada, Manitoba, and Winnipeg. The

Portage Place development is managed by a corporation which, unlike Harbourfront, represents all three levels of government. The Forks exhibits an even more intricate corporate structure: it is managed by a corporation that is a subsidiary of the corporation responsible for Portage Place and includes representatives from the three levels of government.[21]

In responding to the challenges posed by suburban development, then, the state, including all levels of government, has been heavily involved in the promotion of commerce and the development of compatible public facilities. To a lesser extent, in the case of the CAI at least, it has intervened to try to address some of the social consequences of its earlier interventions in the expansion of cities. As we shift our attention from the mechanisms promoting suburban development to those that were fashioned in an attempt to revitalize inner cities, we see a very different set of arrangements but a common theme as well: political economy in a nexus of complex intergovernmental interactions. Here, as in our observations on suburban development, we find the three levels of the state interacting and responding to diverse private interests as they mobilize their resources to support a wide variety of business ventures in the inner city and, to a much smaller extent, to address the problem of unemployment and the many other social ills of an inner city abandoned in the flight to the suburbs.

## *Inner-City Housing*

As noted, CAI was based on the premise that the results of downtown redevelopment are very likely to be unsatisfactory if the social aspects of inner-city decay are not addressed. That premise has an honourable history. Perhaps the most memorable statement of it is in the classic *Death and Life of Great American Cities*, by Jane Jacobs.[22] One of the central contentions of that intricate, richly textured work is that diversity is a key to urban vitality: neighbourhoods and cities can thrive if they contain a mixture of different types of housing, businesses, and public facilities, while uniformity—for example, a concentration of businesses, with no housing nearby or only housing for the very wealthy or the very poor—robs them of the attractiveness that ultimately stimulates investment. A variety of examples lend weight to Jacobs's argument. The glitzy towers of the Renaissance Centre in Detroit, and the attractive Hart Plaza located nearby, have helped to spawn a number of impressive commercial developments, but they have failed utterly to halt the radical decay of downtown Detroit. Likewise in Baltimore, the lively, urbane Harbourplace market, with an adjacent shopping mall and public park, have stimulated the development of commercial buildings and up-scale housing, but none of this has alleviated the unemployment and housing problems of much of the inner city's population.[23] Many similar examples could be offered.

Interest in avoiding such a state of affairs is not limited to those who deplore the spectacle of a downtown featuring mirrored office towers and plush condominium development surrounded by, and barricaded off from, abandoned buildings, substandard housing, and "down-scale" establishments of one kind or another. It is shared by those segments of the business community that could profit from a more diverse social environment and therefore a more varied market, one that includes such things as middle-level restaurants, movie theatres, and retail stores catering for others besides the very rich and the very poor. Such a varied environment would also improve security for everyone living and doing business downtown and revive the property market.

In response to such reflections as these, both the Canadian federal government and a number of Canadian cities have attempted to incorporate moderate- and low-income housing into their plans for countering inner-city decay. Perhaps the best-known, and probably the most significant, of these initiatives date to the 1970s. They were the federal government's Residential Rehabilitation Assistance Programme (RRAP) and Neighbourhood Improvement Programme (NIP), both initiated in 1973, the City of Vancouver's False Creek development, and the City of Toronto's St Lawrence Neighbourhood.[24] NIP was a scheme for the improvement of parks, community centres, sidewalks, and other public facilities in neighbourhoods threatened by physical and social deterioration. RRAP was a federal government program of partially forgiveable loans for the renovation of homes in need of repairs. Available to cities across the country, it was widely utilized in the upgrading of older inner-city housing.[25]

Toronto's St Lawrence Neighbourhood is a mixed-income housing project located in the most improbable of areas. Adjacent to Toronto's skid row area, and within walking distance of the office towers of the commercial core, it sits on a former strip of junk yards blanketed with debris, between the Gardiner expressway and a rail line on one side and a traffic artery on the other. The project was initiated by the City of Toronto, with strong backing from city officials concerned with housing and from the so-called reform caucus, a left-wing group on city council. The objective of the project was to turn the junk yards into a high-density housing area for families, with shopping and community facilities conveniently located, and accommodating a varied group of residents that reflected the income mix of Metropolitan Toronto as a whole, in proportions similar to those of the larger community.

It is remarkable that Toronto's city council had the hubris to attempt such a development in the mid-1970s, in the face of an overwhelming middle-class bias in favour of suburban housing. What is even more remarkable is that the project was largely successful.[26] An evaluation by David Hulchanski, written in a spirit of scepticism, nevertheless culminated in the assertion that "on the basis of almost any evaluative criteria, it can only be concluded that the City has been very successful. Certainly the spirit, and to a very large degree even the specific details of the original goals and objectives have been achieved . . . The primary goal of the St. Lawrence project—to significantly increase the supply of housing close to downtown for all income groups, particularly low and moderate income groups—has been achieved with great success."[27] This perception is widely shared. No less an expert than Jane Jacobs has written warm words of approval,[28] and the neighbourhood, together with a nearby market development, also publicly initiated, have stimulated the transformation of the former skid-row district into an area of fashionable shopping and posh housing. Both urban experts and investors have been favourably impressed by the project.

Vancouver's False Creek project was also an initiative of municipal government and had objectives broadly similar to those of the Toronto scheme. As in Toronto, the project was backed by a liberal-left coalition on council, the Electors' Action Movement (TEAM), and by city officials, in this case planners. Located in a decayed industrial area on the shores of a polluted backwater, it too was designated for residential development with some public facilities. False Creek included a restaurant, a large park, a recreational waterfront area, and a small shopping complex. Like St Lawrence, it was to accommodate a mix of subsidized, moderate-income, and upper-income housing. Despite their considerable similarities, and despite the fact that each succeeded in its own way, the outcomes of the two projects were different. False Creek was developed at lower residential densities than St Lawrence and with more generous public space allowances. That, together with a splendid waterfront and a magnificent view of mountains and the city skyline, had an ironic result: the project was so successful financially that both the middle- and upper-income dwellings soon came to be perceived as intensely desirable properties, and False Creek came more nearly to resemble a playground for the affluent than a mixed-income housing development.

Nevertheless, it did accommodate some residents of modest means in co-operative and non-profit housing. In addition, if we view both it and the St Lawrence Neighbourhood as part of the response to inner-city problems stemming from suburban development, both schemes helped lend plausibility to the suggestion that life downtown could be made attractive to families of all income levels. In other words, the projects held out the hope that flight to the suburbs and the decay of inner cities need not necessarily become the inevitabilities of the late twentieth and early twenty-first centuries, provided the state matched its continuing fervour to promote suburban development with a newly conceived determination to restore the viability of inner cities. And that, if we take the lessons of NIP, RRAP, St Lawrence, and False Creek seriously, is a necessary proviso. All four schemes relied on state initiative to accomplish objectives that private initiative would not have pursued unassisted.

NIP and RRAP were federal government ventures, but since the schemes brought federal finance to bear upon the renovation of city neighbourhoods, they necessarily required the approval and participation of both local and provincial governments. In developing St Lawrence Neighbourhood, the City of Toronto drew on its own resources and also on assistance from both the federal and Ontario governments.[29] The City of Vancouver required a federal low-interest loan to cover start-up costs, assistance from the federal Winter Works

Programme for the construction of a sea wall, loans from the CMHC, and a change in the provincial Strata Titles Act to permit the construction of condominiums on leased land.[30] Both projects relied on social-housing funds to subsidize co-operative and non-profit housing, including money from the CMHC and a joint federal-provincial rent supplement program. By the same token, in the case of both St Lawrence Neighbourhood and False Creek, the senior governments would not have been able to accomplish what they did if it had not been for municipal initiatives. In Hulchanski's words, "Though neither project would have been possible without the federal social housing supply programmes, it is also true that the federal programmes would not have had the impact on the Toronto and Vancouver areas they have had without the municipalities initiating the two new neighbourhoods."[31]

So, in looking at housing development in the inner city, we arrive at the same findings as we did in our review of downtown commercial and public developments and suburban development: in all cases, governments are heavily involved, and we cannot get a full understanding of government involvement until we look at the state as a whole, rather than maintaining a perspective that is bounded by one or even two levels of government.

The four housing initiatives also reinforce another of our themes: none of them can be understood as a simple government reaction to voter demands. All must be seen as the product of interactions among power centres. Certainly this is true of the St Lawrence and False Creek projects. As we have noted, St Lawrence was driven, in the first instance, by a left-wing coalition then on city council, False Creek was promoted by a liberal-left coalition. Both schemes owed a great deal to initiatives from municipal officials: planning and housing officials in Toronto, planning officials in Vancouver. The success of both presupposed the discovery and consolidation of common ground among the agendas of government agencies at all three levels of government. In addition, both offered benefits to developers, retail business people, wealthy and middle-class home-buyers, and advocates of non-profit housing. Although detailed documentation is not available for this study, similar observations could undoubtedly be made about NIP and RRAP.

A further conclusion may be drawn. If our observations in this chapter are a reliable guide, state initiatives have become more explicitly interventionist with the passage of time and the institutions that carried them forward have become more complex and more intricately structured. A comparison of suburban development with the more recent downtown initiatives makes that point clear. In order to detect the hand of the state in suburban development, we had to look closely to find the reality behind the appearance of purely private market ventures. The obvious thing about suburban development was the functioning of the private market, the operation of individual choice in the selection of housing, and the role of the automobile. It was only through careful consideration that we were able to identify the critical contributions of federal regulators of insurance companies, the CMHC, and the provincial and municipal planning regimes. Downtown redevelopment is a very different matter: it fairly bristles with state involvement. Even the most casual observer recognizes that the major housing projects, commercial developments, and the enhancement of public facilities downtown are not only heavily regulated by the state, but initiated by it, usually through the agency of two or three levels of government.

## *Infrastructure Restoration?*

Early in this chapter, we identified three warnings of the ill effects of low-density, automobile-dominated suburban development: the decline of transit, the decay of inner cities, and the infrastructure crisis. As we have seen, in the 1970s the state gave up trying to address transit decline as a separate issue and instead focussed on inner-city decay—not enough to solve the problem, or even ameliorate it significantly, but enough to have a noticeable impact. In contrast, the seriousness of the infrastructure crisis did not dawn gradually upon the state until the closing years of the 1980s. Not surprisingly, it was municipal leaders who first issued urgent calls for action, and once again it was co-ordinated action by all three levels of government that was seen as the solution. In the late 1980s and early 1990s the Federation of Canadian Municipalities was trying to persuade the federal government to initiate a $15-billion program of infrastructure renewal, equally shared by the three levels of government. The Liberal government that took power in 1993 offered to put up $2 billion, on the condition that provinces and municipalities supply $4 billion from their own resources. The first step in the program was a series of negotiations with provincial and municipal authorities across the country to determine what projects would be funded. Thus, once again, all the elements of the political economy of the state in the city were at work, reflecting a variety of governmental and private-sector interests.

Just as other schemes have not solved the problems of transit decline and inner-city decay, this program is unlikely to solve the problem of over-extended infrastructure. Winnipeg offers as good an example as any of some of the pitfalls. There, before any federal funds had even been approved, two muncipal politicians, including the mayor, dropped their opposition to the immediate commencement of a new suburban bridge-building project; undoubtedly, they did so partly on the basis of their belief that federal funds would now be available for desperately needed renewal of older infrastructure, thereby making available for the suburbs money that would otherwise have gone to inner-city renewal. Significantly, however, the federal program had always been billed as a creator of jobs in the construction industry during a period of high unemployment, not as an urban initiative. At the present time, it is beginning to look as if the federal government is not prepared to see the infrastructure program used primarily as a means of restoring the deteriorating inner city. Once again, and despite the infrastructure program, suburban development seems destined to continue at the expense of the inner city. Indeed, all of the problems outlined in this chapter remain with us, despite substantial state initatives, which have generally been partially successful but left the root causes of urban decline firmly in place.

## *Conclusions*

Fragmented views of city politics, which treat the levels of government as separate entities and consider city government largely or wholly apart from the social context within which it functions, have generally played a dominant role in the Canadian literature on cities, and that literature has suffered as a result. Not that a broader perspective has been entirely absent. A number of studies representing such a perspective have been cited in this chapter and more could be named. Nor is there is any objection as such either to institutional studies of local government or to studies that concentrate on a single level of government or on an interaction between two levels. On the contrary, such studies are important: they are like magnifying glasses that allow us to make minute examinations of various parts of the bigger picture. Yet, without a clear view of the whole, studies of this kind leave us with a distorted version of reality. In the study of Canadian city politics, the balance between the two approaches has slighted the overview in favour of minutiae. As a result, many important issues have been neglected and, not incidentally, students have been driven away in droves from the study of city politics.

A political-economy perspective and a comprehensive view of the operations of the state in the city offer insights, not only into cities, but also into the wider society in which cities play such an important role. Perhaps the most useful contribution of the present study is the observation that the state, in addition to playing a major role in the growth and decay of Canadian cities, has grown in influence and complexity. That is not the conventional view of our times. We tend to see ourselves as willing or unwilling heirs to the legacy of Margaret Thatcher and Ronald Reagan, and to view our society as being marked by shrinking governments and a burgeoning private sector. Undoubtedly, there is a great deal of truth in that picture, but, as this chapter suggests, the whole truth is probably a good deal more complex. If it is true that some aspects of the state are shrinking, it is also true that in other respects the state is becoming more omnipresent in our lives. We are obviously going through a period of massive change, in which much that we have taken for granted, including many elements of our public life, is undergoing a transformation. But whether the new world will be characterized by the simplified, stripped-down state of Margaret Thatcher's dreams or by a state with ever-increasing power and influence, is not at all clear.

Nor is it clear that the dominance of suburban life, which is the main theme of the events reviewed in this chapter, will remain the order of the day. Dispersal of cities continues, but in recent years a great deal of growth has taken place beyond the metropolitan fringe, not only in exurban communities, but in small towns and rural areas. Modern communications technology has the potential of setting people free to live anywhere and work anywhere; for example, one can play the Toronto stock market in front of a computer terminal located in a cabin in the Laurentians, or the Rockies. Some bold commentators are already predicting the decline of the suburbs.[32] In the meantime, some inner cities have experienced modest revivals in the 1980s and early 1990s.[33] In short, much is possible and little is certain. What is certain is that we will not understand either our cities or the crucial role they play in the evolution of our society unless we keep the big picture—the entire state and the full social context—clearly in view.

## *Notes*

1. My thanks to Jim Lightbody and Jeffrey Patterson for thoughtful and constructive critiques of an earlier draft, to the Social Sciences and Humanities Research Council, to the University of Winnipeg and the Institute of Urban Studies for material support and encouragement, to Shairoze Damji for research assistance, and to Allison Sproul Dixon, Sandy Brown, Heather Mathieson, and Lynne Schultz for the fastest, most efficient, and most courteous inter-library loan service in the western hemisphere. The mistakes, unfortunately, are wholly my own.
2. Robert Fishman, *Bourgeois Utopias* (New York: Basic Books, 1987); William Severini Kowinski, *The Malling of America: An Inside Look at the Great Consumer Paradise* (New York: William Morrow, 1985); *Variations on a Theme Park: The New American City and the End of Public Space,* Michael Sorkin, ed. (New York: The Noonday Press, 1992); John C. Bacher, *Keeping to the Marketplace: The Evolution of Canadian Housing Policy* (Montreal: McGill-Queen's University Press, 1993); Peter Freund and George Martin, *The Ecology of the Automobile* (Montreal: Black Rose Books, 1993); Marc A. Weiss, *The Rise of the Community Builders: The American Real Estate Industry and Urban Land Planning* (New York: Columbia University Press, 1987); John Sewell, *The Shape of the City: Toronto Struggles with Modern Planning* (Toronto: University of Toronto Press, 1993); Jack Lessinger,

*Penturbia: Where Real Estate Will Rise after the Crash of Suburbia* (Bellingham, Wash.: Socioeconomics Press, 1993).

3. Framing an enquiry that is both credible and broad enough to do justice to the subject is one of the most difficult challenges in the study of the city. Even purely theoretical treatments tend to limit themselves by over-emphasizing one aspect of the subject—for example, the powerful influence of multinational corporations or the importance of the automobile. For a thoughtful discussion of this problem see Mark Gottdiener, *The Social Production of Urban Space* (Austin: University of Texas Press, 1985).
4. Kenneth G. Crawford, *Canadian Municipal Government* (Toronto: University of Toronto Press, 1954), 18.
5. Frances Frisken, "Canadian Cities and the American Example: A Prologue to Policy Analysis," *Canadian Public Administration*, vol. 29 (1986), 345–76.
6. Lionel D. Feldman and Katherine A. Graham, *Bargaining for Cities: Municipalities and Intergovernmental Relations: An Assessment* (Toronto: Institute for Research on Public Policy, 1979); Christopher Leo and Robert Fenton, "'Mediated Enforcement' and the Evolution of the State: Development Corporations in Canadian City Centres," *International Journal of Urban and Regional Research*, vol. 14 (1990), 185–206; James Lorimer, "The High Cost of Suburban Housing," in James Lorimer and Evelyn Ross, *The Second City Book: Studies of Urban and Suburban Canada* (Toronto: James Lorimer and Company, 1977), 56–67; John Sewell, "Where the Suburbs Came from," ibid., 10–17.
7. Sewell, ibid. and *The Shape of the City.*
8. Donald J.H. Higgins, *Local and Urban Politics in Canada* (Toronto: Gage, 1986); C.R. and S. Nobes Tindal, *Local Government in Canada*, 3rd. ed. (Toronto: McGraw-Hill Ryerson, 1990).
9. Paul E. Peterson, *City Limits* (Chicago: University of Chicago Press, 1981), ch. 11; Dennis R. Judd and Todd Swanstrom, *City Politics: Private Power and Public Policy* (New York: Harper Collins, 1994), chs. 5–7 and passim. John Mollenkopf, *The Contested City* (Princeton, N.J.: Princeton University Press, 1983).
10. James Lorimer, *A Citizen's Guide to City Politics* (Toronto: James, Lewis and Samuel, 1972).
11. John R. Logan and Harvey L. Molotch, *Urban Fortunes: The Political Economy of Place* (Berkeley: University of California Press, 1987).
12. *The Politics of Urban Development,* Clarence N. Stone and Heywood T. Sanders, eds. (Lawrence, Kansas: University Press of Kansas, 1987).

13. Humphrey Carver, *Houses for Canadians* (Toronto: University of Toronto Press, 1948), 127.
14. Sewell, "Where the Suburbs Came from"; Hans Blumenfeld, *The Modern Metropolis* (Cambridge, Mass: MIT Press, 1967); John C. Bacher, *Keeping to the Marketplace.*
15. Bacher, ibid.; Sewell, "Where the Suburbs Came from" and *The Shape of the City*; Carver, *Houses for Canadians.* A comparable view of United States suburban development may be found in Weiss, *The Rise of the Community Builders.*
16. Federation of Canadian Municipalities, *Municipal Infrastructure in Canada: Physical Condition and Funding Adequacy*, vol. 4, no. 1 (Ottawa: 1985); Federation of Canadian Municipalities, *Proceedings: First Canadian Conference on Infrastructure* (Edmonton: 1987).
17. The service consisted of small buses operating out of shopping centres that picked passengers up at their doors in response to a telephone call.
18. More detail on this subject can be found in Leo and Fenton, "'Mediated Enforcement,'" 194–5, 201–2.
19. Lest this account sound absurdly glowing, it must be added that the CAI and North Portage also presided over a failed attempt at high-tech industrial development, a job-creation scheme that turned out to be much less than met the eye, and the deterioriation of a previously thriving business district across the street from the new shopping mall.
20. This phenomenon is documented in more detail in Leo and Fenton, "'Mediated Enforcement and the Evolution of the State.'"
21. The CAI was shut down in 1992, but, at this writing, a successor of some description seems likely to be created, and once again all three levels of government probably will be involved.
22. New York: Vintage Books, 1961. A more recent work that builds on Jacobs's book is Edmund P. Fowler, *Building Cities That Work* (Montreal: McGill-Queen's University Press, 1992). See also William H. Whyte, *City: Rediscovering the Centre* (New York: Doubleday, 1988).
23. Marc V. Levine, "Downtown Redevelopment as an Urban Growth Strategy: A Critical Appraisal of the Baltimore Renaissance," *Journal of Urban Affairs*, vol. 9, no. 2 (1987) 103–23.
24. David Hulchanski, *St Lawrence and False Creek: A Review of the Planning and Development of Two New Inner City Neighbourhoods* (Vancouver: School of Community and Regional Planning, University of British Columbia, 1984).

25. Social Policy Research Associates, *An Evaluation of RRAP* (Toronto: Canada Mortgage and Housing Corporation, 1979); Canada Mortgage and Housing Corporation, *Final Report on the Public Consultations on Residential Renovation in Canada* (Ottawa: CMHC, 1989). The funding for RRAP was discontinued by the Conservative government, but its Liberal successor has since promised to revive it.
26. The fact that the bias in favour of suburban housing was undoubtedly weaker in the City of Toronto than in most other Canadian centres helps to explain why the development succeeded there, but in no way detracts from the achievement. A mere glance at the extent and continuing speed of low-density development in the Toronto area confirms that, here as elsewhere in North America, the inner city is, to put it mildly, not the residential area of choice for most middle-class people.
27. Hulchanski, *St Lawrence False Creek*, 28, 31.
28. Jane Jacobs with Kate Sutherland, "Streets that Work: Seven Hints to Help Keep Our Cities' Lifelines Viable," *Canadian Heritage*, May–June 1987, 31–34.
29. Hulchanski, *St Lawrence and False Creek*, ch. 5.
30. Ibid., ch. 11.
31. Ibid., 11.
32. Lessinger, *Penturbia.*
33. L.S. Bourne, "Population Turnaround in the Canadian Inner City: Contextual Factors and Social Consequences," *Canadian Journal of Urban Research*, vol. 1 (June 1992), 66–85, offers a good discussion of this phenomenon.

## *Selected Sources*

Bacher, John C. *Keeping to the Marketplace: The Evolution of Canadian Housing Policy* (Montreal: McGill-Queen's University Press, 1993).

Feldman, Lionel D. and Katherine A. Graham. *Bargaining for Cities: Municipalities and Inter-governmental Relations, An Assessment* (Toronto: Institute for Research on Public Policy, 1979).

Fowler, Edmund P. *Building Cities That Work* (Montreal: McGill-Queen's University Press, 1992).

Frisken, Frances. "Canadian Cities and the American Example: A Prologue to Policy Analysis," *Canadian Public Administration*, vol. 29, no. 3 (1986), 345–76.

Jacobs, Jane. *The Death and Life of Great American Cities* (New York: Vintage, 1961).

Judd, Dennis R. and Todd Swanstrom. *City Politics: Private Power and Public Policy* (New York: Harper Collins, 1994).

Lorimer, James and Evelyn Ross, eds. *The Second City Book: Studies of Urban and Suburban Canada* (Toronto: James Lorimer, 1977).

Peterson, Paul E. *City Limits* (Chicago: University of Chicago Press, 1981).

Sewell, John. *The Shape of the City: Toronto Struggles with Modern Planning* (Toronto: University of Toronto Press, 1993).

Stone, Clarence N. and Heywood T. Sanders, eds. *The Politics of Urban Development* (Lawrence, Kansas: University Press of Kansas, 1987).

Weiss, Marc A. *The Rise of the Community Builders: The American Real Estate Industry and Urban Land Planning* (New York: Columbia University Press, 1987).

# 3

## *The Origins of Canadian Municipal Government**

Engin F. Isin

THE GOVERNANCE OF OUR CITIES is inextricably bound up with their history. Canadian municipal governments, as well as the practices and legislation associated with them, took their current shape through a long and arduous process of evolution. At present, any aspect of local government, from what powers such government can exercise to how money is raised for its operations, can be likened to a layer of sediment in that it holds historical evidence—in its case, evidence of political struggle stretching back at least two hundred years. Even beyond that, certain layers, to continue with our geological metaphor, can be traced to American and English municipal institutions that originated as early as the twelfth century.

Yet one period requires special attention—the eighty years between American independence in 1783, when the British North American colonies began to be settled with some urgency, and the achievement of confederation in 1867. These years were formative ones for Canadian

*I would like to thank Frances Frisken, James Lemon, and Andrew Sancton for their comments regarding earlier drafts. Also, I wish to acknowledge a Social Sciences and Humanities Research Council grant, which supports a research program that this paper draws upon.

political and legal institutions, including local government. It was in this period that Canadian municipal government inherited, shaped, and redefined American and English local institutions to suit the needs of a rapidly growing and expanding British North America. This chapter is an overview of the political and legal conditions under which Canadian municipal government evolved.

When Canadian municipal government first emerged, the British North American economy was pre-industrial, perceptions of space and time as defined by transportation and communications technology were fundamentally different from those prevailing today, and culture and society were dominated by a governing elite whose interests were directly connected to imperial policies drawn up in Britain. The entire territory was laid out in townships, a settlement model that had been devised in the eighteenth century with the goal of maintaining social and political stability in the American colonies.[1] These townships, which would later constitute the basis for municipal institutions, were small in size and so reflected the society's reliance on boats and horses for transportation and communication.[2] The colonial statesmen and administrators who drew up these plans could not have anticipated either the emergence of new technologies or the immense population increase and urbanization of later eras. Nor could they have foreseen the fundamental changes that colonial societies were about to experience because of industrialization and liberalism.

The world-economy within which the British North American colonies emerged was also fundamentally different from that of the late twentieth century. When the first cities were established in British North America, Britain's colonial policy was concerned both with keeping colonies subservient to its economic needs and demands and with maintaining its geopolitical presence on the North American continent after the American revolution. Today, Great Britain has very little influence on not only Canada but also other post-colonial societies, such as Australia and New Zealand. The modern world-economy is dominated by multinational corporations, which are much more effective in using and dominating nations and societies than the British colonial apparatus could have ever imagined. They deploy techniques and technologies that allow them to move commodities with incredible speed and precision across the entire world-economy. As a result, the industrial societies of the nineteenth century are no longer the ones where industrial production is concentrated. At the same time, as national boundaries are crumbling, new regional, urban, and ethnic identities are surfacing, and old political and legal institutions are under tremendous strain to adapt to changing conditions. Despite the dramatic changes Canadian society has undergone, however, our municipal governments continue to reflect their colonial origins between 1783 and 1867. This chapter is offered primarily in the spirit of rekindling our sense of local government—how, in a world much different from our own, municipal governments began and what they were expected to accomplish by the authorities who established them. Such rekindling, in turn, should provide a perspective on local government that will aid efforts to reform our contemporary system of local government.

It is through analyzing the specific circumstances in which Canadian local government emerged and the concerns and dictates that shaped it that we can lay the groundwork for imagining an alternative role for municipal government in Canadian federalism—a role that must correspond to current realities. Understanding the origins of municipal government will also allow us to imagine an alternative role for us as citizens.

## *What Is Municipal Government?*

The British North America Act, which established the Canadian federation in 1867, provided that each provincial government had exclusive powers in relation to "Municipal Institutions."[3] The modern Canadian municipal government is therefore a corporation created by each province for the purposes of local government. Municipal government refers to the governing body of the corporation—the council—and its administrative machinery. The only duties a municipal government can perform and the only powers it can exercise are the ones explicitly mentioned in its founding act or charter.

An act that creates a municipal corporation typically begins with a clause declaring that the inhabitants of the town or the city are constituted as a body politic and corporate. Then it grants this body corporate capacities of perpetual succession, meaning the power to hold lands, to pass regulations and by-laws, to sue and be sued, and to hold a common seal. The act next defines the territorial boundaries of the town or city thus incorporated and the powers vested in the governing body of the corporation, styled as the town or city council. The governing body is composed of the mayor and aldermen or councilmen. The head of council is either chosen from among the elected councilmen or elected directly by the voters. The corporation is divided into wards, which have prescribed boundaries, and each ward elects one or more aldermen. Both voters and members of the governing body are usually required to be Canadian citizens. (The right to vote and hold municipal office was originally restricted to male property owners who were residents of the municipality. There were also property qualifications, which were greater for office holders than for voters. The qualifications were carefully calculated to control participation in city politics.) The mode of holding elections is always specified. Provision is made for the election of a mayor, and his duties are defined: the most important and symbolic of his responsibilities is to act as a magistrate. The act contains a minute and detailed enumeration of the council's powers which are often numerous and listed in one clause. The most important are the authority to carry debts, to levy and collect taxes, to appoint corporate officers, to enact ordinances regarding public health, to establish a police force, to establish a correction and punishment system, and to administer justice. The act of a corporation is its constitution, and it gives all the authority and specific powers that the municipal government possesses. As noted above, the corporation cannot exercise powers and authority that are not prescribed by its constitution.

The act of incorporation also presupposes a number of political principles. First, the modern municipal corporation is created at the pleasure of the legislature, and, while the legislature may obtain the consent of the people of the municipality to be affected by the incorporation, such consent is not necessary. The act of incorporation is not a contract between the provincial legislature and the corporation. The legislature can erect, change, divide, and abolish a corporation at its pleasure, as it deems appropriate. Secondly, the authority and power conferred on the modern municipal government are not merely local in nature but supra local: the act of incorporation empowers the municipal council to exercise those powers falling within provincial jurisdiction. And, thirdly, the principle of franchise enables the legislature to legitimatize the central authority and power to be exercised in municipalities. It is on the basis of all these legal and constitutional attributes that we can call the modern municipal government an apparatus of governance: it enables the provinces to govern bodies of people in a functionally decentralized manner. Or, to put it in other words, the incorporation of the municipal government means the creation of a body politic with an elaborate and written document, which forms and empowers a governing body to bear both the economic and the political costs of meeting a community's needs. By instituting fields of power in which the liberty to act is granted to citizens only within the limits defined and the rules specified, municipal government balances authority and autonomy. At the same time, the corporation empowers citizens to participate in their own governance within the prescribed limits of politics. Overall, the provincial legislatures have at their disposal an apparatus of governance that is adaptable to differences in specific local political conditions.[4] The question is how and under what political conditions such a legal institution was invented.

## *European and American Origins of Canadian Municipal Government*

Although the history of Canadian municipal government has unique features, its origins are principally European, especially English, and, to some extent, American. A brief outline of the European and American background is therefore necessary in order to appreciate the broader history that envelopes Canadian municipal government.

The municipal corporation emerged in European laws in the twelfth century. Its actual constitution varied in different counties, notably in England, France, Italy, and Germany, but in general terms the twelfth-century municipal corporation was autonomous. This means that the municipal corporation had powers and rights that were not necessarily derived from a higher authority. Such municipal corporations can be designated *de facto*; that is, if their powers existed in practice, they were recognized in law.[5] Of course, there were tensions between these various municipal corporations and the ruling elite.

In Germany, for example, *Stadtluft macht frei* (city air makes people free) became a legal maxim and spread throughout continental Europe and England; charters, which were the founding legal documents of the municipal corporation, stipulated that after a year and day of breathing the town air a serf could not be returned to bondage, for he had become a *citizen*.[6] The municipal corporations emerged as an enemy of feudal lordships and kingships. The medieval concept of citizenship was articulated through association with other people, a principle elaborated by the corporation as a mutually dependent sworn association of people.[7]

As Belgian historian Henri Pirenne argued, the birth of the autonomous corporation was closely associated with the revival of industry and trade in the West after the collapse of the Roman Empire.[8] The city became an economic association of merchants, craftsmen, and artisans, who created the corporation as a means of seeking relief from surrounding feudal lordships, kingdoms, and other jurisdictions of all sorts. The autonomous corporation and citizens were naturally in conflict with the nascent royal and territorial powers. But the autonomous corporation was also a potential source of revenue for the emerging monarchical bureaucracies of Western Europe: kings and lords often established new cities to encourage trade and so accumulate tax revenue. Monarchs also waged wars against the old cities to coerce them into their tax schemes. The charter was in fact a contract between the law-making authority and the citizens as a corporation.[9] Failure by either party to honour the contract would result in conflict or even war.[10] The level of autonomy embodied in the charter was an outcome of a constellation of forces: the city itself, surrounding feudal lordships (ecclesiastical and lay), and the monarch or prince. As mentioned, the result was a considerable variation in autonomy in different regions of Europe—from Italian city republics with immense powers to English boroughs with moderate liberties under the suzerainty of a strong monarchy.

As is well known, medieval municipal corporations were by and large subsumed under the emerging nation-states between the fifteenth and the eighteenth centuries. Accordingly, European law changed to reflect the new reality. The municipal corporation was redefined as a legal institution created by the state to attend to its local affairs. These newly defined municipal corporations may be characterized as *de jure*: they could no longer exercise powers not explicitly granted to them.[11] The difference between *de facto* and *de jure* municipal corporations is important, for it reveals the modern tension between municipal governments and their "creators," states (or provinces in Canada).

By the nineteenth century, however, the municipal corporations had gained a new lease on life and emerged as significant elements of the new system of government—democracy—that was adopted by many European states. In England, the Municipal Corporations Act of 1835, which followed a royal commission on municipal corporations, described the modern municipal government as a corporation that had a clear mandate from the state to *govern* "its" inhabitants. How did this change come about? Since the middle of the eighteenth century, jurists, political theorists, and "social reformers" had become convinced that a great need of the times was to reform, if not to recast, the oppressive body of laws that had been inherited from the absolutist regimes of the sixteenth and seventeenth centuries. In the Age of Enlightenment, these laws were seen not only as barbaric in substance and often chaotic in form but also as inefficient: they attached an exaggerated importance to the severity of punishment while ignoring the value of clarity and precision in the form of the law and of certainty in its *positive* application. It was argued that government by command, edict, and proclamation—in short, government by force—was not effective; instead, government on the basis of calculated, coherent legislation was defined as the proper domain of politics. Governing, in this sense, meant that those invested with authority would control the conduct of subjects through laws, rules, and regulations.[12]

The new vision of government became apparent in England during the 1830s, when there was a shift of emphasis from *punitive* law (although such did not disappear entirely) to *institutional* and enabling law. Central to the latter was a form of government that relied on political institutions for the enforcement and implementation of state policies. According to this view, municipalities governed inhabitants partly through the exercise of powers they had been explicitly granted and partly by enabling *some* inhabitants to choose their governors. In other words, *domination* was no longer the means through which governance was accomplished. Rather, the municipal corporation was a calculated and precise apparatus of government.[4] It was an integral part of the prevailing system of governance and was given an elaborate constitution, which enabled the governing body (the mayor and the council) to establish institutions, laws, rules, and regulations to direct the conduct of its inhabitants.

Tension between *de facto* municipal corporations and the states that claimed to govern them was common in the American colonies, where the British authorities were always sceptical of *de facto* powers exercised by certain colonial towns and cities. When colonial America was opened up for settlement in the seventeenth century, the British colonial governors and administrators were presented with the problem of "government at a distance"; how could the colonies be governed from London as subordinate polities? The answer was by no means obvious, for the New England colonies had already been established as corporate entities. From the beginning these colonies exercised *de facto* powers in order to organize their political culture according to their own needs, and one of the results was the emergence of the much heralded "New England town"—an institution of local government with considerable *de facto* powers. These towns and cities exercised *de facto* corporate powers in two senses. First, because the colonies themselves, being of corporate status, could not create corporations, the towns and cities fashoned their own priorities, policies, rules, and regulations. And, secondly, corporate colonies organized their towns and cities according to their needs and the dictates of local politics and culture.

As soon as the British colonial governors set out to subordinate the colonies, a new form of colonial government became predominant: the royal colonies. These colonies placed increasing reliance on royal governors, councils, legislatures, written commissions and carefully prescribed powers, and one of their other characteristics was the prevalence of *de jure* municipal corporations. Between the 1660s and the 1730s there was considerable effort to create *de jure* cities in the royal colonies to facilitate the exercise of "government at a distance." Many of these were "close" corporations resembling the early-modern municipal corporations of England: they were governed by self-perpetuating councils without elections. By 1776 there were between twenty-four and thirty-six *de jure* corporations in colonial America. After the rebellion of the Thirteen Colonies, it became a standard interpretation among British statesmen and colonial agents that one of the important causes of the crisis had been the failure to create more *de jure* corporations and to subordinate *de facto* ones. As we shall see, this diagnosis was the backdrop against which corporations were later conceptualized and created in British North America.

## *Early Settlement and Municipal Government*

The formative eighty-four years of Canadian local government can be divided into two periods: from early settlement in 1783 until the Durham report in 1839; and from 1839 until 1867, the year of the British North America Act.

In the first period, political conditions in the British North American colonies were much different from those that had prevailed in the Thirteen Colonies before the revolution. To begin with, the territory that became British North America was acquired through conquest and the diplomatic bargaining that ended with the Treaty of Paris in 1763. The fact that the American colonies were not acquired by conquest, but had originated as settler communities with charter privileges, was of the highest significance for the problem of "government at a distance."[13] By contrast, since New France had been conquered, the existing liberties and customs of its inhabitants were open to interpretation, as it were, by the British colonial apparatus.[14] Hence, as Gordon Stewart has noted, between the 1760s and 1790s British North America had the most extreme form of statist and centralist constitution.[15] By the close of the eighteenth century the constitutional model followed throughout the region was that of the royal colony with royal governors, appointed councils, and representative assemblies.

Still, in the aftermath of the rebellion of the Thirteen Colonies, the British colonial apparatus was in a state of disarray and reorganization: in the minds of colonial administrators and governors, it was not at all clear or obvious that Britain was going to build a new empire of colonies from the 1820s onwards.[16] Instead, it was a period of questioning and reordering of priorities. The Board of Trade and Plantations was abolished in 1782 and was not replaced with the Colonial Office until 1801, and, as Phillip Buckner has stated, "Until the 1820s, the

Colonial Office had neither the expertise, the knowledge, nor the desire to supervise effectively the work of distant governors."[17]

From the 1780s to the 1820s, the Colonial Office was haunted by the prospect of another colonial rebellion. The consequences of this fear for British North American political and legal culture were far-reaching: the colonial governors and their councils formed a distinct oligarchy and exercised unchecked power within the colonies, protected by the provisions of royal constitutions.[18] At the same time, the ruling elite deeply distrusted municipal corporations on the grounds that they fostered disloyalty. Its attitude towards local government has been noted time and again by historians since the late nineteenth century. J.B. Bourinot, for example, noted that the statesmen "appear to have quietly acquiesced in a state of things calculated to repress a spirit of local enterprise and diminish the influence of the people in the administration of public affairs. Indeed, we have some evidence that the government itself was prepared for many years to discourage every attempt to introduce into Canada anything that had so long existed in New England."[19] He also claimed that the elite's hostility towards democracy can be traced back as far as 1770, when a resolution was passed in Nova Scotia declaring all town meetings illegal.[20] Adam Shortt, displaying his liberal belief in British institutions, stated that the colonial administrators Frederick Haldimand, Guy Carleton (Lord Dorchester), and John Graves Simcoe "professed to fear another revolution as the natural and inevitable consequence of granting them [the colonists] British freedom; and in this they were probably not far astray, assuming that their views of what a colony should be are correct."[21] James Aitchison, in a more recent and comprehensive historical survey of municipal government in Upper Canada, joined the earlier historians in pointing out that "when the first townships on the upper St. Lawrence were surveyed in 1783, the surveyors were instructed not to call them townships but royal seigneuries, and to number, not name them. The intention was to consider them merely as divisions like the concessions and lots into which they were subdivided and thus to avoid any suggestion that they were to form units of local administration."[22] David William Smith, the surveyor general of Upper Canada, expressed this fear of town meetings quite succinctly: "As I conceive these meetings to have been the cause of the late unhappy rebellion and must always be attended with riot and confusion, I think the majority of the people should never be called together but to choose their representatives for a House of Assembly."[23] William Smith, chief justice of Upper Canada, expressed a similar sentiment when he said, "I trace the late revolt and rent to a remoter cause, than those to which it is ordinarily ascribed. The truth is that the country had outgrown its government. All America was thus abandoned to democracy and [to] little republics."[24] Of course, the words "democracy" and "little republics" in this statement refer to the practices of autonomous governance. The rebellion of the Thirteen Colonies, then, influenced not only the early British North American culture in general but also attitudes toward towns, since they were thought to have played a decisive role in the rebellion.

Shortt grasped this point when he wrote, "We observe the conflict of the two rival American systems typified by New England and Virginia, the one seeking to vest in the people the election of their local officers and the regulation of their local affairs, the other seeking to confine these rights to the justices of the peace in Quarter Sessions, who again derived their positions from the Governor-in-Council."[25] The tension that Shortt notes between the New England and Virginia systems is important because of his use of New England (corporate colonies) and Virginia (a royal colony) as examples of decentralized and centralized forms of political and legal organization. British fear of the New England model was rooted in a concern about the powers that cities and towns might acquire, powers that could make the government of subjects difficult.

For a more detailed examination of the conflict between local autonomy and centralized control that helped shape political and legal practice until the 1890s, we will now focus on the first incorporation of a city in British North America: Saint John, New Brunswick.

## *Saint John, New Brunswick: 1785*

On 30 April 1785 a royal charter was granted to the inhabitants of the two districts on both sides of the Saint John River incorporating them into a city.[26] The inhabitants were loyalists who had arrived from New

England colonies three years earlier.[27] Their campaign for municipal incorporation had begun with a petition that they had presented to the new governor of New Brunswick, Thomas Carleton. In this petition the settlers promised that "their prudent use of the liberties so to be granted them will justify the favour."[28]

The petition indicates two important things at once: the acquaintance of the New Englanders with the institution of corporation and their recognition of the reluctance of the colonial authorities to grant it.[29] The text of the charter does not further elaborate the reasons for incorporation, but an important letter by Governor Carleton makes some of the reasons explicit. Dated 25 June 1785, the letter was addressed to the then colonial secretary, Lord Sydney, at Whitehall. Carleton wrote that "the sudden increase of Inhabitants at this port and the confusion incident to so novel a situation have induced me to comply with the general wish in granting them a charter of incorporation."[30] And he added that, "although every useful liberty is given to the citizens, there is a sufficient influence retained in the hands of Government for the preservation of Order and securing of perfect Obedience."[31] Carleton's reasoning demonstrates that the charter was granted in response to the demands of the inhabitants. In the absence of such a demand the city would not have been incorporated, while, at the same time, the purpose of the charter was to oblige the inhabitants to recognize the authority of colonial agencies. This is understandable because of the crisis of authority in colonial governance and the desire of British statesmen to ensure that the new ideas nurtured by the rebellion should not hold sway in British North America.

The charter constituted qualified inhabitants as a body corporate and politic.[32] Only freemen and freeholders were considered qualified. The freeholders were those who held real property in the city, and freemen were defined and admitted by the city council on the basis of not only property but also status, family, and privileges. According to T.W. Acheson, freemen and freeholders made up about one-fourth of the total population of the city.[33] The city possessed corporate capacities of perpetual succession.

The charter ordained that the officials should include a mayor, six aldermen, six assistants, one sheriff, one coroner, one common clerk, one chamberlain, one high constable, six constables, and two marshals. Of these, the mayor, the recorder, the common clerk, and the sheriff were to be appointed by the governor of New Brunswick. The aldermen were to be elected by the qualified inhabitants from six wards that were specified in the charter. The mayor, the aldermen, and the three assistants were constituted as the Common Council of the city with executive capacities within the corporation. For judicial purposes the city was also constituted as a county, which meant that the administration of justice did not require justices of the peace of a higher level. From the charter we can see the "sufficient influence" that Carleton spoke about: the mayor and other important officials of the city were to be appointed by the governor.

Although the demand for incorporation came from the prominent inhabitants, the charter itself does not contain any provision that would encroach upon the royal prerogative, or, as the attorney general who confirmed the charter put it, the charter contained nothing "prejudicial to the interest of His Majesty."[34] Carleton's remark concerning the charter—"although every useful liberty is given to the citizens, there is a sufficient influence retained in the hands of Government for the preservation of Order and securing of perfect Obedience"—demonstrates this interesting aspect of the incorporation. For whose benefit was liberty given to the people? What is the nature of the liberty implied here? The constitution of a body politic and corporate meant that some authority and tasks of the colonial government were delegated to the corporation. The explicit stipulation that the city of Saint John could enact local ordinances provided these were neither repugnant nor contradictory to higher laws and statutes indicates the subordinate nature of the body politic that was created.

Until the 1830s no other cities were incorporated in British North America. This was not because there was a lack of a similar demand such as that which had precipitated the Saint John charter. There were unauthorized town meetings (as in Adolphustown, Upper Canada), governor-initiated attempts (as in Niagara, Upper Canada), and local petitions for incorporation (as in Kingston, Upper Canada, and Halifax, Nova Scotia).[35] But the principle that all local communities were subject to centralized control and supervision remained intact until the 1830s and the 1840s. We shall next see how the British colonial apparatus was, at times careful, deliberate, and calculating in circumventing potential rights and powers in towns and cities by retaining central control of such mundane local matters as the establishment of markets.

## *Township and Parish Officers Act, Upper Canada*

The earliest act concerning local polities was passed on 9 July 1793 in Upper Canada.[36] Significantly, this act replaced a bill that had proposed a limited form of town meetings. Simcoe thought that in proposing this bill legislators seemed "rather to have a strong attachment to the elective principle for all Town affairs, than may be thought altogether advisable."[37] Later, however, he revised his opinion somewhat and became resigned not to "withhold such a gratification, to which they had been accustomed, it being in itself not unreasonable, and only to take place one day in the year."[38] The outcome was that he agreed to town meetings in a limited form while at the same time claiming that this would only facilitate the obedience of town inhabitants in matters of policy.[39] The 1793 act provided that each town, township, or parish should elect two town wardens to represent the inhabitants in the quarter sessions of the district in which it was located. But, as soon as a church was built in the town, the minister was empowered to choose another person to act as a town warden. The town warden or the church warden were defined as a corporation.[40] This act was amended twice, in 1806 and 1808, and the word "corporation" disappeared altogether from the new provisions.[41]

## *Simcoe and Portland on Corporations*

There was an interesting correspondence between Simcoe and the Duke of Portland, the Home secretary, on the subject of corporations. On 21 December 1794 Simcoe asked Portland for authorization to incorporate the cities of Kingston and Niagara.[42] The Constitutional Act of 1791 had not conferred any power on governors to incorporate bodies politic, and so Simcoe was obliged to ask for such authorization. Believing that these two cities had reached a stage where they should be bodies corporate and politic, he proposed that the new corporations "should consist of a Mayor and six Aldermen, Justices of the Peace *ex officio*, and competent number of Common Council, to be originally appointed by the Crown, and that the succession to vacant seats might be made in such a manner as to render the Elections as *little popular* as possible."[43]

Portland responded on 20 May 1795, claiming that the idea of delegating powers to corporations would tend to diminish the powers of the central colonial authorities.[44] These corporations "may be disposed to use it in obstructing the Measures of Government, and in all events, will require to be courted and managed, in order to secure the right direction of the Influence thus unnecessarily given them."[45] The crux of the matter becomes clear when Portland adds that there are some institutions "which we permit to continue here [in England] only because they already exist, and are interwoven with other parts of the Government, but which, perhaps, if we had a choice, we should not now be disposed originally to introduce—Such, in the Opinion of many, are Corporations, and separate Jurisdictions of all sorts." Here, Portland is expressing a common sentiment of the late eighteenth century not only about the imprudence of creating a perfect image of the English constitution in the colonies but also about the inadvisability of transplanting corporations to the New World. The following letter from Whitehall to Simcoe reveals that Portland was by no means alone in his opinion:

> You suggest an idea of incorporation—the policy of such a measure after the experience we had at home—together with the conduct of the Mayor and Corporation of New York in the colonies is no longer a matter of doubt. Repeated experience has proved it to be a *most powerful engine* in the hands of an unprincipled *demagogue.* The *prevailing opinion* is that charters do not tend to promote but rather to check trade and manufacture, they are useful for *purposes of police*—but more useful for the purpose of faction—it was one of the few subjects on which I spoke to Mr. Dundas—he did not approve of incorporations. Nor does your humble servant for reasons aforesaid.[46]

It is clear that imperial authorities opposed the creation of "separate jurisdictions of all sorts" because, in their view, such jurisdictions or corporations would tend to foment disobedience and disloyalty. The rebellion of the Thirteen Colonies formed a backdrop against which these claims were justified. It is impossible to ascertain what would have happened if Simcoe had been authorized to incorporate Kingston and Niagara and whether he would have incorporated other cities. Nor is it clear why he was confident that the incorporations he proposed would not, as Portland feared, be "misused." At any rate, the incorporation of cities was not to occur for another three decades and was then set in motion by the new liberal idea of colonialism—an idea that, interestingly enough, closely resembled Simcoe's agenda of creating the perfect image of the English constitution in British North America.

## *Markets and Police Towns, Upper Canada*

Another series of laws demonstrates that the powers to establish markets and police were entrusted to the justice of the peace in quarter sessions as opposed to town inhabitants. When the colonies were settled in the aftermath of the American rebellion, Upper and Lower Canada were divided into districts for the administration of justice and for settlement purposes. Each district was administered by quarterly sessions of appointed magistrates who, until the 1840s, retained considerable power in affairs concerning towns and townships. Two of these powers were to establish markets and to appoint police in towns.

The right to establish and regulate markets within towns was conferred upon the justices of the peace of the districts of six towns in Upper Canada. In 1801 a market was established in Kingston by an act of the legislature which also provided for its regulation by justices of the peace.[47] Similar statutes were later passed to establish markets in York (1814), Niagara (1817), Cornwall (1818), Perth (1822), and Amherstburg (1831).[48] In these statutes the power to regulate and to prescribe a fine for breach of regulations was given to the quarter sessions of the district in which the town was located.

The first act to empower the justices of the peace to appoint police was passed in 1816 for Kingston.[49] The second act was passed in 1817 and empowered the justices of the peace to establish and "to regulate the police within the towns of York, Sandwich and Amherstburg."[50] Such acts included the powers "to make, ordain, constitute and publish, such prudential rules and regulations as [the justices of the peace] may deem expedient provided that such rules and regulations shall not be contrary with the laws and statutes of this Province." Another act was passed in 1819 that authorized the justices of the peace to establish and regulate police in Niagara.[51] These five communities were designated "towns having a police established by law," or, more briefly, "police towns."[52]

It is clear that in these early acts regarding markets and police the legislature was careful to retain power through the justices of the peace. The towns were held under centralized control. To put it differently, police towns were considered as polities for the administration of subjects. And these towns did not possess the liberties of incorporated bodies politic.

## *Boards of Police, Upper Canada*

Yet another series of laws passed between 1832 and 1840 established boards of police in nine towns in Upper Canada. With these laws, the institution of the municipal corporation was reintroduced in a quite distinct British North American pattern, a pattern that demonstrated continuing caution by the legislature toward the formation of corporations: only the members of the boards were incorporated, not the town inhabitants. The boards of police also constituted a departure from the policy that placed police towns under the control of justices of the peace. The boards of police consisted of members elected from among and by *qualified* town inhabitants.

The first incorporation of a board of police took place in 1832 in the town of Brockville, and the event amply reflected the new principle of establishing authority in local polities by delegating powers to an elected body.[53] The preamble of the act stated the increase of population as the reason for establishing the corporation. The rights and capacities of a corporation to perpetual succession were conferred on the board, whose main duty was to prevent vice and to preserve good order in the said town.[54] The members of the board of police would be elected. For the purposes of election, the town was divided into two wards, the boundaries of which were indicated. Each ward was to elect two members of the incorporated board. Once elected, the board was to appoint a fifth member. And then a president was to be chosen from within the board.

The qualification to be a member of the board required that the town inhabitant be a freeholder or a householder paying a certain amount of rent per annum for his dwelling. An elite was therefore formed whose obligation was to govern the town. The qualification to be a voter in the election required that the town inhabitant be a male householder, a subject of the king, and in possession of a freehold estate. These qualifications for board membership and voting demonstrate the calculated restrictions that were put upon participation in town politics.

Boards of police appeared in other towns in Upper Canada with almost identical clauses and provisions of incorporation: Hamilton (1833), Cornwall (1834), Port Hope (1834), Prescott (1834), Belleville (1834), Cobourg (1837), Picton (1837), and London (1840).[55] What these incorporated boards of police suggest is that the Upper Canada legislature was cautious in conferring corporate capacities on towns: the boards of police had more duties and obligations than rights and liberties. Or, stated another way, these bodies politic were constituted so as to make them accept the delegated powers of the state; and, by empowering a qualified elite to govern through taxation, these communities also relieved the state of the costs of governance.

## *Beginnings of Modern Municipal Government*

We have seen so far that the attitude of British colonial authorities towards municipal corporations was one of unmistakable scepticism, if not outright animosity. But in the 1830s, partly in response to the local requirements of governance, colonial policy took a new direction with the incorporation of a series of cities in British North America. The first cities to be incorporated after Saint John in 1785 were Quebec (1832), Montreal (1832), Toronto (1834), Halifax (1841), Kingston (1846), and Hamilton (1846). The hiatus between the incorporation of Saint John in 1785 and that of Quebec and Montreal reflected continuing uncertainty about the governance of cities. Until the 1840s the British colonial apparatus had not developed an effective response to the problem of how to govern colonies through towns and cities without allowing these municipal institutions to develop rights and powers.

In this section we will discuss in detail the legislative acts that transformed many British North American towns into modern cities in the 1830s and 1840s. We will also discuss the ideas that the law-making authorities held about the incorporations.

## *Montreal and Quebec, Lower Canada: 1832 and 1840*

Montreal and Quebec were first incorporated by a temporary ordinance in 1832. Interestingly, the colonial authorities, anticipating the rebellions of 1837–38 and already being nervous about the potential emergence of municipal powers, included an expiration date in the ordinance: it was valid for four years after which time, if considered appropriate, it would be renewed. But the Lower Canada legislature, wracked by political differences, refused to renew the incorporation when it expired in 1836.[56] Between 1836 and 1840 both cities were governed by the justices of the peace of their respective counties. Then, in 1840, Quebec and Montreal were incorporated by separate ordinances but with identical clauses.[57] Contrary to the prevailing practices, the preambles to these ordinances made no mention of the earlier ordinances of incorporation. Rather, both ordinances were drafted as if they were the first in both Montreal and Quebec.

As in Saint John, the governor was to appoint the first mayor, who was to hold office for about two years (until 1 December 1842). But in contrast to the situation in Saint John, the governor was also to appoint six aldermen and twelve councilmen, who were to hold office also until 1 December 1842. Montreal and Quebec, then, were still not entrusted with civic elections. Only after 1842 were elections to be held in a manner that was prescribed in the legislation. The property qualifications in Montreal and Quebec for aldermen and councillors, although somewhat reminiscent of those in Saint John, were exceptionally high, as we shall see, when compared with the qualifications in other incorporations during the same period. The aldermen had to own or rent property assessed at £1000, the councilmen had to own or rent property at £500. It is difficult to be precise but this qualification must have been even more restrictive than the one in Saint John, where, according to Acheson's estimate, only 25 per cent of the inhabitants could hold municipal office.[58] These provisions demonstrate that the local authorities devised the ordinances of incorporation so as to limit city politics to an elite group and to maintain considerable power in the hands of the governor.

The similarities between the Saint John charter and Montreal and Quebec ordinances are quite remarkable. But two differences stand out. First, whereas in 1785 the royal governor was reluctant to grant incorporation, in 1840 it was becoming an acceptable practice. Was it acceptable because state policies had become more liberal in conferring "autonomy," or because the state was now confident that it could use cities as instruments of government? The answer involves both explanations: the state was more liberal on the subject of incorporation because it was more confident in its own powers. Secondly, Saint John was incorporated by a royal charter that was drafted and confirmed by the Privy Council in Whitehall; Montreal and Quebec, in contrast, were incorporated through local legislation.

## *Toronto, Upper Canada: 1834*

In 1826, eight years before the incorporation of Toronto, William Lyon Mackenzie, a member of the House of Assembly of Upper Canada, urged that "an act incorporating this city is much wanted for the encouragement of order and regularity."[59] Two years later he asked: "Would it not be of the greatest advantage to our townsfolk if an act for the incorporation of this town (after the most approved principle now in operation in towns in Great Britain) could be passed into a law during the ensuing session of parliament?"[60] The remark concerning Great Britain is significant in that it shows Mackenzie's close interest in legal and political developments immediately before the Reform Act of 1832 and the Municipal Corporations Act of 1835.

The first proposal of incorporation was made in the very year that Mackenzie delivered his speech. When the bill was introduced in the

House of Assembly, however, it faced opposition. A member of the assembly, Francis Collins, argued that "York is too little as yet for a Corporation, commerce and manufactures must grow and attract a more dense and intelligent community, a community independent of, and too powerful for the tools of office, before a Corporation can be with safety established."[61] He added: "Indeed it is almost too ridiculous to talk about turning such a paltry little dirty hole as Little York into a corporate city."[62] A year later Collins noted that, "We have seen enough grinding taxation of corporations in the old country to make us almost tremble at the name—this town is too young to bear the burden."[63] Collins's view, therefore, was that the size of the city is a precondition of incorporation.

Mackenzie also opposed the bill but on different grounds, namely that it created a "close" corporation; the bill provided an "unnatural union of extensive patronage with legislative judicial executive powers in the same body of Individuals, without any check to prevent the natural disposition of man to abuse power for his own advantage," a view of the act that he maintained when it was passed in 1834.[64] In taking this position, Mackenzie displayed a genuinely modern, liberal attitude toward the city as a corporation; he was certainly not against incorporation of the city but he did reject its incorporation on elitist terms. We will later see the full development of this modern conception of the city as a corporation in the context of liberal colonial politics.

On 6 March 1834 the City of Toronto was incorporated.[65] The act noted that, with "the rapid increase of the population, commerce and wealth of the Town of York, a more efficient system of police and municipal government than that now established has become obviously necessary [and] none appears so likely to attain effectively the objects desired as the erection thereof into a City and the incorporation of the inhabitants, and vesting in them the power to elect a Mayor, Aldermen and Common Councilmen." For purposes of elections, the city was divided into five wards. The mayor, aldermen, councilmen, and inhabitants of the city were incorporated as a body politic with capacities of perpetual succession. The property qualifications for aldermen and councilmen were lower than those in Montreal and Quebec but higher than those in Kingston, Hamilton, and Halifax. The aldermen had to own or rent property assessed at £200; the councilmen, property assessed at £150.

## *Kingston, Upper Canada: 1838 and 1846*

Kingston was incorporated in 1838 as a town and was subsequently incorporated as a city in 1846. The 1838 act stated that "the incorporation of the town of Kingston, in consequence of its increase, has become advisable and necessary for the improvement and prosperity of the town."[66] Although the act constituted the town as a body politic and corporate, three aspects of such bodies politic were excluded. First, the corporate capacities did *not* include the right to perpetual succession. This meant that the town could easily be abolished with little legal complication. Secondly, the town was not fully separated from its district in the administration of justice in that some authority was retained by the quarter sessions of the Midland District. Finally, the familiar clause that prescribed the erection and regulation of a workhouse and a house of correction was omitted from the act. Aside from these three aspects, the act constituted the town as a corporation in quite similar terms and conditions as those in the city of Toronto. The property qualifications for aldermen and councilmen were quite low when compared with Toronto's: they had to own or rent property assessed at £60. The property qualification specified for mayor was also very low at £75. Residence qualifications for the mayor was ten years, however, and for aldermen and councilmen it was seven years. For electors, the property qualification was £10 and the residence qualification three months.

The incorporation act of 1846 that erected Kingston into a city included those clauses and provisions of a body politic previously excluded.[67] The act stated that "from the increase in the trade and population of the said Town it is found that the provisions of the said Act are insufficient, and it is expedient for the better protection and management of the local interests of the inhabitants that the said Town should be incorporated into a City." These insufficiencies were remedied by activating the three clauses mentioned above: the city now could have perpetual succession; the mayor could act as a justice of the peace; and the council could establish and regulate a police, and establish and regulate workhouses, houses of correction, and almshouses. Both property and residence qualifications for aldermen and councilmen were reduced. For aldermen, the property qualification was now £40 and the residence requirement four years. For councilmen, the property qualification was lowered to £25 and the residence requirement to three years.

## *Hamilton, Upper Canada: 1833 and 1846*

An interesting feature of Hamilton's early history is that it was first incorporated in 1833 as a board of police, an arrangement that, as discussed earlier, governed some towns in Upper Canada from 1832 to 1840. This system was found insufficient, and after 1840 communities that had been incorporated as boards of police were incorporated as towns, or, in the case of Hamilton, as cities.[68] A number of towns that had been incorporated as boards of police were incorporated as towns in 1846 and 1847 with special acts. With such an act the Cornwall Board of Police was incorporated as the Mayor and Town Council of the Town of Cornwall.[69] This act stated that the Board of Police was no longer adequate for the community's needs, "and it is expedient for the better protection and management of the local interests of the inhabitants that the said Act should be amended." It was added that "such change of the corporate name shall not be construed to make the said Corporation a new Corporation, but merely to continue the former Corporation with another name and with new powers."[70] This special act was repeated for Hamilton (1846), Cobourg (1847), and London (1847), all of which had first been incorporated as boards of police. On the other hand, in 1847 an act was passed which conferred limited corporate powers on those towns that had not yet been incorporated, thereby erecting them into corporate towns.[71]

The Hamilton act provided similar clauses for the constitution of the city as those in Toronto and Kingston. But there were slight differences. The lieutenant governor of Upper Canada was to appoint a police magistrate for Hamilton (who was also to serve as a justice of the peace).[72] The qualifications for aldermen, councilmen, and electors were moderately low. The property qualification for aldermen and councilmen was £40 and the residence requirement two years. The elector had to own or rent property assessed at £5, with a residence requirement of three months.

## *Halifax, Nova Scotia: 1841*

Halifax was founded in 1749 but was largely settled by people who came from New England during and after the American revolution.[73] As in other British North American colonies, imperial policy in Nova Scotia revealed a tension between *de facto* corporate autonomy on the part of towns and the necessity of central control. We have alluded above to a 1770 statute in Nova Scotia where town meetings, which New England colonists were accustomed to, were declared unlawful. Similarly, attempts by a number of colonists settled in Halifax to incorporate the city were consistently resisted by the legislature and the governor-in-council: a petition in 1785 for the incorporation of Halifax as a town was rejected by the executive council as being neither "necessary" nor "expedient."[74] In 1790 another attempt was made by the speaker of the House of Assembly, who drafted an act of incorporation. Yet it, too, was not acted upon by the governor-in-council.[75]

In the 1830s the issue of incorporation resurfaced, undoubtedly owing to the atmosphere of political change in other British North American colonies. There were a number of petitions and counter-petitions for incorporation. On 10 April 1841 Halifax was incorporated as the first modern city in Nova Scotia by an act passed by the legislature.[76] The act of incorporation was similar to those discussed above. The governance of the city was vested in the city council: the constitution of the city council, procedure for elections, qualifications of voters and councilmen, the ward system, an elaborate powers-clause designating fields of regulations and the institution of corporate powers—all resembled the terms in other acts of incorporation in British North America.

There were, however, some differences. One was that the corporation was created for a five-year term, as opposed to perpetuity, which suggests some feeling of experimentation on the part of the legislature.[77] Another was that the appointment of the mayor (which was to be made by elected councilmen) was subject to approval by the governor-in-council.[78] Also, the by-laws of the council were to be approved by the governor-in-council.[79] The qualifications for mayor, aldermen, and councilmen were within the same range as those in Kingston, Toronto, and Hamilton. The property qualification for mayor and aldermen was £50 while the residence requirement was one year. The property qualification for councilmen was £30, with a one-year residence requirement. The property qualification for electors was very high—£20—and the residence requirement was one month.

## *The New Emphasis on Municipal Corporations*

As these specific laws were passed to incorporate towns and cities in the 1830s, there was also a new movement towards rationalizing municipal corporations throughout the colonies. The source of this movement was twofold. First, there was a dramatic shift in England towards new forms of governance, which included municipal corporation as their cornerstone. As mentioned earlier, reforms of 1832 restructured the entire English electoral system and also affected many towns and cities. In 1835 municipal government was again reformed with general legislation, which abolished some municipal corporations and created others. In these reforms, it was clearly stated that governing England would not be possible without adequate local administration of state affairs. The second source of the drive to overhaul municipal government was increasing political unrest, which eventually resulted in the Rebellions of 1837–38. The rapid growth and increasing diversity of the local population, combined with liberal ideas that reached the colonies from abroad, made centralized and autocratic governance more and more difficult and less practical.

So concluded one of the most important reports in the history of British North American colonies: Lord Durham's report of 1839.[80] As John Russell, the secretary of state for colonies, stated in 1839, the bill that was introduced in parliament to unite Upper and Lower Canada embodied "the results of deliberate reflection on the various suggestions contained in the report of the Earl of Durham."[81] The immense influence of the report can be partly attributed to its approach: it clearly rejects the old system of colonialism; arguments are often set against the background of England and the United States. Durham's goal was nothing less than the transformation of the British North American colonies into self-governing societies.

With respect to towns and cities, Durham's report played a critical role in preparing the way for new municipal corporations. The theme that runs through the report was that the municipal corporations were instruments through which the colonies could make a greater contribution to the economic growth of Britain. "In the British colonies," Durham said, there is no "effectual system of municipal government. The great business of the assemblies is, literally, parish business; the making of parish roads and parish bridges."[82] As Lord Durham himself admitted, he was less informed about Upper Canada than Lower Canada. For this reason, but also because Lower Canada posed more political problems, he often isolated the municipal conditions in Lower Canada. His report observed that "Lower Canada remains without municipal institutions of local self-government, which are the foundations of Anglo-Saxon freedom and civilization; nor is their absence compensated by any thing like the centralisation of France."[83] Durham was surprised to find that the territorial institutions of the province did not serve the purposes of governance but were mere judicial and electoral districts and remained "during the present suspension of representative government, useless geographical divisions. There are no hundreds [medieval English institutions] or corresponding sub-divisions of counties."[84] In short, the districts and counties were not territorial institutions with duties, obligations, and perhaps liberties, all of which were considered essential elements of towns; nor were they connected with one another in a system of government and jurisdictional obligations. As for the Eastern Townships of Lower Canada, they were "inhabited entirely by a population British and American in origin; and may be said to be divisions established for surveying, rather than any other purposes. The Eastern townships present a lamentable contrast in the management of all local matters to the bordering state of Vermont, in which the municipal institutions are the most complete, it is said, of any part even of New England."[85]

The conclusion Lord Durham reached was that "the utter want of municipal institutions giving the people any control over their local affairs, may indeed be considered as one of the main causes of the failure of representative government, and of the bad administration of the country."[86] He reasoned that the lack of municipal institutions required the concentration of power; and that was an inefficient way of exercising power and also occasioned the formation of its polar opposite, resistance and rebellion: "The true principle of limiting popular power is that apportionment of it in many different depositories which has been adopted in all the most free and stable states of the Union."[87] To put it another way, Durham believed that diffusion of power was the best protection against popular resistance and rebellion. Hence, "the establishment of municipal institutions for the whole country should be made a part of every colonial constitution; and the prerogative of the Crown should be constantly interposed to check any encroachment on the functions of local bodies, until the people should become alive, as most assuredly they almost immediately would be, to the necessity of protecting their local privileges."[88]

## *Sydenham and a System of Municipal Government*

Upon his appointment as the governor general of British North America in 1839, Lord Sydenham was told by Lord John Russell that "the establishment of Municipal Institutions for the management of local affairs, will be among the most important of the subjects to which your attention will be called."[89] Russell stated that the bill introduced in the British parliament for the union of the Canadas included many suggestions of Lord Durham, among which was the introduction of municipal institutions. And Russell added that "on the importance of such institutions I need not enlarge. Your acquaintance with the system of municipal government in [England] will point out to you that there is no mode in which local affairs can be so properly administered, and that they form, at the same time, the most appropriate means of training the great body of people to the higher branches of legislation."[90] This clear expression of the importance of municipal institutions as a means of both administration and governance is indicative of the influence of Durham's report. The British colonial apparatus had never expressed the need for and use of municipal corporations with such urgency and clarity.

When the Canadas were united under one legislature in 1840, however, the act of union did not include any provisions for municipal corporations.[91] Sydenham was immensely disappointed when he received a copy of the act from Russell.[92] But, at the same time, his disappointment prompted one of the most explicit statements on municipal corporations and governance by a colonial statesman.

Sydenham stated that upon reading the report he had been convinced that municipal institutions must become a part of the colonial constitution.[93] This conviction was reinforced after Sydenham had an opportunity to study conditions in the British North American colonies; he now had no doubt that "the cause of nearly all the difficulty in the government of every one of them is to be found in the absence of any well-organised system of local government."[94] His interpretation of the rebellions from the point of view of the absence of properly constituted authority in towns and cities was without question one of the reasons for the creation of new municipal corporations. Sydenham was aware, of course, that in Upper Canada some municipal incorporations existed at the time. Yet they were by no means adequate and other colonies also needed such institutions. Sydenham believed that, if a successful system was introduced first in the Canadas, New Brunswick and Nova Scotia would soon follow.[95] In a letter to a friend, Sydenham also stated his often-quoted view that "the establishment of Municipal Government by Act of Parliament is as much a part of the intended scheme of Government for the Canadas as the union of two legislatures, and the more important of the two."[96] Sydenham took seriously the importance of municipal corporations. Nevertheless, as we shall now see, the resultant act was quite undeveloped and inadequate to embody *liberal* principles of municipal government.

## *Modern Canadian Municipal Government*

By 1840, then, two processes were at work: growing experience in the incorporation of cities and towns, and a changing attitude towards colonies within the British colonial apparatus which was fuelled by new political and economic conditions in England and by the rebellions in Upper and Lower Canada. British North American colonies had already put into practice some of the principles that were formulated by political economists and administrators in the 1830s and the 1840s. What the new liberalism did was to make some of these practices of incorporation explicit and to give a more solid purpose to them. It was the District Councils Act of 1841 that set out to establish authorities in localities where such did not yet exist.[97] The act stated that the provisions did not affect the established rights, capacities, or powers of the corporations or other authorities of towns and cities within which the board of police might be established.[98] Therefore, the act kept intact existing established power over any such corporate city or town by the justices of the peace of the district within which it was located.

By 1849, on the eve of the Municipal Corporations Act, there were in Upper Canada three incorporated cities (Kingston, Hamilton, and Toronto), six incorporated towns (Cornwall, Bytown, Dundas, Cobourg, London, and Brantford), five incorporated boards of police (Brockville, Port Hope, Prescott, Belleville, and Picton), and twenty-two incorporated district councils. The Municipal Corporations Act was passed on 30 May 1849.[99] Applying to Upper Canada alone rather than to the two Canadas, it established all inhabitants of villages, townships, towns, counties, and cities as a body corporate and politic with certain conditions and endowed them with the essential attributes of a corporation. With respect to Upper Canada's sister colony, an act passed on 29 March 1845 had introduced in Lower Canada a graded system of corporate powers and capacities encompassing townships at the bottom of the pyramid, cities and towns in the middle, and counties at the top.[100] But in 1847 this act was repealed and all parish and township municipalities were abolished and replaced with county municipalities.[101] This act introduced a distinction between rural municipalities (counties and their constituent parishes and townships) and villages, towns, and boroughs. In 1855 the system was again changed by the Lower Canada Municipal and Road Act.[102] This measure, which did not apply to incorporated cities, refined the graded system of corporate capacities by constituting the inhabitants of counties, parishes, townships, towns, and villages as bodies corporate and politic.

Outside the Canadas, Halifax was the only incorporated city in Nova Scotia until 1855. That year the inhabitants of the counties of Annapolis, Yarmouth, King's, and Queen's were incorporated as bodies politic and corporate and were placed under municipal government.[103] Halifax was excluded from the scope of this legislation.[104] The act created county councils which, somewhat like the district councils in the Canadas, were to be composed of elected councilmen from the townships. This measure was followed by two further acts in

1856 which created a municipal system similar to those in Upper and Lower Canada. First, townships were constituted as bodies politic with limited corporate power and liabilities.[105] Each county or district incorporated was under obligation to establish townships.[106] And secondly, the 1855 act was amended so as to apply to all other counties in the province. With these stipulations, corporate local power took root in Nova Scotia as an integral part of the system of governance.

## *Conclusion*

The emergence of the modern municipal corporation in Canadian history is associated with the rise of modern *liberal* governance, a mode of exercising power that relies less on a punitive and negative system of law and more on institutional and enabling law. The centralized and statist policies of the British colonial apparatus between the 1780s and the 1830s had not succeeded in containing the tension between local autonomy and central authority. The rebellions in 1837 and 1838 made this point abundantly and painfully clear to British statesmen and administrators, who, above all, wanted to avoid the catastrophe of another revolution. As a solution, they gradually turned to the modern program of governance which managed to contain the tension between localism and centralization by conferring upon municipal corporations the authority to govern "their own affairs" by specifying the domains in which the corporations must establish institutions, and by setting basic parameters and criteria for municipal government. In other words, modern municipal law forged an effective balance between municipal autonomy and central authority by constituting the modern corporation as an apparatus of governance. The modern municipal corporation became an apparatus of governance inasmuch as it was encouraged and empowered to manage local affairs.

Municipal government was constituted through local elections and on the basis of specified property and residence qualifications. The latter gave legislatures considerable power to influence the composition of local councils beyond the direct appointment of the first council of a newly incorporated municipality. We have seen how the property qualifications for mayor, aldermen, councilmen, and their electors were adjusted carefully from one city to another to influence the composition of the governing body. Another set of legal components had to do with the requisite qualifications in British North America for voters and electoral candidates. Although the property qualifications were moderately low in comparison with those in Britain under the municipal franchise of 1835, the practice itself reveals that not everybody was thought fit to participate in elections. By adjusting the property qualifications the legislature could determine the level of participation in the municipal government. The latter was essentially conceived as an instrument to serve and further the interests of the property class, and it would be financed by taxes levied on the property of those who were served by it.

The governing body of an incorporated city could sell and buy property, appear before a court, and pass by-laws to regulate, directly or indirectly, the conduct of the people. It exercised these powers as the executive of the corporation, authorized by a superior legislature ("from above") and by the qualified people ("from below"). Accordingly, the source of the governing body's authority was twofold. First, it was the legislature that created the modern municipal government as a corporation and that empowered its governing body. And, secondly, it was the qualified inhabitants who elected the members of the governing body. But voters could authorize the governing body to exercise *only* those powers that were prescribed by the legislature. The modernity of Canadian municipal government as a corporation, then, consists of rules specified by the provincial legislatures within which a governing body elected by eligible voters exercises its rights and fulfils its governmental obligations. Municipal government in British North America was not autonomous in the sense that citizens were unable to make decisions about the conditions of their municipality independent from state or other external prerogatives. On the contrary, many obligations of citizens were specified by the provincial legislature. The rights granted to corporations were by no means unconditional or unspecified; powers were always specified and qualified with the clear understanding that, if the governing body went beyond the powers thus granted, the corporation could be punished. To conclude, beneath the arrival of "democracy" and "responsible government" in British North American colonies in the 1840s, tirelessly announced by liberal historians, there emerged a tight network of institutions for discipline, governance, and policing, the core of which was the modern municipal government as a corporation.

The conclusions of this chapter on the origins of Canadian municipal government cast considerable doubt on interpretations that would have us believe that by the 1840s a democratic, autonomous municipal government had emerged. We have seen that there are dramatic differences between what liberal statesmen such as Durham and Sydenham proposed in their writings and the actual legislation and practices that followed. Although liberal writers give the impression that Canadian municipal government was conceived as somehow autonomous and democratic, actual legislation such as the Baldwin Act embodied a restrictive, calculating, and centralized mode of municipal government. Similarly, this chapter seriously questions the notion that democratic municipal government suddenly emerged in the 1840s. Rather, there was considerable continuity from the 1780s to the 1840s, a period when Canadian municipal government as an apparatus of governance was gradually but fitfully invented and improved. The Canadian municipal government that emerged in the 1850s embodied theories and practices that had first arisen between the 1780s and the 1840s.

If these are the conclusions we can draw from the birth of the modern Canadian municipal government, what comparisons and contrasts can we make with regard to corporations in England and America that would shed some light on the modernity of the municipal corporation in general? British North American political and legal conditions, although circumscribed within broader English and American conditions, still diverged from them and led to new departures. Perhaps the most striking and influential were the general municipal corporations acts. At the time these acts were passed, neither England nor any of the states in the American republic possessed similar counterparts. In England, the Municipal Corporations Act of 1835 addressed the problems of "close" corporations and industrial cities. Only in 1882 were the remaining boroughs constituted as modern municipal corporations, and it was not until 1888 and 1894 that England instituted a municipal system similar to that of British North America in the 1840s. Similarly, in the early American republic all incorporations were accomplished by special acts of state legislatures and it was not before the late nineteenth century that general acts were passed. Furthermore, legal and political thought in the American republic was mostly preoccupied with the relations between the commercial oligarchies that controlled the cities and the landed gentry that dominated the colonial legislatures.

By contrast, the problems of "close" corporations and of *de facto* corporations did not exist in British North America. From the very beginning, carefully calculated statist policies succeeded in circumventing autonomous municipal government. Therefore, the practice of establishing a general municipal system was an original synthesis of two contemporary developments. First, of course, the developments in English corporate law constituted a precedent. And, secondly, the early American legal practice that incorporated localities such as villages, counties, and townships with special-act charters also constituted a model.[107] The modernity of the municipal corporation was thus first fully crystallized in British North America, where the municipal corporation became an apparatus of governance as early as the 1840s. More research on colonial societies is needed to explore the origins of the city as a modern corporation.[108]

## Notes

1. For an overview of this settlement-scheme see Don W. Thomson, *Men and Meridians: The History of Surveying and Mapping in Canada* (Ottawa: Department of Mines and Technical Surveys, 1966), and L.M. Sebert, "The Land Surveys of Ontario, 1750–1980," *Cartographica*, vol. 17 (1980), 65–106.
2. The size of townships was envisaged as about 14 kilometres wide and varying in depth from 14 to 19 kilometres. See David J. Wood, "Grand Design on the Fringes of Empire: New Towns for British North America," *Canadian Geographer*, vol. 26 (1982), 243–55.
3. British North America Act, 1867, section 92; Constitution Act, 1982. See also Jacques L'Heureux, "Municipalities and the Division of Powers," in *Intergovernmental Relations*, Royal Commission on the Economic Union and Development Prospects for Canada, Ivan

Bernier, A. Cairns, and D.C. Smith, eds., vol. 63 (Toronto: University of Toronto Press, 1985).

4. Before we proceed farther, a word on terminology is in order. The term "municipal government" was introduced into the Anglo-American legal systems only in the 1830s. Before then the act of establishing a place as a corporation was often equated with the creation of a city. According to the *Oxford English Dictionary*, prior to the nineteenth century the term "municipal" was not in common use, and when used it meant, very interestingly, something pertaining to the internal affairs of a state. This was the case both in England after the fifteenth century and in colonial America. Therefore, although the term "corporation" appears in European law as early as the twelfth century, its designation as a municipal corporation is a modern, nineteenth-century phenomenon. Nevertheless, we will use the term "municipal corporation" to denote all classes of corporations including cities, towns, boroughs, counties, and urban villages throughout the period discussed in this chapter.
5. See Engin F. Isin, *Cities without Citizens: Modernity of the City as a Corporation* (Montreal: Black Rose Books, 1992), ch. 2.
6. Max Weber, *Die Stadt*, written c.1911–13, posthumously published 1921; English translation by Don Martindale and Gertrud Neuwirth (New York: Free Press, 1958); Henri Pirenne, *Medieval Cities* (Princeton, N.J.: Princeton University Press, 1925).
7. Weber stated this very clearly in his *General Economic History:* "In the middle ages, the distinguishing characteristic of [a city] was the possession of its own law and court and an autonomous administration of whatever extent. The citizen of the middle ages was a citizen because and insofar as he came under this law and participated in the choice of administrative officials." Quoted in Derek Heater, *Citizenship: The Civic Ideal in World History, Politics, and Education* (London: Longman, 1990), 21.
8. Pirenne, *Medieval Cities*, 295.
9. A charter is a document recording and providing proof of a juridical act, such as a deed, contract, constitution, privilege, or mandate. The name comes from the Latin *c(h)arta* or *c(h)artula,* originally meaning a sheet of papyrus, with something written on the papyrus, parchment, or paper (a document, letter, or booklet). The charter is associated with the emergence of legal systems in Western Europe in the late eleventh and twelfth centuries. Most charters (those issued by authorities such as popes, emperors, kings, and rulers) were produced in the author's chancery, the agency responsible for composing and

copying the written text. A charter had two main parts: protocol and text. The first included at the beginning the names and titles of the author (whose legal disposition was being recorded) and the recipient (in whose favour the charter was issued), a greeting, and possibly an invocation, and at the end it might include subscriptions of the author, witnesses, chancery officials, and scribes, along with the dating, a prayer, a seal, and other signs of validation. The text usually had a notification and exposition, and possibly a preamble preceding the disposition which might itself be followed by various concluding clauses. For more details see *Dictionary of Middle Ages*, 13 vols, Joseph R. Strayer, ed. (New York: Scribner, 1982–89).

10. Mumford, *The City in History: Its Origins, Its Transformation, and Its Prospects* (London: Harcourt Brace Jovanovich, 1961), 302.
11. See Isin, *Cities without Citizens*, ch. 2.
12. See an important chapter by Roberto M. Unger, "Law and Modernity," in his *Law in Modern Society: Toward a Criticism of Social Theory* (New York: Free Press, 1976).
13. Gordon T. Stewart, *The Origins of Canadian Politics: A Comparative Approach* (Vancouver: University of British Columbia Press, 1986), 20.
14. See Instructions to James Governor Murray, 7 December 1763, Archives of Ontario *Third Report* (1905), article 51.
15. Stewart, *Origins of Canadian Politics,* 21.
16. The best and the most comprehensive account of this period is by Helen T. Manning, *British Colonial Government after the American Revolution, 1782–1820* (New Haven, Conn.: Yale University Press, 1933). See also John W. Cell, British *Colonial Administration in the Mid-Nineteenth Century: The Policy-Making Process* (New Haven: Yale University Press, 1970), which contains a brief discussion of the organization of the Colonial Office in the 1800s. Klaus Knorr, *British Colonial Theories, 1570–1850* (Toronto: University of Toronto Press, 1944), contains a discussion of the prevalent ideas in this period.
17. Phillip A. Buckner, *The Transition to Responsible Government: British Policy in British North America, 1815–1850* (Westport, Conn.: Greenwood Press, 1985), 51.
18. See Stewart, *Origins of Canadian Politics*, ch. 1.
19. John George Bourinot, *Local Government in Canada: An Historical Study* (Baltimore: John Hopkins University Press, 1887), 26.
20. Bourinot said in *Local Government*: "We have abundant evidence that at this time the authorities viewed with disfavour any attempt to establish a system of town government similar to that so long in operation in New England. On the 14th of April 1770, the Governor and Council

passed a resolution that 'the proceedings of the people in calling town-meetings for discussing questions relative to law and government and such other purposes, are contrary to law, and if persisted in, it is ordered that the parties be prosecuted by the attorney-general'" (44).

21. Adam Shortt, "The Beginning of Municipal Government in Ontario," *Transactions of the Canadian Institute*, vol. 7, (1902), 410.
22. James H. Aitchison, "The Development of Local Government, 1783–1850" (PhD thesis, University of Toronto, 1953), 188. Also, see C.F.J. Whebell, "Robert Baldwin and Decentralization, 1841–1849," and G.T. Glazebrook, "The Origins of Local Government," in *Aspects of Nineteenth Century Ontario*, F.H. Armstrong *et al.*, eds. (Toronto: University of Toronto Press, 1974).
23. D.W. Smith to John Askin, 2 October 1792, in *The Correspondence of Lieut. Governor John Graves Simcoe . . .* [hereafter *Simcoe Papers*], 5 vols., E.A. Cruikshank, ed. (Toronto: Ontario Historical Society 1923–31). vol. 1: 231.
24. Chief Justice William Smith to Dorchester, 5 February 1790, *Statutes, Treaties and Documents of the Canadian Constitution, 1713–1929*, P.M. Kennedy, ed. (Oxford: Oxford University Press, 1930), 290.
25. Shortt, "The Beginning of Municipal Government," 422.
26. *Canada's First City: The Charter of 1785 and Common Council Proceedings under Mayor G.G. Ludlow, 1785–1795* (Saint John, New Brunswick, 1962), 3–46.
27. *First Report of the Commission on Municipal Institutions*, Ontario Legislative Assembly, *Sessional Papers*, no. 42 (1888) 26.
28. *Canada's First City*, 3.
29. *Canada's First City*, 3.
30. The letter is transcribed in ibid., 50.
31. Ibid.
32. Ibid., 4–5.
33. T.W. Acheson, *Saint John* (Toronto: University of Toronto Press, 1985), 32.
34. *Canada's First City*, 45.
35. Shortt, "The Beginning of Municipal Government," 409; George M. Betts, "Municipal Government and Politics," in *To Preserve and Defend: Essays on the Nineteenth-Century Kingston*, G.J.J. Tulchinsky, ed. (Montreal: McGill-Queen's University Press, 1976); T.B. Akins, *History of Halifax City* (Halifax: Nova Scotia Historical Society, 1895).
36. "An act to Provide for the Nomination and Appointment of Parish and Town Officers within this Province," *Statutes of Upper Canada*, 9 July 1793, 33 George III, c.2.

37. Simcoe to Dundas, quoted in Aitchison, *Development of Local Government*, 190.
38. Simcoe to Dundas, 16 September 1793, *Simcoe Papers*, vol. 2: 54.
39. Aitchison, *Development of Local Government*, 189.
40. 33 George III, c.2, clause vii.
41. 46 George III, c.3 (1806); 48 George III c.5 (1808).
42. Simcoe to Portland, 21 December 1794, W.P.M. Kennedy, *Statutes*, 215–16 .
43. Ibid., 215.
44. Ibid., 217.
45. Ibid.
46. William Osgood to Simcoe, 30 January 1795 ("secret and most confidential"), quoted in Aitchison, *Development of Local Government*, 548 (emphasis added).
47. *Statutes of Upper Canada*, 41 George III, c.3,
48. *Statutes of Upper Canada*, "An Act to Empower the Commissioners of the Peace for the Home District, in Their Court of General Quarter Sessions Assembled, to Establish and Regulate a Market in and for the Town of York," 14 March 1814, 54 George III, c.15; "An Act to Establish a Market in the Town of Niagara, in the Niagara District," 57 George III, c.4.
49. *Statutes of Upper Canada*, 56 George III, c.33.
50. *Statutes of Upper Canada*, "An Act to Establish a Police in the Towns of York, Sandwich and Amherstburg," 7 April 1871, 57 George III, c.2.
51. *Statutes of Upper Canada*, "An Act for Establishing a Police in the Town of Niagara, in the District of Niagara, and for Other Purposes therein Mentioned," 12 July 1819, 59 George III, c.5.
52. Aitchison, *Development of Local Government*, 553.
53. *Statutes of Upper Canada*, "An Act to Establish a Police in the Town of Brockville, in the District of Johnstown," 28 January 1832, 2 William IV, c.17. See also Canada (Upper Canada, 1791–1840) House of Assembly, *Report of the Committee of Conference on Brockville Police* Bill (York: King's Printer, 1832).
54. 2 William IV, c.17, clause xviii.
55. *Statutes of Upper Canada*, "An Act to Define the Limits of the Town of Hamilton, in the District of Gore, and to Establish a Police and Public Market therein," 13 February 1833, 3 William IV, c.16; "An Act to Incorporate the Village of Prescott, and to Establish an Elective Police therein," 6 March 1834, 4 William, c.27; "An Act to Establish a Police in the Town of Cornwall, in the Eastern District," 4 William

IV, c.25; "An Act to Define the Limits of the Town of Port Hope, and to Establish a Police therein," 4 William, c.26; "An Act to Establish a Board of Police in the Town of Belleville," 6 March 1834, 4 William IV, c.24; "An Act to Establish a Police in the Town of Cobourg, and to Define the Limits of the Said Town," 4 March 1837, 7 William IV, c.42; "An Act to Incorporate the Villages of Hallowell and Picton, by the Name of the Town of Picton, and Establish a Police therein," 4 March 1837, 7 William IV, c.44; "An Act to Define the Limits of the Town of London, in the District of London, and to Establish a Board of Police Therein," 10 February 1840, 3 Victoria, c.31.

56. Ontario, Royal Commission on Municipal Institutions, *First Report; Sessional Papers,* no. 42 (1888), 25.
57. *Lower Canada Ordinances,* "An Ordinance to Incorporate the City and Town of Quebec," 3 & 4 Victoria, c.35 (1840); "An Ordinance to Incorporate the City and Town of Montreal," 3 & 4 Victoria, c.36 (1840).
58. Acheson, *Saint John,* ch. 2.
59. *Colonial Advocate* (York), 30 March 1826; see also Edith G. Firth, *The Town of York, 1815–1834: A Further Collection of Documents of Early Toronto* (Toronto: University of Toronto Press, 1966), 270.
60. *Colonial Advocate,* 18 December 1828; Firth, *Town of York,* 278.
61. *Canadian Freeman* (York), 1 January 1829; Firth, "Introduction," *Town of York,* lxxiii–lxxiv.
62. *Canadian Freeman,* 1 January 1829; Firth, *Town of York,* 280.
63. *Canadian Freeman,* 11 November 1830; Firth, *Town of York,* 284.
64. *Colonial Advocate,* 20 March 1834; Firth, *Town of York,* 300.
65. "An Act to Extend the Limits of the Town of York; to Erect the Said Town into a City; and to Incorporate It under the Name of the City of Toronto," 6 March 1834, 4 William IV, c.23.
66. *Statutes of Upper Canada,* "An Act to Incorporate the Town of Kingston, under the Name of the Mayor and Common Council of the Town of Kingston," 6 March 1838, 6 Victoria, c.27.
67. *Statutes of The Province of Canada,* "An Act to Incorporate the Town of Kingston as a City," 18 May 1846, 9 Victoria, c.75.
68. *Statutes of the Province of Canada,* "An Act to Alter and Amend the Act Incorporating the Town of Hamilton, and to Erect the Same into a City," 9 June 1846, 9 Victoria, c.73.
69. *Statutes of the Province of Canada,* "An Act to Amend the Act of Incorporation of the Town of Cornwall, and to Establish a Town Council therein, in Lieu of a Board of Police," 9 June 1846, 9 Victoria, c.72.

70. 9 Victoria, c.72, clause ii.
71. "An Act to Confer Limited Corporate Powers on the Towns and Villages of Canada West, Not Specially Incorporated," *Statutes of Canada*, July 28, 1847, 10 & 11 Victoria, c. 42.
72. 9 Victoria, c.73, clause xlii.
73. Akins, *Halifax.*
74. D.J.H. Higgins, *Local and Urban Politics in Canada* (Toronto: Gage, 1986), 37.
75. Akins, *Halifax*, 88; Higgins, *Urban Politics*, 37.
76. *Nova Scotia Statutes*, "An Act to Incorporate the Town of Halifax," 4 Victoria, c.55.
77. 4 Victoria, c.55, clause lxxxiv.
78. 4 Victoria, c.55, clause lvii.
79. 4 Victoria, c.55, clause lii.
80. See Ged Martin, *The Durham Report and British Policy: A Critical Essay* (Cambridge: Cambridge University Press. 1972). For a close reading of the text of the report see Janet Ajzenstat, *The Political Thought of Lord Durham* (Montreal: McGill-Queen's University Press, 1988).
81. Russell to Sydenham, 7 September 1839, Kennedy, *Statutes*, 516.
82. *Report on the Affairs of British North America*, 2 vols., Charles Lucas, ed. (Oxford: U.K.: Claredon Press, 1912), 2: 92.
83. Ibid., 98–99.
84. Ibid., 114.
85. Ibid.
86. Ibid., 113.
87. Ibid., 287.
88. Ibid.
89. Russell to Sydenham, 7 September 1839, Kennedy, *Statutes*, 519.
90. Ibid.
91. *Statutes of Canada*, "An Act to Re-unite the Provinces of Upper and Lower Canada, and for the Government of Canada," 3 & 4, Victoria, c.35.
92. Sydenham to Russell, 16 September 1840, Kennedy, *Statutes*, 551–4.
93. Ibid.
94. Ibid.
95. Ibid.
96. Sydenham to a friend, 1840, Kennedy, *Statutes*, 555.
97. *Statutes of the Province of Canada*, "An Act to Provide for the Better Internal Government of That Part of This Province Which Formerly Constituted the Province of Upper Canada, by the Establishment of

Local and Municipal Authorities therein," 27 August 1841, 4 & 5 Victoria, c.10.

98. 4 & 5 Victoria, c.10, clause lxii.
99. *Statutes of the Province of Canada*, "An Act to Provide, by One General Law, for the Erection of Municipal Corporations, and the Establishment of Regulations of Police, in and for the Several Counties, Cities, Towns, Townships and Villages in Upper Canada," 30 May 1849, 12 Victoria, c.81.
100. *Statutes of the Province of Canada*, "An Act to Repeal Certain Ordinances therein Mentioned, and to Make Better Provision for the Establishment of Local and Municipal Authorities in Lower Canada," 29 March 1845, 8 Victoria, c.40.
101. *Statutes of the Province of Canada*, "An Act to Make Better Provision for the Establishment of Municipal Authorities in Lower Canada," 28 July 1847, 10 & 11 Victoria, c.7.
102. *Statutes of the Province of Canada*, "Lower Canada Municipal and Road Act," 30 May 1855, 18 Victoria,, c.100.
103. *Statutes of Nova Scotia*, "An Act for the Municipal Government of Counties," 18 Victoria, c.49, 1855.
104. 18 Victoria, c.49, clause lxxxix.
105. *Statutes of Nova Scotia*, "An Act for the Municipal Government of Townships," 19 Victoria, c.11, 1856.
106. 19 Victoria, c.11, clause i.
107. Ernest Griffith and C. Adrian, *A History of American City Government: The Formation of Traditions, 1775–1870* (Washington: University Press of America), 34–9.
108. See, for an example of comparative research in this field, David Hamer, *New Towns in the New World: Images and Perceptions of the Nineteenth-Century Urban Frontier* (New York: Columbia University Press, 1990).

## *Selected Sources*

Aitchison, J.H. "The Municipal Corporation Act of 1849," *Canadian Historical Review*, vol. 30 (1949), 107-22.

Brittain, Horace Leslie. *Local Government in Canada* (Toronto: Ryerson Press, 1951).

Durham, John Lambton. *Report on the Affairs of British North America,* 3 vols., Charles Lucas, ed. (Oxford, U.K.: Clarendon Press, 1912).

Isin, Engin F. *Cities without Citizens: Modernity of the City as a Corporation* (Montreal: Black Rose Books, 1992).

Kitchen, Harry and L. Melville. "Local Government and Canadian Federalism," Royal Commission on the Economic Union and Development Prospects for Canada, vol. 63 *(Intergovernmental Relations),* Ivan Bernier, A. Cairns, and D.C. Smith, eds. (Toronto: University of Toronto Press, 1985).

L'Heureux, Jacques. "Municipalities and the Division of Powers," Royal Commission on the Economic Union and Development Prospects for Canada, vol. 63 *(Intergovernmental Relations),* Ivan Bernier, A. Cairns, and D.C. Smith, eds. (Toronto: University of Toronto Press, 1985).

Martin, Ged. *The Durham Report and British Policy: A Critical Essay* (Cambridge, U.K.: Cambridge University Press, 1972).

Stewart, Gordon T. *The Origins of Canadian Politics: A Comparative Approach* (Vancouver: University of British Columbia Press, 1986).

Taylor, John H. "Urban Autonomy in Canada: Its Evolution and Decline," in *The Canadian City: Essays in Urban and Social History,* G.A. Stelter and Alan F.J. Artibise, eds. (Ottawa: Carleton University Press, 1984).

Williams, John C. "The Invention of the Municipal Corporation: A Case Study in Legal Change," *American University Law Review,* vol. 34 (1985), 369-438.

# 4

## *Politics Where We Live: Women and Cities*[1]

Linda Trimble

> Interviewer: Why did you run for mayor?
> Cynthia Hill, mayor, Inuvik, Northwest Territories: "They shot my dog."
> Elsie Wayne, mayor, Saint John, New Brunswick: "The council was corrupt. I got flooded out from lousy town planning."
> Pat McMahon, mayor, Yellowknife, Northwest Territories: "Council wanted to build an apartment building on our ball field."[2]

WHAT COMES TO MIND when we hear the words "women and the politics of equality"? Most people think about matters that are generally labelled "women's issues" and seen as the responsibility of the federal and provincial governments, matters such as pay equity, affirmative action, abortion, sexual assault, and child care. But other issues are involved in "women and the politics of equality." Recreational facilities for children, affordable housing, the safety of the streets at night, community services for those in need, public transportation—such issues and others like them preoccupy women and fall squarely within the jurisdiction of municipal governments. For instance, city councils plan transportation routes, set bus rates, provide lighting on city streets, and write the zoning laws which regulate the type of housing that is built in a given area. Along with community groups, city councils also decide whether or not to support low-income housing projects, food banks, after-school programs, shelters for the homeless and for battered women and children, and rape-crisis centres. The manner in which these various issues are handled helps to determine how, and often where, we live.

Given the importance of "politics where we live," it should not be surprising that women have been extremely active at the municipal level of government. This chapter presents data on women's participation in elected offices at the city level and demonstrates that women are represented in city governments in greater numbers than in provincial, territorial, and federal governments. The chapter also challenges two commonplace explanations for women's higher levels of representation at the municipal level. The first explanation holds that, because municipal politics are less competitive and important than provincial or national politics, the city electoral game is more "open" to women candidates.[3] The second explanation is based on gender roles; it contends that the roles associated with elected office at the city level are more congruent with women's responsibilities and interests.[4] Both these explanations are based on incorrect and unflattering assumptions about the nature of politics in general, city politics in particular, and women's participation in the political process.

## *Women As City Office Holders*

The election of women to public office in more than token numbers is a relatively recent phenomenon. Janine Brodie's study of female candidates for municipal, provincial, and federal office between 1945 and 1975 identified only 1003 candidates, almost half of whom contested office between 1971 and 1975.[5] Between 1921 and 1967, women comprised (on average) 2.4 per cent of the candidates for federal office and won 0.8 per cent of the seats in parliament; the 10 per cent mark was not passed until the 1988 federal election, when women won thirty-nine seats (13.2 per cent of the total).[6] As Chantal Maillé observes, the election of women in significant numbers to parliament, provincial and territorial legislatures, and municipal councils was not evident until the 1980s.[7] It is still rare for women to comprise more than a quarter of the elected representatives in any political institution.

Available data on women and municipal politics is relatively recent and incomplete. However, three observations can be made. First, the representation of women in city governments, along with their representation at the provincial and federal levels, surged over the course of the 1980s and early 1990s. Donald J. Higgins found that in 1984 women held only 15 per cent of council seats in major Canadian municipalities (fifty-six cities altogether).[8] As Table 1 indicates, however, by 1993 women held 24 per cent of the council seats in eighty-eight Canadian cities, an increase of 8 per cent. While Higgins discovered that seven Canadian cities had elected no women, 1993 data show that only three municipalities (Cambridge and Kitchener, Ontario, and Matsqui, British Columbia) have no women on council.

Nine years ago, women held 25 per cent of council seats in only eleven of fifty-six cities (19.6 per cent). Yet, as of December 1993, women constituted one-quarter or more of the city councillors in slightly more than half of the cities (forty-five of the eighty-eight cities, or 51 per cent). Further, as of 1993, women have equal representation in four cities and are in the majority in two cities. In Delta, British Columbia, women comprise 57 per cent of council members (one of these women holds the office of mayor), and in Richmond Hill, Ontario, the number is 66 per cent. Finally, Higgins found only seven female mayors in fifty-six cities (12.5 per cent); my research discovered that the number had increased by 8 per cent (eighteen female mayors in eighty-eight cities, or 20 per cent).

*Table 1*
*Representation of women on city councils in Canada (from lowest to highest percentage of women)*†

| *City (* = female) mayor)* | *Date of most recent election* | *Number of councillors* | *Number of women councillors* | *Percentage women on council* |
|---|---|---|---|---|
| * Cambridge, ON | 1991 | 10 | 0 | 0.0 |
| Kitchener, ON | 1991 | 10 | 0 | 0.0 |
| Matsqui, BC | 1993 | 6 | 0 | 0.0 |
| Dartmouth, NS | 1991 | 14 | 1 | 7.1 |

† Calculation of number of councillors and number of women on council does not include the mayor.

*Table 1 – (continued)*

| *City (* = female) mayor)* | *Date of most recent election* | *Number of councillors* | *Number of women councillors* | *Percentage women on council* |
|---|---|---|---|---|
| * Kingston, ON | 1991 | 14 | 1 | 7.1 |
| * Sainte-Foy, PQ | 1993 | 12 | 1 | 8.3 |
| Charlesbourg, PQ | 1992 | 12 | 1 | 8.3 |
| Chicoutimi, PQ | 1993 | 12 | 1 | 8.3 |
| Fredericton, NB | 1993 | 12 | 1 | 8.3 |
| St-Leonard, PQ | 1990 | 12 | 1 | 8.3 |
| Sault Ste Marie, ON | 1991 | 12 | 1 | 8.3 |
| Trois-Rivières, PQ | 1990 | 12 | 1 | 8.3 |
| Brandon, MB | 1992 | 10 | 1 | 10.0 |
| Brantford, ON | 1991 | 10 | 1 | 10.0 |
| East York, ON | 1991 | 9 | 1 | 11.1 |
| St Catharines, ON | 1991 | 18 | 2 | 11.1 |
| Burlington, ON | 1991 | 16 | 2 | 12.5 |
| Hamilton, ON | 1991 | 16 | 2 | 12.5 |
| * Red Deer, AB | 1992 | 8 | 1 | 12.5 |
| Sarnia-Clearwater, ON | 1991 | 8 | 1 | 12.5 |
| * Vaughan, ON | 1991 | 8 | 1 | 12.5 |
| St-Laurent, PQ | 1990 | 14 | 2 | 14.3 |
| Whitby, ON | 1991 | 7 | 1 | 14.3 |
| Coquitlam, BC | 1993 | 6 | 1 | 16.6 |
| * Halifax, NS | 1991 | 12 | 2 | 16.6 |
| LaSalle, PQ | 1991 | 12 | 2 | 16.6 |
| Markham, ON | 1991 | 12 | 2 | 16.6 |
| Montréal-Nord, PQ | 1990 | 12 | 2 | 16.6 |
| Nepean, ON | 1991 | 6 | 1 | 16.6 |
| * Oakville, ON | 1991 | 12 | 2 | 16.6 |
| Sherbrooke, PQ | 1990 | 12 | 2 | 16.6 |
| Thunder Bay, ON | 1991 | 12 | 2 | 16.6 |
| Charlottetown, PEI | 1992 | 10 | 2 | 20.0 |
| Moncton, NB | 1992 | 10 | 2 | 20.0 |
| North Bay, ON | 1991 | 10 | 2 | 20.0 |
| Peterborough, ON | 1991 | 10 | 2 | 20.0 |
| Regina, SK | 1991 | 10 | 2 | 20.0 |
| * Saint John, NB | 1992 | 10 | 2 | 20.0 |
| St John's, NF | 1993 | 10 | 2 | 20.0 |
| * Winnipeg, MB | 1992 | 15 | 3 | 20.0 |

*Table 1 – (continued)*

| *City (* = female) mayor)* | *Date of most recent election* | *Number of councillors* | *Number of women councillors* | *Percentage women on council* |
|---|---|---|---|---|
| Laval, PQ | 1993 | 24 | 5 | 20.8 |
| Jonquière, PQ | 1991 | 14 | 3 | 21.4 |
| Sudbury, ON | 1991 | 9 | 2 | 22.2 |
| Guelph, ON | 1991 | 12 | 3 | 25.0 |
| Hull, PQ | 1991 | 12 | 3 | 25.0 |
| Kelowna, BC | 1993 | 8 | 2 | 25.0 |
| Lethbridge, AB | 1992 | 8 | 2 | 25.0 |
| Longueuil, PQ | 1990 | 20 | 5 | 25.0 |
| Quebec, PQ | 1993 | 20 | 5 | 25.0 |
| Saanich, BC | 1993 | 8 | 2 | 25.0 |
| Scarborough, ON | 1991 | 20 | 5 | 25.0 |
| Sydney, NS | 1991 | 12 | 3 | 25.0 |
| * Ottawa, ON | 1991 | 15 | 4 | 26.6 |
| Ajax, ON | 1991 | 7 | 2 | 28.6 |
| Beauport, PQ | 1992 | 14 | 4 | 28.6 |
| * Toronto, ON | 1991 | 24 | 7 | 29.2 |
| * Barrie, ON | 1991 | 10 | 3 | 30.0 |
| Saskatoon, SK | 1991 | 10 | 3 | 30.0 |
| Waterloo, ON | 1991 | 10 | 3 | 30.0 |
| Windsor, ON | 1991 | 10 | 3 | 30.0 |
| York, ON | 1991 | 10 | 3 | 30.0 |
| Etobicoke, ON | 1991 | 16 | 5 | 31.3 |
| Montreal, PQ | 1990 | 50 | 16 | 32.0 |
| Corner Brook, NF | 1993 | 6 | 2 | 33.3 |
| * Edmonton, AB | 1992 | 12 | 4 | 33.3 |
| * Mississauga, ON | 1991 | 9 | 3 | 33.3 |
| Moose Jaw, SK | 1991 | 6 | 2 | 33.3 |
| Niagara Falls, ON | 1991 | 15 | 5 | 33.3 |
| North Vancouver, BC | 1993 | 6 | 2 | 33.3 |
| North York, ON | 1991 | 21 | 7 | 33.3 |
| Whitehorse, YT | 1991 | 6 | 2 | 33.3 |
| * Yellowknife, NT | 1991 | 6 | 2 | 33.3 |
| Calgary, AB | 1992 | 14 | 5 | 35.7 |
| Brampton, ON | 1991 | 16 | 6 | 37.5 |
| * Gloucester, ON | 1991 | 8 | 3 | 37.5 |

*Table 1 – (continued)*

| *City (* = female) mayor)* | *Date of most recent election* | *Number of councillors* | *Number of women councillors* | *Percentage women on council* |
|---|---|---|---|---|
| Kamloops, BC | 1993 | 8 | 3 | 37.5 |
| Prince Albert, SK | 1991 | 8 | 3 | 37.5 |
| Prince George, BC | 1993 | 8 | 3 | 37.5 |
| Richmond, BC | 1993 | 8 | 3 | 37.5 |
| London, ON | 1991 | 18 | 7 | 38.9 |
| Verdun, PQ | 1993 | 13 | 5 | 38.5 |
| Gatineau, PQ | 1991 | 12 | 5 | 41.6 |
| * Delta, BC | 1993 | 6 | 3 | 50.0 |
| Langley, BC | 1993 | 6 | 3 | 50.0 |
| Surrey, BC | 1993 | 8 | 4 | 50.0 |
| Vancouver, BC | 1993 | 10 | 5 | 50.0 |
| Victoria, BC | 1993 | 8 | 4 | 50.0 |
| * Richmond Hill, ON | 1991 | 8 | 5 | 62.5 |
| Total | | 1032 | 246 | 23.8 |

Sources: *Canadian Almanac and Directory, 1992* and telephone correspondence with various city halls.

The second observation to be made about women's election to city governments is that the representation of women varies by region and city size. As Table 2 indicates, the representation of women in major and capital cities is, in many cases, significantly higher than the Canadian average of 24 per cent. Women comprise more than a quarter of the councillors (including the mayor) in twelve of the eighteen large or capital cities. As well, seven of the eighteen mayors in major and capital cities are women (39 per cent). Since several of Canada's capital cities are relatively small (Charlottetown, for example), the representation of women on council in cities with a population of 250 000 or more was calculated. Eighty-three of the 278 elected representative in these fourteen cities[9] are women (30 per cent). As well, five of the mayors in Canada's fourteen largest cities are women (35.7 per cent).

Maillé reports that women are better represented in Quebec's larger cities. As of March 1993, women comprised 18 per cent of

*Table 2*
*Number and percentage of women serving on municipal councils in major Canadian cities and capital cities, 1993*

| City (* = female mayor) | Total number representatives† | Date of most recent election | Number of women councillors and % of total† | % change from previous election |
|---|---|---|---|---|
| Vancouver | 11 | Nov. 1993 | 5 (45.5) | + 18.2 |
| Victoria | 9 | Nov. 1993 | 4 (44.4) | + 11.1 |
| * Yellowknife | 7 | Oct. 1991 | 3 (42.9) | 0.0 |
| * Edmonton | 13 | Oct. 1992 | 5 (38.5) | - 15.3 |
| * Saint John | 11 | May 1992 | 4 (36.4) | + 9.2 |
| Calgary | 15 | Oct. 1992 | 5 (33.3) | - 6.7 |
| * Toronto | 25 | Oct. 1991 | 8 (32.0) | + 4.0 |
| Montreal | 51 | Nov. 1990 | 16 (31.4) | + 6.4 |
| * Ottawa | 16 | Nov. 1991 | 5 (31.3) | 0.0 |
| Whitehorse | 7 | Nov. 1991 | 2 (28.6) | 0.0 |
| Saskatoon | 11 | Oct. 1991 | 3 (27.3) | - 9.0 |
| * Winnipeg | 16 | Oct. 1992 | 4 (25.0) | + 5.0 |
| Quebec City | 21 | Nov. 1993 | 5 (23.8) | - 3.4 |
| * Halifax | 13 | Oct. 1991 | 3 (23.1) | + 7.7 |
| St John's | 11 | Nov. 1993 | 2 (18.2) | - 11.8 |
| Regina | 11 | Oct. 1991 | 2 (18.2) | 0.0 |
| Charlottetown | 11 | Nov. 1992 | 2 (18.2) | 0.0 |
| Fredericton | 13 | May 1992 | 1 (7.7) | 0.0 |
| Totals | 272 | | 79 (29.0) | |

† Includes mayors.
Sources: *Canadian Almanac and Directory, 1992* and telephone correspondence with various city halls.

councillors at the local level (towns, municipalities, and cities) and 27 per cent of councillors in large cities.[10] It appears that women are more likely to win elected office in larger municipalities than in smaller ones, and are more likely to be elected in urban than in rural areas. This phenomenon is also evident at the provincial level, as Gary

Moncrief and Joel A. Thompson discovered in their analysis of provincial MLAs serving in 1988: "There was a marked difference in the proportion of women MLAs elected in urban ridings (19.2%) compared to those representing rural ridings (6.0%). To put it another way, the ratio of male-to-female legislators for rural ridings was almost 16:1; for urban ridings it was closer to 4:1."[11]

In addition to the factor of city size, Brodie's study of female candidates for elected office noted that women are more likely to contest public office west of Ontario.[12] Women won suffrage in western Canadian provinces first, and the first female legislator was elected in Alberta.[13] (The first woman to win public office in Alberta was Bessie Nichols, who won a seat on the Edmonton public school board in 1912.[14]) Table 3 shows significant differences in the level of representation of women in city government as we move from west to east. British Columbia currently has the most women on city council (37.5 per cent on average), while the Atlantic provinces have the fewest (18 per cent). Indeed, the percentage of female *mayors* in the Atlantic provinces (22.2 per cent) is higher than the percentage of female *councillors.*[15] Women are also well represented in the mayor's office in the prairie provinces (30 per cent) and in Ontario (27.8 per cent), where

*Table 3*
*Representation of women in city councils by province/region, 1993*

| *Province/Region* | *Number of cities* | *Number of councillors (including mayor)* | *Number of women on council (and % of total)* | *Number of female mayors (and % of total)* |
|---|---|---|---|---|
| British Columbia | 13 | 109 | 36 (37.5) | 1 (7.7) |
| Territories | 2 | 14 | 5 (35.7) | 1 (50.0) |
| Prairie provinces | 10 | 111 | 29 (26.1) | 3 (30.0) |
| Ontario | 36 | 474 | 110 (23.2) | 10 (27.8) |
| Quebec | 18 | 307 | 65 (21.2) | 1 (5.5) |
| Atlantic provinces | 9 | 105 | 19 (18) | 2 (22.2) |

Sources: *Canadian Almanac and Directory, 1992* and telephone correspondence with various city halls. Data represent the most recent elections, those in November 1993.

the phenomenon of electing women as "boom town mayors" has been noted in the press.[16]

To appreciate the extent of women's involvement in municipal politics, it is useful to examine their representation at the federal and provincial levels. The October 1993 election brought a record number of women to parliament. Women now hold 53 of the 295 parliamentary seats (18 per cent), a significant increase from the 1988 level of representation (thirty-nine MPs, 13.2 per cent).[17] Women now hold 18.2 per cent of the seats in Canada's provincial and territorial legislatures, as Table 4 shows. Provincial representation of women ranges from a low of 5.8 per cent in Newfoundland to a high of 25.3 per cent in British Columbia.

*Table 4*
*Female representation in provincial and territorial legislatures**

| *Province/territory* | *No. of members* | *No. of women members* | *% of women* | *% change since last election* |
|---|---|---|---|---|
| British Columbia | 75 | 19 | 25.3 | + 13.7 |
| Prince Edward Island | 32 | 7 | 21.9 | + 9.4 |
| Ontario | 130 | 28 | 21.0 | − 2.0 |
| Manitoba | 57 | 11 | 19.3 | + 5.3 |
| Alberta | 83 | 16 | 19.3 | + 4.9 |
| Quebec | 125 | 23 | 18.4 | + 2.6 |
| Saskatchewan | 66 | 12 | 18.2 | + 10.4 |
| Yukon | 17 | 3 | 17.6 | − 7.4 |
| New Brunswick | 58 | 10 | 17.2 | + 5.2 |
| Northwest Territories | 24 | 3 | 12.5 | + 4.2 |
| Nova Scotia | 52 | 5 | 9.6 | + 3.8 |
| Newfoundland | 52 | 3 | 5.8 | + 2.0 |
| Total | 771 | 140 | 18.2 | |

* The numbers are for the most recent provincial and territorial elections, to December 1993.

Sources: Government of Ontario, *Female Representation in the Senate, House of Commons, and Provincial Legislatures* (Legislature Research Service, March 1992), and newspaper reports on the most recent elections.

These figures lead to our third observation—namely, that women, as we noted at the outset of this chapter, have higher levels of representation in city governments than in federal and provincial ones. The city mean is 23.8 per cent compared to the federal number of 18.3 per cent and the provincial/territorial average of 18.2 per cent. Whereas gender parity at the provincial or federal level is not likely to be reached within the next few decades, women already comprise half or more of the elected representatives in six Canadian cities. There is also evidence to indicate that women are reaching the 50 per cent mark on Canadian school boards. As of October 1991, 49 per cent of those elected to school boards in Nova Scotia were women, and, as of 1990, 43 per cent of school board trustees in Quebec were women.[18]

Janine Bodie found, in her study of women who contested public office between 1945 and 1975, that women were significantly more likely to win municipal than provincial or federal office.[19] Whereas 33 per cent of the municipal candidates she surveyed achieved election, only 9 per cent of the provincial or federal candidates were successful. Given the increased numbers of women on city councils across Canada, it is likely that Brodie's findings would be confirmed by surveys of candidates since 1975. In general, women are more likely to seek, and win, public office at the municipal level.

Why is this so? To date, much of the thinking about women and politics has been based on a distinction between public and private spheres, and this analysis has been used to explain women's extraordinary involvement in community politics and their comparatively insignificant presence at the federal and provincial levels. The next section explores the public/private disjunction and sets the stage for a new analysis of women's participation in city government.

## *Where Public Meets Private*

To account for the unequal distribution of wealth and power between the sexes, feminist theorists often point to the frequently drawn distinction between the *public sphere* of business and government and the *private sphere* of home and family.[20] Until very recently men have dominated roles in the public sphere of paid work and politics, while women have largely been confined to private-sphere roles as wives, unpaid caregivers, and mothers. This division of roles (and power) is fostered and maintained by patriarchal thinking, which sees women as naturally subordinate to men.[21] Patriarchal thinking also assumes that men and women exhibit different personality characteristics and capabilities. Men are assumed to be innately rational, objective, competitive, and intelligent, and as a result they are naturally capable in public-sphere roles. On the other hand, because women are inherently irrational, emotional, and subservient, they are naturally suited to private-sphere roles.

The separation of public and private spheres is embedded in the structure and operation of social, economic, religious, and political institutions. For instance, cities are designed with the public-private split in mind; as Gerda R. Wekerle puts it, zoning "requires the segregation of home and work. It excludes home occupations from residential neighborhoods, thereby making it more difficult for women and men to combine work and family roles."[22] Suburbs epitomize the public/private distinction, since they provide the quintessential "safe haven" of the private sphere within commuting distance of public-sphere activity.

From this perspective, the ubiquity of the public/private dichotomy helps explain the social and attitudinal barriers to women's full participation in public life. To put it bluntly, politics is considered a "man's game." Further, because of the entrenched distinction between public and private, many issues of concern to women are considered private and therefore not relevant to business or government. One of the primary goals of feminist scholars and activists in the women's movement is to point out that there is nothing natural or inevitable about the separation of public and private spheres. In fact, the spheres are interdependent, in three ways. First, men, as husbands and fathers, participate in private life. By the same token, women (especially working-class women) have been involved in the paid labour force since confederation, and women's participation in political parties and other aspects of political life pre-dates the granting of suffrage; for instance, women were active in Winnipeg city politics before they had the vote.[23]

Secondly, the spheres are not naturally separate and distinct. For one thing, each sphere profoundly affects the other. Male domination of public life and public-sphere roles would not be possible without the supportive infrastructure of home and family; women's productive and reproductive labour in the private sphere provides a foundation for the capitalist economy and liberal-democratic institutions. In addition, women's confinement to the private sphere is clearly not a natural outcome of social behaviour, for the Canadian state has seen fit to limit women's participation in the public sphere. Indeed, a significant amount of government intervention is necessary to maintain traditional gender roles. Early in Canadian history women were prevented, by law, from using birth control, earning wages, owning property, voting, and seeking public office.[24] Most formal, state-imposed barriers to women's participation in the public sphere have been removed, but both business and the state continue to intrude into the private sphere by virtue of work arrangements and public policies which assume and reinforce women's primary responsibility for care of the home and children. For example, many businesses and services are structured around the "9 to 5" workday, thus assuming the availability during these hours of a homemaker, usually a woman. State policy reinforces women's private-sphere roles by, for instance, regulating fertility and reproduction and granting tax benefits to families with "dependent" spouses.

Thirdly, the interdependence of spheres is illustrated by the so-called "privatization" of women.[25] Women are privatized in the sense that their interest and participation in public life is viewed as merely a function or expression of their private roles and interests. This phenomenon has two effects; first, women's interests and areas of activity are labelled private and are thereby considered unimportant and apolitical (outside the realm of political action). In this way, children are seen as "private goods" and potholes, malls, and sports teams are regarded as matters of public concern. The second outcome of privatization is that women's political participation is seen as motivated by a concern for the organization and welfare of the family—an attitude particular to them—rather than by a more universal concern with the welfare of society as a whole. Thus when women are politically active, they are engaging in "public housekeeping,"[26] that is, using the tools and resources of the public sphere to improve life in the private sphere.

Many aspects of city politics are privatized in much the same way that so-called "women's issues" are privatized. City politics, after all, are concerned with neighborhoods, education, housing, safety, and the environment, aspects of public life that clearly overlap with the private sphere. That city politics are regarded as less important and influential than provincial or federal politics may not be a coincidence. As an illustration, R.H. Wagenberg comments on "the widespread attitude that municipal government is somehow non-political."[27] Because what city activists and city officials do is often closer to the private sphere than the public sphere, city politics are regarded as less significant and less political.

And so we return to the subject at the heart of this chapter, the involvement of women in municipal politics. One of the explanations given for women's significant representation at the city level is that municipal government is less important, less competitive, and therefore more "open" to women than the federal and provincial governments are. In other words, the "relative lack of power of municipal governments in Canada reduces competition for positions at this level."[28] There are two assumptions supporting this argument: citizen disinterest in city politics reflects its lack of importance; and voter apathy at the city level is based on a rational assessment of the constitutional status of city governments. That Canadians are not overly concerned about the selection of municipal representatives is illustrated by the fact that turnout for municipal elections tends to range between 20 and 50 per cent.[29] On the other hand, there is considerable anecdotal evidence to suggest that citizens are particularly active in the municipal decision-making process when the contested issue affects them directly. For example, public hearings in January 1994 about a controversial housing project in an Edmonton neighborhood were so packed with concerned citizens that the talks continued into the early morning hours.[30] Many other examples could be offered, from many cities, all pointing to extensive citizen involvement in community decision making. The fact that city *elections* are seen as less important than federal or provincial elections does not necessarily mean that city *politics* are seen as less important.

The second assumption—concerning the cities' subordinate status in relation to federal and provincial governments—reflects a formal, legal view of Canadian politics. It disregards political convention. There is plenty of evidence that the written constitution does not necessarily shape everyday politics; one simply has to contrast the

British North America Act, which emphasizes the role of the crown and is silent about the prime minister and the cabinet, with the real world of contemporary Canadian politics. In many cases the formal division of powers is far less important that what governments *actually do*. This is evident in cities; city governments do a lot, spend a lot, and have a lot of power to make decisions that affect our everyday lives. As Wagenberg states, "If one reflects not on the constitutional subservience of municipalities but rather on the question of their role in the quality of life of most Canadians, then some very good reasons emerge to be concerned with municipal government."[31]

What lies behind the assessment of city politics as less powerful? The perception that political power and influence is hierarchical in Canada, with cities at the bottom of the heap and the federal government at the top, clearly requires some rethinking. Who decides which level of government and which policy decisions are more important, and on what basis? What are the criteria? A feminist analysis is useful here, because it advances a broader definition of the political and urges a reconsideration of the public/private dichotomy. For instance, feminists see political action as extending far beyond the formal institutions and mechanisms of decision making to include informal political action such as volunteerism and community activism. A reevaluation of the importance of city politics must take a similar path. As well, rethinking the contribution of municipal politics should consider the true interdependence of public and private spheres. City decisions matter to people because they affect our daily (private) lives.

The other aspect of privatization is also evident in literature about women and city politics. Women are believed to be drawn to municipal politics because it is more congruent with their private-sphere roles, interests, and responsibilities. This argument is likewise based on two assumptions: that it is easier for women with private-sphere responsibilities to hold city-level political office, and that the nature of city decision making allows women to bring their private-sphere roles and ideals into the public sphere. The first assumption is valid, for obvious reasons. It is more convenient for women with children, especially homemakers with young children, to hold office where they live. Part-time residence in a provincial or the federal capital can be very difficult for women, even when their families are supportive.[32] Brodie found, in her study of female candidates, that municipal office holders were more likely than legislators to have children and to be homemakers at the time of their first campaign. Further, she discovered that women "competing at the municipal rather than the legislative level were less often delayed by considerations of children's ages."[33]

This is not the whole picture, however. The choice of electoral arena is not merely a pragmatic decision based on one's family situation. Citizens active at the elite level do not make casual decisions to run for office; entering into political candidacy requires considerable interest, enthusiasm, motivation, and resources. Brodie's survey results indicate that women run at the municipal level because they are interested in city policy issues and community goals. In particular, involvement with volunteer groups, especially community-improvement groups, stimulated women's municipal candidacy.[34] Thus women's candidacy at the city level may be a natural outcome of their community activism.

Women's interest in local politics is often stimulated by their involvement with the community. As Wekerle argues, women's activism at the local level is a natural result of their private-sphere roles: "Women's concern with the home has led them to become more active in community issues and self-help movements to improve living conditions related to housing, childcare, food cooperatives, and neighborhood planning."[35] The problem here, Wekerle goes on to point out, is that women's political interests can be trivialized by interpreting them as "private" in nature; that is, there is always a private explanation for public posturing. For instance, Kathryn Kopinak says that women "are drawn into elected office [at the city level] to humanize the polity by performing tasks in public which they have traditionally carried out in the home."[36] Accordingly, women's participation in city politics represents "one step backwards for women" since it restricts their participation in "higher" levels of public office and does not advance the cause of women's equality.[37] In other words, women's participation in city governance is motivated by particular, private-sphere interests as well as by their natural sense of duty and inclination to self-sacrifice. This assumption reflects patriarchal thinking, since it draws a firm line between public and private spheres. It implies that women's motivations for seeking elected office and their subsequent political activities are really *apolitical*, particularistic, and subordinate both to male authorities and to higher levels of government. Each of these implications can be challenged.

The idea that women's political activity is apolitical represents a narrow and unworkable definition of the political. As we have seen, there is considerable overlap between the public and private spheres of activity, with political decisions having dramatic effects on private life. Wekerle provides a good example to illustrate this point—city transportation policy:

> Transportation services are designed primarily to carry workers to and from their jobs during peak commuting hours. Planning does not take into account the fact that the journey to work for women workers is often more time consuming, more costly, and more complicated than men's. Women frequently use public transportation for shopping and household errands, and women workers combine these trips with the journey to work to save precious time. Yet fare structures and the location of transit lines do not accommodate this trip pattern. In addition, mothers are generally responsible for taking children to child-care facilities and picking them up. These trips are not reflected in transportation models even though they require an extra trip twice a day, sometime in a direction away from work.[38]

Obviously, the design of transportation policy (and housing policy, education, and so on) affects our private lives in direct and measurable ways. Thus any effort to articulate, in the political arena, how policy affects us and how it should be changed is a political act. One of the compelling reasons for women's involvement in political life is illustrated by the example of transportation—policy decisions often do not take women's different needs and interests into account. In sum, women's activity in city and community politics is both public and private; it is political work which considers the impact of political decisions on the home, the family, and the neighborhood.

To argue that women's political activity is particularistic is to imply that home and family interests are not part of the common good. Such a view is based on a radical bifurcation of public and private spheres in which children are seen as private goods and development projects as public ones. It implies that women are rooted to the private sphere and cannot fully participate in the universal discourse of political life. But how can political life address the common good if the interests of women and children are ignored? Women's political involvement is often aimed at illustrating how the well-being of people lies at the heart of the well-being of society in general, and city governments are the linchpin of community-family relationships. For instance, the Federation of Canadian Municipalities currently urges all cities "to look at all municipal services, including housing, transportation, policing, recreation and infrastructure, to see whether they help families."[39]

The privatization argument implies that women's political participation is subordinate to that of men. Kopinak, for instance, notes that female municipal office holders do not use their political experience to "move up" the political ladder to provincial or federal office.[40] Also, Kopinak is concerned about the increasing concentration of women on school boards. According to this line of thinking, women "settle" for municipal office even though it is less powerful, and their increased numbers on city councils and school boards do little to undermine women's overall political subservience. Brodie's study of female candidates supports the assertion that women do not see municipal office as the first rung on the political ladder. Her data show that about 77 per cent of female candidates contesting municipal office in their first campaign remained at the municipal level in subsequent campaigns. According to Brodie, "These data refute the conventional wisdom that municipal candidacy acts as a training ground or stepping stone for provincial and federal office. In fact, more women filtered down from legislative to municipal candidacy (28%) than shifted up from the municipal to legislative level (23%)."[41]

Yet it is possible that women seek (rather than settle for) municipal office. Perhaps women's involvement at this level reflects a realistic assessment of their ability to use politics to change and improve their lives and the lives of other members of the community. Perhaps women seek city office because they want to exercise power. There is some historical evidence to suggest that women sought municipal office and were active in community politics at a time when city governments were relatively more active than provincial and federal governments (that is, prior to the development of the welfare state). Mary Kinnear's study of women candidates in Winnipeg's municipal elections between 1918 and 1939 found that these individuals wanted the influence associated with elected office. They ran for office because it mattered: "School trustees had an extensive list of duties—to keep the school and school equipment in proper condition, employ necessary and suitable teachers, [and take] proper steps to ensure the health of the pupil." Aldermen's responsibilities ranged from zoning and property regulation to health control and unemployment relief. The city government directly and intimately affected the daily lives of both the prosperous and the poor."[42] And, as Jill McCalla Vickers argues, *both men* and *women* "cared far less what happened in Ottawa or the provincial capitals until the state at those levels was connected by an exercise of powers to the public life of their communities."[43]

Finally, the idea that women's involvement in city politics does little to promote equality for women can also be questioned in light of historical material on women's political behaviour. Mary Kinnear discovered that female candidates in Winnipeg city politics during the interwar years focussed on gender-equality issues and made deliberate appeals to voters on the basis of gender: "Gender was invoked in three ways. They [female candidates] appealed to the right of women to participate fully in the political arena, and to the value of women's kind of service, which, they argued, would benefit the entire community . . . they concerned themselves especially with issues thought to affect women and children. They emphasized a desire to be in partnership, not conflict, with men."[44] As well, contesting electoral office at the local level was a strategy of the women's movement in pre-suffrage years. For instance, in 1892 Toronto feminists won a significant victory in the suffrage campaign when three women were elected school board trustees.[45]

Do contemporary female councillors, who in many cities form a "critical mass" of elected officials (more than 20 per cent), make a difference in political office? We simply do not know. Research on the ideas, style, and impact of women councillors has not yet been conducted.

## *Conclusion*

Women are increasingly well represented on city councils and other elected offices at the municipal level; indeed, they are better represented on city councils than in provincial, territorial, and federal legislatures.

Women sit in the mayor's chair in several large Canadian cities, such as Toronto, Ottawa, and Edmonton. The female mayor of Toronto is responsible for more citizens than are the premiers of Canada's smaller provinces and its territories; moreover, she is also directly accountable to city residents because she is directly elected by them. City governments collect large sums of money in the form of property taxes and spend it in ways that affect people directly. They play a large role in planning transportation routes, regulating housing, providing essential services such as water and garbage removal, and contributing to the life of communities by developing parks and playgrounds. City governments support industrial development, the arts, and sports. School boards, utilities, and police commissions allocate budgets and influence policy at the grass roots. The list could go on; these examples simply show that city politics are "politics where we live." City politics are important, and powerful, *because* they are close to home, because they reflect our daily interests and needs.

Women's involvement in city politics demonstrates a rational assessment of the importance of municipal-level policy decisions. The fact that women choose city politics does not indicate their relative powerlessness, as some argue. Instead, it reflects a political strategy which is cognizant of the overlap between public and private spheres and which recognizes community politics as a useful arena for political change. Women become involved in city government because of its profound influence on their lives; that is, women choose city politics because it is powerful in ways that matter to them. Politics at the city level—"politics where we live"—is arguably more tangible, more immediate, and more rewarding than political action at the federal and provincial levels.

## *Notes*

1. I gratefully acknowledge the help of PhD student Paul Hamilton, who collected secondary-source material for this chapter, and MA student David Wright, who conducted telephone interviews in French.

2. Sherrill MacLaren, *Invisible Power: The Women Who Run Canada* (Toronto: Seal, 1992), 215. Elsie Wayne was elected to the House of Commons on 25 October 1993.
3. Jill McCalla Vickers, "Where Are the Women in Canadian Politics?" *Atlantis*, vol 2. (1978), 46.
4. This is a fairly commonplace assumption; see, for instance, Kathryn Kopinak, "Women in Canadian Municipal Politics," *Canadian Review of Sociology and Anthropology* vol 22, no. 3 (1985), 407, and Chantal Maillé, *Primed for Power* (Ottawa: Canadian Advisory Council on the Status of Women, 1990), 14.
5. Janine Brodie, *Women and Politics in Canada* (Toronto: McGraw-Hill Ryerson, 1985), 16. The study was limited to twenty-two Canadian cities, and so the number of candidates does not include all of the municipal office-seekers.
6. See Maillé, *Primed for Power*, 6.
7. Ibid., 1.
8. Donald J. Higgins, *Local and Urban Politics* (Toronto: Gage, 1986), 364.
9. The cities with populations of 250 000 or more are Calgary, Edmonton, Etobicoke, Hamilton, Laval, London, Mississauga, Montreal, North York, Ottawa, Scarborough, Toronto, Vancouver, and Winnipeg.
10. Chantal Maillé, "Women in Quebec Politics" (presentation at a round-table discussion on women and representation, Canadian Political Science Association meetings, Learned Societies Conference, Carleton University, 2 June 1993).
11. Gary Moncrief and Joel A. Thompson, "Urban and Rural Ridings and Women in Provincial Politics in Canada: A Research Note on Female MLAs," *Canadian Journal of Political Science*, vol 24, no. 3 (December 1991), 835. A provincial riding was considered an urban riding if it was "contained wholly or partially within a city or metropolitan area with a population of at least 50,000."
12. Brodie, *Women and Politics in Canada*, 19.
13. See Alison Prentice *et al.*, *Canadian Women: A History* (Toronto: Harcourt Brace Jovanovich, 1988), 196–7, for possible explanations.
14. Gordon Kent, "Trustee blazed a trail for women in politics," *Edmonton Journal* (24 February 1992). Ms Nichols was elected before full female suffrage was granted; in Edmonton at that time, only unmarried female property owners were allowed to vote for aldermen and school trustees.

15. A 1991 newspaper article reported that more than half of Nova Scotia's mayors were women. See Gail Lethbridge, "Women make their mark in municipal politics," *Halifax Chronicle-Herald*, 26 October 1991, C1, C2.
16. Kim Zarzour, "Boom town mayors," *Toronto Star*, 2 January 1992, E1, E4. For instance, Hazel McCallion is the mayor of Mississauga, and Lorna Jackson is the mayor of Vaughan.
17. See Kirk Makin, "Voters send 54 women to shake up old boy's club," *Globe and Mail*, 27 October 1993, A13. Also, it should be noted that Deborah Grey won a 1989 by-election, bringing the number of women in the House of Commons to forty prior to the 1993 election.
18. Lethbridge, "Women make their mark," and Maillé, "Women in Quebec Politics."
19. Brodie, *Women and Politics in Canada*, 21.
20. Many feminist writers note the prevailing distinction between the public and private spheres. See, for instance, Virginia Sapior, *The Political Integration of Women* (University of Illinois Press, 1984), 6, and 30–1.
21. Lorraine Code, "Feminist Theory," in *Changing Patterns: Women in Canada*, 2nd ed., Sandra Burt *et al.*, eds. (Toronto: McClelland and Stewart, 1993), 22–5.
22. Gerda R. Wekerle, "Women in the Urban Environment," *Signs*, vol 5, no. 3 (spring 1980 supplement), 202.
23. Sylvia Bashevkin, *Toeing the Lines: Women and Party Politics in English Canada*, 2nd ed. (Toronto: Oxford University Press, 1993), 6–7, and Mary Kinnear, "Post-Suffrage Prairie Politics: Women Candidates in Winnipeg Municipal Elections 1918–1939," *Prairie Forum*, vol. 16, no. 1 (spring 1991), 41–57.
24. Sandra Burt, "Legislators, Women, and Public Policy," in *Changing Patterns: Women in Canada*, Burt *et al.*, eds. (Toronto: McClelland and Stewart, 1988), 129–33.
25. Jean Bethke Elshtain, "Moral Woman and Immoral Man: A Consideration of the Public-Private Split and Its Political Ramifications," *Politics and Society*, vol 4, no. 4 (1974), 473.
26. This phrase is used in the context of women and cities by, for instance, Susan Saegert, "The Adrogenous City: From Critique to Practice," in *Women, Housing and Community*, Willem Van Vliet, ed. (Avebury, England: Aldershot and Brookfield, 1988), 29.
27. R.H. Wagenberg, "Issues in Municipal Government," in *Introductory Readings in Canadian Government*, Robert M. Krause and R.H. Wagenberg, eds. (Toronto: Copp Clark Pitman, 1991), 367.
28. Vickers, "Where are the Women?" 46.

29. Higgins, *Local and Urban Politics,* 261.
30. Marta Gold, "Riverdale issue debated into night," *Edmonton Journal,* 18 January 1994, B3.
31. Wagenberg, "Issues in Municipal Government," 348.
32. See Rosemary Brown, *Being Brown* (Toronto: Random House, 1989), especially 137.
33. Brodie, *Women and Politics in Canada,* 91.
34. Ibid., 52–3.
35. Wekerle, "Women in the Urban Environment," 211.
36. Kopinak, "Women in Canadian Municipal Politics," 407.
37. Ibid., 406–7.
38. Wekerle, "Women in the Urban Environment," 205.
39. Vivian Smith, "Family nearing community forefront," *Globe and Mail,* 7 February 1994, A4.
40. Kopinak, "Women in Canadian Municipal Politics," 403–4.
41. Brodie, *Women and Politics in Canada,* 22–3.
42. Kinnear, "Post-Suffrage Prairie Politics," 52.
43. Jill McCalla Vickers, "Feminist Approaches to Women in Politics," in *Beyond the Vote,* Linda Kealey and Joan Sangster, eds. (Toronto: University of Toronto Press, 1989), 22.
44. Kinnear, "Post-Suffrage Prairie Politics," 41–8.
45. Prentice *et al., Canadian Women: A History,* 179.

## *Selected Sources*

Brodie, Janine. *Women and Politics in Canada* (Toronto: McGraw-Hill Ryerson, 1985).

Higgins, Donald J. *Local and Urban Politics* (Toronto: Gage, 1986).

Kinnear, Mary. "Post-Suffrage Prairie Politics: Women Candidates in Winnipeg Municipal Election 1918–1939," *Prairie Forum,* vol. 16, no. 1 (spring 1991), 41–57.

Kopinak, Kathryn. "Women in Canadian Municipal Politics: Two Steps Forward, One Step Back," *Canadian Review of Sociology and Anthropology,* vol. 22, no. 3 (1985), 394–410.

Maillé, Chantal. *Primed for Power* (Ottawa: Canadian Advisory Council on the Status of Women, 1990).

Prentice, Alison *et al. Canadian Women: A History* (Toronto: Harcourt Brace Jovanovich, 1988).

Saegert, Susan. "The Androgenous City: From Critique to Practice," in *Women, Housing and Community,* Willem Van Vliet, ed. (Avebury, England: Aldershot and Brookfield, 1988), 23–37.

Vickers, Jill McCalla. "Where Are the Women in Canadian Politics?" *Atlantis,* vol 2. (1978), 40–51.

Wagenberg, R.H. "Issues in Municipal Government," in *Introductory Readings in Canadian Government,* Robert M. Krause and R.H. Wagenberg, eds. (Toronto: Copp Clark Pitman, 1991), 347–69.

Wekerle, Gerda R. "Women in the Urban Environment," *Signs,* vol. 5, no. 3 (spring 1980 supplement), 188–214.

# 5

## *When "They" is "We": Movements, Municipal Parties, and Participatory Politics*

Tim Thomas

THIS CHAPTER traces the attempts of Canadian reformers to encourage greater participatory democracy at the municipal level. More specifically, it focusses on three cities, Vancouver, Winnipeg, and Montreal, where urban reform movements were led by political parties. Despite their differences, these parties all advocated changes that would bring municipal government "closer to the people."

Reform ideas achieved their greatest success in Montreal where the decentralist party, the Montreal Citizen's Movement (MCM), was elected in 1986. Yet an examination of the MCM's years in office from 1986 until 1994 reveals that the constraints of power as well as those associated with political parties (the logic of electoral competition) rendered any attempts at institutional reform relatively ineffective. Montreal's experience, along with Vancouver's and Winnipeg's, points to an inescapable conclusion: even at governmental levels closest to the people in settings whose political cultures strongly favour participatory democracy, the political party has proven to be an inadequate vehicle for activists interested in expanding public participation in the democratic process.

## The Setting

For Canadians concerned with participatory democracy, it would seem logical to abandon the non-ideological, electorally driven, brokerage parties that dominate politics on the federal and provincial levels and instead focus on the level of government that many believe most directly affects everyday life. Indeed, long-time municipal activist Dimitrios Roussopoulos most explicitly contemplated this possible connection between participatory democracy and municipal politics when he wrote, "The force of localism and the direct access of city politics may very well make city hall as an institution the most vulnerable to the people's rage."[1]

With the possible exceptions of Winnipeg, Vancouver, and Montreal, however, there is little evidence of growing popular interest in municipal government. For the most part, local government is still regarded by Canadians as an administrative tool for the implementation of policy decided by more important levels of government, rather than as an effective forum for policy innovation and political change in general. Yet, while this perspective is the dominant one, it is also true that new urban problems have increased the sensitivity of many segments of the population to the role of municipal government. From the 1960s on, citizen groups concerned about a variety of issues have been a feature of the urban landscape, and one of the common characteristics of these groups is a powerful sense of mission. Writing of the 1960s and 1970s, Donald Higgins observed that, even though detailed knowledge of occurrences in other cities was often absent, "to the activists as well as to some less impassioned observers, there was a sense of there being an urban reform "movement"—a feeling of shared experiences and objectives."[2]

Generally, Higgins argues that this urban reform or "citizen" movement in Canadian city politics had three main elements.[3] First, spontaneously formed groups sought to preserve their neighbourhoods from unwanted intrusions (expressways, high-rise/density development proposals). Included in these citizen groups were people whose leadership was more heavily drawn from professional occupations with linkages beyond the community than had been the case with traditional neighbourhood leaders. They advocated city-wide policy measures such as the provision of more public housing and day-care facilities, the drafting of municipal development plans, improved public transit, better protection for minorities and tenants, and more effective public participation in municipal decision making.

Secondly, an increasing number of "reform" politicians won election to city councils and transformed the composition of these bodies by increasing their percentage of women councillors and by lowering the average age of their members. These reform councillors had close ties to citizen groups and possessed operational styles that emphasized consultation, public hearings, and streams of reports to the public. Some were connected to the New Democratic Party or reformist municipal parties, a sharp break with traditional "non-partisan" city politics, and most were seen by large elements of the public as leftists or even anarchists.

The third group making up this so-called urban reform movement was the alternative press and periodicals such as *This Magazine*, *Our Generation*, and *City Magazine*. The simultaneous emergence of all of these actors in metropolitan areas across the country, combined with the fact that they proclaimed similar messages, accounts for the use of the term "movement" to describe them. Yet there were other factors that allowed for such terminology. The three components of the reform movement seemed to share a concern for process and a commitment to politics in the broadest sense. Higgins notes: "Perhaps the one factor that has made urban group politics close to being a movement in the late Sixties and the Seventies is a broadening of what is considered 'political.' 'Politics,' it seems, is a more respectable word to apply to city government than was the case a decade or so ago."[4]

The most common kinds of policy thrusts championed by progressive urban politicians were public housing, public transit, day care, energy, and—in order to make the tax burden more equitably shared—property tax reform. Alongside this agenda was a struggle by organized labour to reduce the power of capital's interests relative to city hall. This struggle was especially intense in Vancouver and Winnipeg, and the experience of the Montreal Citizen's Movement is a more recent example of the same conflict.

Higgins argues that perhaps all these aspects of the progressives' orientation can be encompassed in the broader issue of democratization of the governance of the city: "The matter of the extent to which power can be dispersed and restructured so that groups of citizens in the different areas of the city maintain an effective control of those aspects of their lives over which municipal government can have a bearing . . . I think that this is the best description of what real progressive urban politics is all about."[5] Still, Higgins concludes that the diversity of progressive urban politics renders the label "movement" inappropriate. "Whether of the elected politician variety, the community group variety, or in terms of the media," Higgins writes, "progressive urban politics is so far from being uniform in direction, pace of evolution, strategy, tactics, kinds of personalities involved, content and so on, that to think of it at all as a movement is misleading and not particularly helpful to those who wish to understand and learn from what has happened."[6]

## *Winnipeg*

In the case of Winnipeg, Higgins claims that "the end of the Seventies saw little of a reform movement left, either electorally or in the form of organized community groups."[7] This was true in spite of the fact that the City of Winnipeg Act (1972) was hailed as a landmark in the reform of municipal institutions. There was to be one council, one tax base, and a unified administrative structure while community committees made up of three or four councillors were created to counter any effects of over-centralization and to supervise zoning and planning initiatives. Furthermore, to guarantee a sufficient degree of local control by private citizens, each community committee area was to have a resident advisory group (RAG) consisting of annually elected resident advisors. These advisors were to meet regularly with councillors and tender advice on matters of local concern.[8]

What ensued, however, was far from what the act had envisaged. With respect to the attempts to decentralize and democratize local governments, the resident advisory system played a minor role in city government and in no way offered an effective counterweight to the centralized administrative system. Although the resident advisory arrangement at times provided an arena for local activists to stop local developments perceived as detrimental to their communities, the RAGs were moribund in the suburbs and, on larger region-wide issues, the impact of the local decision-making units was far less successful.[9]

Surprisingly few councillors emerged out of the RAGs. Instead, "once it became clear that the RAGs themselves had so little institutionalized power as to be irrelevant," progressives in Winnipeg relied on a strategy that was not only purely electoralist but of the "top-down variety."[10] Rather than using the RAGs and initiating reform from the grass roots, Winnipeg progressives pinned their hopes on the career aspirations of Lloyd Axworthy, now a Liberal MP and cabinet minister, who was perceived as a type of "saviour from above." When it became apparent that Axworthy was not interested in becoming the city's mayor, much of the momentum for municipal reform was lost.

M.O. Dickerson and others assert that, because local governments tend to function without political parties or any other devices for building working majorities which can yield coherent policy, municipal politics remain an ineffective area for substantive policy change and are useful only for piecemeal problem-solving related to specific issues.[11] Even in Canadian cities such as Winnipeg that have avoided such patterns and have implemented competitive party structures, the drive to reform municipal government has been short-lived and municipal politics has tended to be propelled by the popularity of certain issues or individuals. This has often occurred at the expense of ideological concerns and desires for grass-roots policy innovation. The case of Vancouver best demonstrates the point.

## *Vancouver*

When problems of urban growth and its social effects were becoming apparent in Vancouver, two events in 1967 served to facilitate communication between a variety of disaffected groups in the city. The first was the election of Mayor Tom Campbell, who came to personify the private-profit motive in civic development and the anti-intellectualism and contempt for citizen participation which was then so common in Canadian cities.[12] The second was the decision by Vancouver's board of administration and council to proceed with the construction of a proposed freeway. This decision was protested by an unlikely mix of downtown business and professional people, ratepayers in affluent areas, planners and architects, teachers and University of British Columbia academics, community workers, and low-income neighbourhood and youth groups.

Two organizations were soon formed to represent these constituencies, the Electors Action Movement (TEAM) and the Citizens Council on Civic Development (CCCD), both of which were motivated by opposition to the freeway and other development projects. "Citizen participation" became the watchword and was perhaps the principal goal of the new reformers. Paul Tennant writes that TEAM and CCCD were reform groups of the "city beautiful" variety, seeking to change certain policies but remaining conservative in their desire to protect that which made their city a pleasant place to live and raise a family.[13]

Later in 1968, however, TEAM was joined in its opposition to the board of administration and council by a second new civic party, the Committee of Progressive Electors (COPE), which was explicitly socialist and which sought not to preserve and protect but to reduce or destroy middle-class control of the city. The years from 1968 to 1972 were exciting ones for TEAM and COPE and were marked by the successful defeat of not only the freeway proposal but many similar development projects. Nevertheless, Paul Tennant observes that "the tremendous energy required to organize and maintain the opposition to the developers, to the bureaucracy . . . could not be carried on indefinitely. Because of their success and their exhaustion the various citizens' groups faded away or, like CCCD, lapsed into routine activities . . . the politically inclined of the citizen reformers gravitated largely to TEAM to continue the battle directly . . . It was thus the case that TEAM grew while the citizen's groups declined."[14]

Consequently, by the time TEAM finally did achieve power in 1973, the energy of citizen reform groups was fading and municipal politics in Vancouver were beginning a return to their old ways. Furthermore, COPE, which had joined with TEAM to oppose major development projects of the previous administrators, now saw little reason for cooperation and began to oppose TEAM bitterly. Leading the way was COPE's lone city councillor, Harry Rankin.

Yet the TEAM victory did result in significant changes to the composition and style of the city's municipal council. The TEAM members of council were on average more than a decade younger than their predecessors. In addition, Tennant writes that few, if any, other cities with open elections have ever produced a council of such high occupational and social status. All of the eleven councillors had university degrees, eight had pursued post-graduate studies, and four were university professors. Control over council passed from business interests to professionals who, by and large, had no business interests.[15] Parallels can be made with the case of the MCM councillors who brought similar educational and professional characteristics to Montreal's city hall.

During its first years in power (1973–74), TEAM worked to implement much of the party's policy platform. Neighbourhood participation in local area planning was encouraged, and the power of the senior bureaucracy was curtailed. TEAM also reduced the former secrecy of the development process; for the most part, though the system is now more subject to delay and personality conflict, it is also much more open than it had been prior to TEAM's reforms. Most council members maintained their party affiliation after their election, but party discipline was not highly developed and the increasing presence of independents on council over time signified less a weakening of the party system than the splintering of TEAM itself.[16] Finally, after 1973 the number of nominations of candidates from ethnic minorities in all three parties rose sharply, and TEAM (like the MCM) nominated and had elected many more women than any other party.

Yet, despite TEAM's achievements Tennant argues:

> In the two remaining areas—those of beliefs about the nature of the city itself and about citizen participation—there has been less change . . . The city is viewed less as a corporate whole than it was previously, but full recognition of neighbourhoods, as only the ward system would allow, continues as a dubious prospect. Most TEAM council members came to office favouring the partial ward system, but once in office they tended . . . to see increasing wisdom in the at-large system which brought them to office.[17]

Tennant concludes that "Vancouver's politics . . . has been the politics of the middle class. Full participatory democracy remains as illusory in Vancouver as in any other Canadian city."[18]

## Montreal

Given these observations concerning Winnipeg and Vancouver, Montreal appears unique because of the relative permanence of its left-libertarianism and the desire of its social-movement constituencies to use municipal government as a means of "decentring the state" by actively involving citizens in issues that have an impact upon their daily lives. This fact is admitted even by Donald Higgins, who writes: "As well as intractable disputes over questions of long-term objectives, there are equally intractable disputes over basic strategy, and the strategic issue of an electoral versus a grass-roots mass organizing strategy came into sharper focus in debates within the MCM than in any other progressive group I have encountered in city politics."[19] In the Montreal context, reformers are concerned with process and are not solely issue-driven or controlled by established social democratic parties. Concerns about participatory democracy are much more firmly imbedded in municipal politics and represent the philosophical underpinnings of a considerable proportion of its municipal candidates. As a result, even though the MCM's left-libertarian, anarchist elements felt ignored by the party, they had sufficient strength and support to form two of their own parties to run against the MCM in Montreal's municipal election of 1990: the Democratic Coalition and Ecology Montreal.

The strength of left-libertarianism and the abiding commitment to participatory democracy in Montreal are perhaps attributable to the large number of urban social movements and community groups within the city. Pierre Hamel notes: "More numerous, strong and dynamic than those of other cities in Quebec or the country as a whole, the urban movements of Montreal have successfully mobilized thousands of citizens around problems that affect the daily existence and the quality of life of populations residing in popular districts of the city."[20] Consequently, it can be safety concluded that Montreal's left-libertarianism and decentralist orientation are not part of a trend common to Canadian municipal politics in general. Yet, even in Montreal, a strong case can be made that the efforts of the MCM and its activists failed to lead to the implementation of the active, participatory form of politics originally envisaged.

From 1970 to 1974 two main forces of opposition surfaced in Montreal to confront Mayor Jean Drapeau and his ruling Civic Party. The first force contained the remnants of FRAP, a political party that Drapeau destroyed by associating its leftist elements with those responsible for the October Crisis of 1970. In 1974 these former FRAP supporters, devoted to attacking Drapeau's failure to provide sufficient housing and social services, merged with a middle-class movement opposed to uncontrolled development in downtown Montreal to form the Montreal Citizen's Movement. One observer notes that "upon its founding in 1974, the goals of the MCM were vaguely socialist and explicitly decentralist. Its program stressed popular participation in decisions, which reflects its own decentralized structure."[21]

Because the MCM rested on an alliance between diverse and often conflicting political and social groups, it avoided attempts to clarify policies when such clarification might lead to confrontation within its membership. Instead, its program of 1974 projected a series of reforms intended to decentralize administration by dispersing decision-making powers throughout the city's neighbourhoods.[22]

Between 1976 and 1978 the MCM attempted to rid itself of divisiveness and internal inconsistencies by adopting a more socialist stance. The 1976 congress adopted a plan to bring together politicized citizens to resist the way capital was transforming their areas.[23] One out of every three platform points was oriented around long-term social change through the mobilization of active popular support. Ironically, the 1978 elections were a disaster for the MCM and it seemed as though the people of Montreal, who had recently experienced the coming to power of the Parti Québécois at the provincial level, did not wish to risk further change by rejecting the stability and authority of the Drapeau machine.

The socialist, ideological phase of the MCM had been discredited and the period in opposition between 1978 and 1986 marked the biggest shift in MCM policy. With electoral success increasingly in sight, goals began to change. In 1978 there was not a single administrator, business person, or manager presented as a candidate, but by

1986 at least one out of every five MCM candidates came from these occupational categories. While the Civic Party instituted its own reforms between 1982 and 1986, the new MCM leader, Jean Doré, advocated a more laissez-faire philosophy. He attempted to establish legitimacy in business circles but continued to stress the MCM's traditional themes of citizen consultation and increased participatory democracy.[24]

Assessing the MCM's years in opposition from 1974 to 1984, Ingrid Peritz observed that the MCM had a powerful influence on both the policy and process of Montreal's municipal government during that ten-year period.[25] With respect to process, Peritz noted that when the MCM first attended council meetings in 1974 citizens and councillors had no forum in which seriously to question the administration on important issues. By 1984 they had obtained a half-hour councillors' question period before each meeting and citizens could address questions in writing. In 1974 an internal auditor examined city hall's books behind closed doors; by 1984 an independent auditor submitted an annual public report scrutinizing the administration's operations.

When the MCM first elected councillors to city hall, there were only four meetings a year which were called at the mayor's discretion and which lasted no more than one night each. Ten years later there was a minimum of ten meetings a year, the most contentious of which could last as long a two weeks. With regard to the MCM's impact on municipal policy during the period, Peritz concluded that "the MCM, along with vocal community groups, can also share credit for improving the face of Montreal over the past decade: housing renovations have replaced rampant demolitions that scarred central city neighborhoods in the 1970s. Beautification programs have transformed nondescript areas into well-lit back lanes and mini-parks. Bicycle paths and pedestrian malls line city streets where cars once dominated."[26]

The MCM's hard work, determination, and shrewd electoral strategies were rewarded in 1986, when the party won all but three council seats. It then had to meet the expectations of its supporters, a task that proved difficult. Within a year and a half of the election, some key issues arose that transformed the attitudes of many Montrealers concerned with enhancing citizen involvement in the governance of the city. The political turmoil involving these issues confirmed the fears of a growing number of dissident councillors within the MCM that the party was becoming oligarchic at the expense of its "movement" constituencies and was no longer the party that it had claimed to be.

The MCM had always seen itself as an organization for the people, the citizen, rather than big capital, big business, big government, big anything. It was its duty to protect the average individual from the awesome power of organized capital in municipal politics. This conviction, central to the MCM's leftist and libertarian heritage, had congealed during the Milton-Park struggle of the early 1970s when more than 600 low-income households joined many of the MCM's founding activists to fight a developer's plan to demolish their community and replace it with high-rises for "the middle-classes on their way back from the suburbs, and for affluent young professionals."[27]

In the late 1980s, the MCM confronted a similar issue, but this time it reacted differently. Like the Milton Park struggle, the Overdale affair revolved around the conflict between tenants' rights and the power of developers, and it symbolized how far the MCM had deviated from its founding *raison d'être*. The MCM's decision to accept a suspect plan by developers to build luxury condos in the Overdale community—and to relocate the local tenants—has been described by Peter Wheeland as "the antithesis of what many activists had fought for over the years."[28] Even more outrageous was the fact that such a thing could occur with the MCM in office.

The demolition of the Queen's Hotel was difficult for MCM veterans as well and, as was the case with Overdale, this event reminded them of the unplesantries of an earlier period. Many early MCM activists were people living in the downtown areas of Montreal who abhorred the Drapeau administration's propensity to think nothing about wiping our large portions of the city's architecture and heritage. At no time was this resentment more evident than in 1973 when the Drapeau administration permitted the demolition of Montreal's magnificent Van Horne mansion on Sherbrooke Street. After that event, however, Montreal's old buildings fared rather well until the MCM's decision in 1988 to condemn "the Queen's," a hotel located across the street from Montreal's Bonaventure (Grand Trunk) station that had fallen into disuse with the decline in the popularity of rail transit. In light of the Queen's demolition, the *Montreal Gazette* published an editorial entitled "Van Horne, 1988 Style," reminding Montrealers of Drapeau's fateful decision in 1973.[29] For many MCM activists, it seemed that the MCM was once again ignoring its roots and committing the same crucial errors in judgment that had led to the collapse of the old Drapeau administration. The year 1988 also witnessed the Matrox affair, which appeared to involve the simultaneous betrayal of two of the MCM's most important "social movement" constituencies—environmentalists and pacifists. The issue arose when Montreal's representatives on the Montreal Urban Community (MUC) Public Planning Commission agreed to let the Matrox company clear twenty hectares of protected forest land in the Bois de Liesse park, the last stand of black maple trees on the island. The company required the land so it could expand its parking facilities after it signed a $300-million military contract with the United States government. Ultimately, the entire controversy showed just how easily the MCM could be separated from some of its founding ideals. "For antimilitary and green-space activists alike, the name of a U.S. contractor in Montréal's West Island suburbs became a one-word milestone of the distance the MCM administration had put between itself and the citizen's groups that gave it its foothold."[30]

The Overdale, Queen's, and Matrox episodes were symbolic of the MCM's willingness to discourage participatory democracy by ignoring the expressed wishes of its long-term supporters once in power. Even more indicative in this regard were the processes of governance implemented by the MCM leadership. The MCM's attempts at municipal democratization and the development of processes to incorporate the views of its grass roots into its policy—goals that had always been regarded as central to the party's *raison d'atre*—were widely criticized as timid and ineffective.

In January 1987 the MCM named public committees on community development, cultural development, planning, housing and public works, economic development, and administration and finance. The committees were responsible for conducting open public consultation in their specific policy areas before any major policy recommendation reached the city's powerful executive committee and then city council. At the time of their creation, some councillors welcomed the committees as an important first step but expressed concern that their mandate was not far-reaching enough. Although the committees did represent an improvement over the methods of the past, they were not nearly as powerful as those of cities such as Toronto where "nothing is presented to city council before a committee—and citizens—get a stab at it first."[31] In Toronto every decision that council makes is preceded by public comment. Montreal's committees, in contrast, "were mandated to develop policy—not screen council items. Nothing binds the committees to let citizens speak about issues like routine zoning changes, the bread-and-butter of public committees in other cities."[32]

Jean Panet-Raymond writes that the Overdale affair exposed these MCM standing committees (sometimes called commissions) as mere consultative mechanisms whose recommendations could easily be ignored by the executive committee. The committees were not allowed to deal with any by-law of a financial nature and, like the Consultation Bureau which is attached to the general secretariat of the city, received their mandates from the executive. Any city department choosing to conduct public hearings also had to get prior approval from the executive and the bureau.[33]

Executive committee chairman Michael Fainstat defended Montreal's committees, claiming that they could not be as extensive as Toronto's because Montreal has a parliamentary system of government in which power is vested in the executive committee (roughly the equivalent of a cabinet) and city council. The executive committee was responsible for scrutinizing matters before they reached council and Fainstat argued that he was opposed to establishing another level of decision making: "We're not trying to slow things down."[34] But after hearing that Montreal was supposed to catch up with the democratization of other cities of North America, some Montrealers found the committees disappointing.

Perhaps the most promising mechanisms proposed to achieve the objective of municipal democratization in Montreal were the district advisory committees (DACS) which, in many ways, resembled the RAGs in Winnipeg. The city was divided into nine districts, each with a neighbourhood advisory committee which, unlike the five public committees, was obliged to hold regular public meetings to discuss such matters as local zoning changes before they went to council. It soon became apparent to many, however, that the DACS had very limited jurisdiction; they did not have any decision-making authority, and they seemed to have their agendas set by the executive committee as well. Any recommendations for the DACS were sent directly to the executive committee for study, a practice that one councillor described as "worrisome in terms of what is says about democracy at city hall."[35] Panet-Raymond concluded that the DACs "are not institutions where people can learn how to wield local power, as one would hope for under true municipal decentralization . . . There was no overall information strategy for the population or the people working within the administraton."[36]

Another process-oriented issue first made itself evident in the month of June 1987 when some councillors voiced disapproval in caucus over the city's decision to purchase an $82 000 Fazioli piano. After some councillors leaked the caucus rift to the press, rules were implemented to enforce caucus "confidentiality."[37] These rules, which effectively silenced some of the MCM's traditionally vocal councillors, were justified by Michael Fainstat in the following words: "There are procedures for expressing dissidence. What happens within the caucus belongs within the caucus."[38]

The issue came to a head when the dissident councillors were ostracized for expressing their disagreements on issues such as Matrox and Overdale in caucus. Councillor Marvin Rotrand stated at the time: "Like several other caucus members, I have felt a growing mood of intolerance in past months. Some of the statements made in caucus recently by executive committee members have shown a complete lack of respect for minority opinion, and for those holding these ideas. The atmosphere in caucus has grown unacceptably intemperate."[39] In addition, many of these dissident councillors also felt that caucus confidentiality was being used strategically to stop them from rallying the population or the MCM membership to oppose certain policies:

> Public dissent was only allowed after the caucus had reached a decision, and caucus usually only reached these decisions a few hours before city council went into session on Monday evenings. Thus the right to dissent, as Sam Boskey put it, "only exists between 5:00 and 7:00." The "gang of four" (Boskey, Goyer, Melançon, and Rotrand) were frequently targeted by motions of censure. Every media leak fed the climate of paranoia, and was

> automatically attributed to the dissidents. In one case, at the instigation of caucus president Sharon Leslie, they even condemned an "anonymous councillor" for having divulged a caucus discussion to the media.[40]

Jean-Hugues Roy writes that the municipal "parliamentarism" the MCM sought to introduce had unfortunate side effects, the most important of which was the rigid belief on the part of many MCM-ers in what can only be called "the party line." He concluded that "ultimately, for many MCM-ers, it seems the party has replaced citizens as their base of allegiance."[41]

That certainly was the view of long-time MCM councillor Pierre-Yves Melançon. In November 1988 Melançon, who was to later lead the Democratic Coalition, quit the MCM caucus. His stiffly worded letter of resignation accused the six-member executive committee of having corrupted the MCM's dream of greater democracy at city hall. According to Melançon, a few people within the MCM had monopolized and centralized power to almost as great an extent as had the former Civic Party administration. He highlighted his frustration over the time it had taken to implement reforms and attributed this problem to the MCM's propensity for placing sensitive issues "under study." In the meantime, groups in need of employment equity (women and visible minorities) were losing valuable jobs and time. For Melançon, the MCM had no intention of ever implementing reforms, particularly those related to the areas of the environment, culture, and sports and entertainment services.[42]

On 12 November 1988, a week after the well-publicized Melançon resignation, a full-page article appeared in the *Gazette* echoing many of his sentiments. The article, written by Lewis Harris, was entitled "Haunted by promises." It argued that, despite its early promise and many promises, the MCM was frequently guilty of some of the Drapeau era's failings. Harris noted that the city had approved at least a dozen projects for downtown Montreal in the absence of a master plan, thus following a practice that it had harshly criticized when in opposition. He denounced the MCM for not preserving the Queen's Hotel and quoted one party member as saying that, although the MCM was a product of community groups, popular movements, and ordinary people, the present administration was working primarily with the business community. Harris's article concluded with the following quotation from Concordia University professor Andy Melamed: "The executive committee of the city has too much power, absolutely. I have a feeling that power does corrupt when you have so many councillors at city hall."[43]

The day after the article appeared in the *Gazette*, a conference was held at the Institut pour une politique alternative de Montréal (IPAM). Not surprisingly, the subject of the conference was "Le MCM au pouvoir—les deux premières années." Composed largely of social activists, academics, and dissenting MCM councillors, the conference observed a growing conservatism and centralization of power within the city government. In a paper presented at the IPAM conference, MCM activist and Concordia University professor Stephen Block also suggested that the MCM was taking on all the trappings of a traditional "cadre-type" party including party discipline and rigid, hierarchical control over policy and the behaviour of its members. Those who resisted or acted independently were dubbed dissenting traitors working to the detriment of the party. Block was quick to point out that the liberty to engage in such behaviour politically used to be the defining purpose of the MCM: "New ideas within this party are almost automatically treated as threats to be defeated. The bottom line is that this party is not about a pledge of allegiance. It should be about tolerating differences of opinion which is an idea which must be reintroduced into our political culture. At risk is the party platform and the ideas and jobs of those who most truly support it."[44]

More recently, Sandro Contenta of the *Toronto Star* reiterated the charges of the MCM's critics. In an October 1990 article assessing Jean Doré's record as mayor, Contenta wrote: "The community and social groups that helped him get elected have become his staunchest critics while the developers and businessmen who feared his coming to power now praise him."[45]

There are opposing viewpoints. Former mayor Jean Doré has argued that the MCM did indeed deliver on promises to make city hall more democratic. While Drapeau used city council as a rubber stamp for his schemes, Doré pointed to the standing committees and district advisory committees established by his administration as evidence of greater democracy and decentralization of power. But perhaps the most democratic reform in Doré's view was the public question period established at the beginning of council meetings, when everything from potholes to taxes could be discussed.[46] Consider the following description of how the question period was used by Montrealers under the MCM regime: "A rock musician shows up with his guitar and sings his question; a multiple sclerosis patient in a wheelchair, unable to speak, types his query. There are question-period regulars—cyclists seeking more bike paths and street artists seeking fewer hassles from the police—and mass turnouts for issues like property taxes and flood damage."[47]

In addition, long-time MCM activist Arnold Bennett vehemently disagreed with attempts to characterize the DACs as nothing more than a "sham and a façade" because they lacked decision-making powers. Bennett argued:

> Though the DACs were a long way from true neighbourhood councils, could only recommend, and were hedged with unacceptable restrictions, they were a formidable consciousness-raising tool. Citizens could do more than merely ask questions or submit petitions at the DAC meetings; they could file *requêtes* that local councillors then had to debate publicly. Community groups quickly learned how to use this request procedure to focus debate on their issues, such as the demand for more public housing in Côte des Neiges. Individuals also used *requêtes* to cut through red tape, and force a quick resolution of problems that otherwise would have been left on the bureaucratic back-burner.[48]

On the whole, it would seem that, although the MCM did not live up to the dreams of its many activists who desired a more participatory form of municipal politics, it did not perform badly as a government. Responding to the criticisms of disillusioned MCM activists, many observers suggested that perhaps these activists were too utopian and unrealistic in their expectations. Yet a fundamental question remains: how long should reformers endure the constraints imposed by power? Following the election of 1984, the MCM executive committee argued that the requirements of everyday practical politics left little latitude for the implementation of many basic MCM policies. MCM ideologue Stephen Block noted that this position put many councillors in a dilemma since resigning from the party signified "a triumph for the executive committee and its clique of loyal insiders."[49] Such sentiments were even more explicitly stated by dissident councilor Pierre Bastien in his letter outlining his reasons for resigning from the MCM:

> Soon after the election, I watched many longtime MCM activists leave . . . I remember having tried to explain to them the constraints of power, and the compromises necessary to exercise it . . . Now I can say that I no longer find you [the MCM executive committee] convincing. For me, power was the means to realise the MCM programme. For you, the MCM was the means to exercise power . . . Since 1989 . . . MCM councillors have had to close ranks behind you, and present an image of solidarity, if they wish to hold on to their seat . . . You take advantage of this to clean house, separating not only those who do not roll over on command, but those who are not faithful at all times.[50]

Bastien was aware of the need to be "realistic" and to temper ideological rigidity in the interests of future policy rewards, but his letter also expressed the belief that he had been obliged to compromise his beliefs to a far greater extent that his own sense of "realism" allowed.

## *Conclusion*

The rise of municipal activism and the creation of competitive party structures in Winnipeg and Vancouver were driven more by the popularity of certain issues and individuals than by a desire to democratize the governance of the city. Once the issues had subsided or key individuals had left municipal politics, municipal government in these two cities resumed its traditional role of smoothly implementing policy decided by more important levels of government. For municipal activists, however, all was not lost. The persistence of libertarian sentiment in Montreal and its embodiment in the MCM made that city's municipal government the last remaining hope for a breakthrough in participatory democracy.

Yet, in the end, the case of the MCM suggests that parties will always become preoccupied with organizational success (re-election) to the detriment of the logic of constituency representation. In the mid-1980s Montreal was a city of strong libertarian sentiment, municipal politics seemed the level of government closest to the people and therefore the one most subject to their influence, and a popular and loosely structured party had been formed to lead the struggle on the part of Montrealers to obtain greater control over administrative decisions affecting their daily lives. However, even in this very promising context, advocates of participatory democracy, despite some positive advances, experienced considerable frustration and ultimately lost their fight for less rigid, top-down decision making. The Queen's Hotel, Overdale, and Matrox episodes highlighted the MCM's willingness to ignore and discourage the expressed desire of its longtime supporters, while the party's intolerance of dissent and reluctance to democratize the governance of the city threw its reformist credentials into doubt.

The experience of Winnipeg, Vancouver, and Montreal, then, lends support to claims that the political party is not the most effective vehicle for addressing the concerns of the grass-roots elements of any political community. Rather than involving themselves in party politics of any form, people advocating participatory democracy would be best advised to lead by example and promote their ideas among the public at large.

## *Notes*

1. Dimitrios Roussopoulos, "Beyond Reformism: The Ambiguity of the Urban Question," *Our Generation,* vol. 11, no. 2 (winter 1976), 50.
2. Donald Higgins, "Progressive City Politics and the Citizen Movement: A Status Report," *City Magazine, Annual Review,* vol. 5, no. 1 (1981), 84.
3. Ibid., 84–94.
4. Ibid., 91.
5. Ibid., 94.
6. Ibid., 86.

7. Ibid., 90.
8. Lloyd Axworthy, "The Best Laid Plans Oft Go Astray: The Case of Winnipeg," in *Problems of Change in Urban Government,* M.O. Dickerson, S. Drabek, and J.T. Woods, eds. (Waterloo, Ont.: Wilfrid Laurier University Press, 1980), 109.
9. Ibid., 117–18.
10. Higgins, "Progressive City Politics," 90.
11. *Problems of Change in Urban Government*, Dickerson *et al.*, eds., 3–4.
12. Paul Tennant, "Vancouver Politics and the Civic Party System," in ibid., 23.
13. Ibid., 24–5.
14. Ibid., 26–7.
15. Ibid., 27–8.
16. Ibid., 28–33.
17. Ibid., 34. On this point it is necessary to explain briefly the ongoing debate over the ward system in Vancouver. This debate revolves around the fact that the ward system would in effect allow the neighbourhoods a form of political autonomy with respect to matters of local concern.
18. Tennant, "Vancouver Politics," 13.
19. Higgins, "Progressive City Politics," 89.
20. Pierre Hamel, *Action collective et démocratie locale (dans les mouvements urbains montréalais)* (Montréal: Presses de l'Université de Montréal, 1991), 97.
21. Henry Milner, "The MCM: Back to the Drawing Board," *City Magazine*, vol. 4, no. 2 (April 1979).
22. Marc Raboy, "The Future of Montreal and the MCM," in *The City and Radical Social Change,* D. Roussopoulos, ed. (Montreal: Black Rose Books, 1982), 241.
23. Milner, "The MCM."
24. Lewis Harris, "Haunted by Promises," *Montreal Gazette,* 12 November 1988, B12.
25. Ingrid Peritz, "MCM Losing Radical Tinge after 10 Years at City Hall," *Montreal Gazette,* 13 October 1984, B5.
26. Ibid.
27. Joyce Napier, "Party Celebrates 15-Year Rescue of Neighbourhood," *Globe and Mail,* 26 September 1983, 10.
28. Peter Wheeland, "The MCM Splinter—The Alternate Parties," in *Montreal: Citizen's Guide to Politics,* Brendan Weston and Jean-Hughes Roy, eds. (Montreal: Black Rose Books, 1990), 190.

29. Luther A. Allen, "The Stones of the Queen's, Is There a Will to Preserve?" *City Magazine,* vol. 10, no. 4 (spring 1989), 5.
30. Brendan Weston, "Militarism—Montreal's Nuclear-Free Zone," in *Citizen's Guide,* Weston and Roy, eds., 144.
31. Ingird Peritz, "MCM Report Card: People Feel Let Down," *Montreal Gazette,* 9 February 1987, A9.
32. Ibid.
33. Jean Panet-Raymond, "Democracy—Decentralisation: Discourse and Reality," in *Citizen's Guide,* Weston and Roy, eds. 149–50.
34. Peritz, "MCM Report Card."
35. Elizabeth Thompson and Lewis Harris, "Neighborhood Committee Bylaw Splits MCM Caucus," *Montreal Gazette,* 14 December 1988, A3.
36. Panet-Raymond, "Democracy," 150.
37. Peritz, "MCM Caucus: Some Feeling Left Out," *Montreal Gazette,* 2 July 1987, A3.
38. Ibid.
39. See the dissident councillors' letters of resignation from caucus, reprinted in *Citizen's Guide,* Weston and Roy, eds. 152–6.
40. Wheeland, "The MCM Splinter," 191.
41. Jean-Hugues Roy, "Promises—the MCM's Credibility Gap," in *Citizen's Guide,* Weston and Roy, eds., 154–5.
42. Pierre-Yves Melançon, "Ma démission comme membre du conseil des élues et élus du R.C.M." (distributed at a conference conducted by the Institut pour une politique alternative de Montréal, 12 November 1988).
43. Harris, "Haunted by Promises," B1.
44. Stephen Block, "The MCM Party Insiders and the Recall Vote," a paper presented at a conference of the Institut pour une politique alternative de Montréal, Montreal 12 November 1988, 3.
45. Sandro Contenta, "Shine Is Off Montreal's Reform Mayor," *Toronto Star,* 28 October 1990, B4.
46. Ibid.
47. Ingrid Peritz, "Democracy at City Hall: It's There for the Asking," *Montreal Gazette,* 25 September 1987, A3.
48. Arnold Bennett, "Dissent—Why I Stayed in the MCM," in *Citizen's Guide,* Weston and Roy, eds. 169.
49. Stephen Block, "The MCM Party Insiders," 2.
50. Pierre Bastien, "Resignations: MCM Councillors' Letters," in *Citizen's Guide,* Weston and Roy, eds., 160–1.

## *Selected Sources*


Allen, Luther A. "The Stones of the Queen's, Is There a Will to Preserve?" *City Magazine*, vol. 10, no. 4 (spring 1989), 5.

Dickerson, M.O., S. Drabek, and J.T. Woods. eds. P*roblems of Change in Urban Government* (Waterloo: Wilfrid Laurier University Press, 1980).

Hamel, Pierre. *Action collective et démocratie locale (dans les mouvements urbains montréalais)* (Montreal: Presses de l'Université de Montréal, 1991).

Hamel, Pierre, Jean-François Léonard, and Robert Mayer. *Les mobilisations populaires urbaines* (Quebec: Les éditions nouvelle optique, 1982).

Higgins, Donald J.H. *Local and Urban Politics* (Toronto: Gage, 1986).

———. "Progressive City Politics and the Citizen Movement: A Status Report," *City Magazine, Annual Review*, vol. 5, no. 1 (1981), 84–95.

Kitschelt, Herbert. *The Logics of Party Formation* (London: Cornell University Press, 1989).

Léonard, Jean-François and Jacques Léveillée, *Montreal After Drapeau* (Montreal: Black Rose Books, 1986).

Milner, Henry. "The MCM: Back to the Drawing Board," *City Magazine*, vol. 4, no. 2 (April 1979), 37–41.

Raboy, Marc. "The Future of Montreal and the MCM," *Our Generation*, vol. 12, no. 4 (1978), 5–18.

Roussopoulos, Dimitrios. "Beyond Reformism: The Ambiguity of the Urban Question," *Our Generation*, vol. 11, no. 2 (winter 1976), 46–58.

Weston, Brendan and Jean-Hugues Roy, eds. *A Citizen's Guide to City Politics* (Montreal: Black Rose Books, 1990), 164–80.

# 6

## *Provincial-Municipal Relations; or Hyper-Fractionalized Quasi-Subordination Revisited*

Caroline Andrew

WHAT WAS THAT TITLE AGAIN? Some readers may think that they have accidentally crossed discipline boundaries and wandered into a textbook on medical pathology. Indeed, when J. Stefan Dupré coined the expression "hyper-fractionalized quasi-subordination" to characterize provincial-municipal relations in Ontario, he did admit that it was a barbarous phrase.[1] Yet, despite its awkwardness, it does capture some of the complexity and even the paradoxical quality of the relations between provincial and municipal governments. The cities of metropolitan Canada develop within a web of provincial-municipal relationships. Provincial governments are senior partners but their domination is neither complete nor constant.

The complexity in the relations comes from those parts of the expression that qualify the subordination of municipal governments—the "hyper-fractionalization" and the "quasi-ness" of the subordination. The hyper-fractionalized nature of the relationship refers to the fact that, both at the provincial and at the municipal level of government, there are a multiplicity of bodies involved in provincial-municipal relations. The department of municipal affairs in each of the provinces is only one of the provincial players and often co-ordination among the various provincial agencies is relatively limited. Similarly, the profusion of ABCs (agencies, boards, and commissions—the whole variety of special-purpose bodies) at the municipal level makes it difficult for any arm of city government to exercise leadership.

The term "quasi" is used to suggest other limits to the subordination of the municipalities. For Dupré, these limits are political in nature and refer to the important role that municipal elected officials often play in provincial political parties. Provincial officials have therefore to calculate the political costs of exercising direction over municipal governments.

The objective of this chapter is to situate current provincial-municipal relations at a point in balance between past and future. We will look first at the historical legacy of provincial-municipal relations to see how these relations have constructed themselves over time. The important moments can be seen as oscillating between structural reforms and administrative/financial ones. Successive periods of municipal reform have witnessed the creation of municipalities (structural), the gradual increase in provincial funding and control (administrative/financial), and the inauguration of regional governments (structural). Perhaps, in a fourth period, municipal reform will involve administrative and financial adjustments (administrative/ financial).

The second part of the chapter will focus on an examination of those factors that may have an impact on provincial-municipal relations in the future. This will allow us to speculate on whether future trends are more likely to lead to greater municipal autonomy or the continuation of provincial dominance.

## *Historical Legacy*

### *Provincial Creation of Municipal Government*

Most authors in the field of Canadian municipal government agree that the creation of municipal institutions had more to do with provincial imposition than with grass-roots mobilization.[2] Basically, the argument runs as follows: Ontario actively set up municipal governments in the period of the Union of the Canadas—1841–67—as a way of increasing public expenditures on infrastructure without increasing the provincial debt burden. Ontario then tried to "sell" this model to other provincial governments and, indeed, the confederation agreement of 1867 accepted the Ontario model of provincial-municipal relations.

This model did include a fair degree of municipal autonomy. Municipalities had the capacity to use local resources for infrastructure spending and indeed for general economic development. The literature on "boosterism" in the nineteenth century has given some splendid examples of "urban-growth coalitions" and of the lengths to which municipal councils were willing to go to encourage economic development. Paul-Andrè Linteau's account of the Montreal-area municipality of Maisonneuve and Ronald Rudin's examination of other Quebec cities, Leo Johnson's history of Guelph, and Alan Artibise's study of prairie cities all indicate that the provincial governments had succeeded in prompting municipal governments to undertake infrastructure spending.[3] The political dimension of these strategies is important and, as Linteau illustrates in *Maisonneuve*, elected officials were often major financial figures at this time. Small businessmen were well represented on municipal councils (as they are still) but so too were the more important business interests.

While boosterism existed outside Ontario, there was widespread reluctance on the part of populations in other provinces to accept municipal structures. Many people, especially in western Canada, saw municipal government as a structure that would lead to increased taxation, and, as this indeed had been the main objective of the Ontario government in setting up municipal governments, it was difficult to counter their perception. The enthusiasm for being able to exercise local discretion was moderated by the thought of having to pay for these local choices. Without suggesting that there was no grass-roots support in Canada for the creation of local government, authors writing on this question take the view that provincial imposition was more important than the demands of citizens.

## *Loss of Municipal Autonomy*

By the end of the nineteenth century, provincial governments were beginning to limit the discretion of municipalities. This process, which would continue throughout the twentieth century, came about through a complex interrelationship among changing technology and material conditions, the growing interventionism of provincial governments, the increasing strength and organization of professionals, perceptions of municipal inefficacy and corruption, and changes in ideology and definitions of citizenship. John Taylor has written about the loss of municipal autonomy, and one of his central themes is the importance of provincial efforts to equalize services across their territories through the regulation of local government.[4] To the present day, notions of equality and of rights to citizenship are behind provincial, and sometimes federal, initiatives that lead either to the elimination of municipal activity or to its increasing regulation.

Dupré's study of provincial-municipal relations in Ontario also illustrates the process of provincial intervention. One of the first areas to fall under provincial control, once the technological revolution of the private automobile was in place, was that of roads. Local finances and local vision became inadequate as the automobile became the pivot for economic development. As Dupré indicates, however, the Ontario government preferred to give grants to municipal governments rather than eliminate them from this area of policy making. Its approach represents one of the major characteristics of the provincial-municipal system of the twentieth century: the provinces' use of conditional grants to prod municipal governments into conforming with their priorities.

It must also be emphasized that municipal governments in general were in favour of provincial-government activity, particularly provincial financing of municipal activities. Indeed, municipal officials sought this support and were not, on the whole, vigorous defenders of absolute local autonomy. Further research needs to be done to uncover more about the political dynamics behind the development of provincial control. We do not know enough about the processes internal to municipalities, through which professional experts working at the local level pressured their provincial counterparts to extend centralized control in the form of provincial regulation. We also do not know enough about the role of the large municipalities in pushing for provincial rules in order to establish local norms. One thing we do know, however, is that the municipalities, as well as dealing on an individual basis with their provincial governments, grouped into provincial organizations of municipalities in order to lobby collectively. The national Federation of Canadian Municipalities was essentially created in order to lobby the federal government for policy changes useful to municipal governments.

Whatever the combination of factors has been, the growth of provincial conditional grants to local governments, both municipalities and school boards, has been enormous. Table 1 gives an idea of the overall growth since the end of the Second World War.

*Table 1:*
*Provincial governments: Transfers to other governments and hospitals, national-accounts basis, 1947–86*

| | *Transfers to local governments (in millions of dollars)* | | | | |
|---|---|---|---|---|---|
| *Year* | *To school corporations* | *Other* | *Total* | *Per cent of local expenditures* | *Transfers to hospitals* |
| 1947 | 67 | 34 | 101 | 16.8 | - |
| 1948 | 86 | 43 | 129 | 18.4 | - |
| 1949 | 107 | 50 | 157 | 19.6 | - |
| 1950 | 118 | 53 | 171 | 19.0 | - |
| 1951 | 131 | 66 | 197 | 17.9 | - |
| 1952 | 146 | 69 | 215 | 16.5 | - |
| 1953 | 157 | 85 | 242 | 18.6 | - |
| 1954 | 177 | 82 | 259 | 17.3 | - |
| 1955 | 224 | 103 | 327 | 19.2 | - |
| 1956 | 254 | 108 | 362 | 19.0 | - |
| 1957 | 301 | 151 | 452 | 21.5 | - |
| 1958 | 358 | 187 | 545 | 23.7 | - |
| 1959 | 415 | 207 | 622 | 23.9 | - |
| 1960 | 467 | 247 | 714 | 25.5 | - |
| 1961 | 547 | 294 | 841 | 28.0 | 694 |
| 1962 | 749 | 314 | 1 063 | 31.3 | 782 |
| 1963 | 808 | 340 | 1 148 | 31.0 | 836 |
| 1964 | 870 | 419 | 1 289 | 33.1 | 953 |
| 1965 | 963 | 477 | 1 440 | 32.0 | 1 120 |
| 1966 | 1 181 | 579 | 1 760 | 33.8 | 1 281 |
| 1967 | 1 397 | 628 | 2 025 | 34.9 | 1 521 |
| 1968 | 1 573 | 689 | 2 262 | 35.3 | 1 750 |
| 1969 | 1 804 | 697 | 2 501 | 34.7 | 1 994 |
| 1970 | 2 274 | 824 | 3 098 | 38.2 | 2 308 |

*Table 1 - (continued)*

*(in millions of dollars)*

| *Year* | *To school corporations* | *Other* | *Total* | *Per cent of local expenditures* | *Transfers to hospitals* |
|---|---|---|---|---|---|
| 1971 | 2 504 | 986 | 3 490 | 39.7 | 2 509 |
| 1972 | 2 751 | 1 160 | 3 911 | 41.2 | 2 912 |
| 1973 | 3 010 | 1 378 | 4 388 | 41.4 | 3 152 |
| 1974 | 3 442 | 1 714 | 5 156 | 41.6 | 3 976 |
| 1975 | 4 220 | 2 340 | 6 560 | 44.9 | 4 780 |
| 1976 | 4 697 | 2 466 | 7 163 | 42.6 | 5 633 |
| 1977 | 5 885 | 2 960 | 8 845 | 47.0 | 6 355 |
| 1978 | 5 855 | 3 221 | 9 076 | 44.3 | 6 643 |
| 1979 | 6 284 | 4 781 | 11 065 | 50.1 | 7 304 |
| 1980 | 7 305 | 3 721 | 11 026 | 44.1 | 8 486 |
| 1981 | 8 360 | 4 528 | 12 888 | 45.4 | 9 608 |
| 1982 | 9 951 | 5 100 | 15 051 | 47.5 | 11 530 |
| 1983 | 10 686 | 5 194 | 15 880 | 47.7 | 12 548 |
| 1984 | 10 606 | 5 404 | 16 010 | 45.7 | 13 493 |
| 1985 | 11 887 | 5 698 | 17 585 | 47.8 | 14 224 |
| 1986 | 12 339 | 6 089 | 18 428 | 47.5 | 11 530 |

Sources: J. Harvey Perry, *A Fiscal History of Canada–The Post War Years* (Toronto: Canadian Tax Foundation, Canadian Tax Paper no. 85, 1989), 433 (Statistics Canada, *National Income and Expenditure Accounts*; CANSIM).

Table 2 offers a portrait of local-government finances, categorized by provinces, for 1990. A comparison between amounts raised through property taxes and those given for a specific purpose by the province illustrates that different patterns exist across the country. New Brunswick stands out from the other provinces in that much more is raised there from property taxes than from provincial conditional grants. In fact, this can be explained by the New Brunswick reforms of the 1960s in which responsibility for education, welfare, health, and the administration of justice were entirely taken over by the province. New Brunswick, then, is the exception to provincial indirect control through conditional grants; in New Brunswick, provincial control has resulted in provincial jurisdiction.

To some extent, the same phenomena are evident in Quebec, where almost all health and welfare expenditures are directly undertaken by the provincial government, and where educational expenditure is more centralized than in other provinces. For this reason, Ontario municipal revenues are more than twice those of the Quebec municipalities even though the difference in the population size of the two provinces is much less. (In 1991 Ontario's population was 9 919 400 and Quebec's 6 850 900.)

## *Regionalization and Provincial Initiative*

The next part of our brief historical overview concerns the period of regional reform that began with the creation of Metropolitan Toronto in 1954 and that flourished throughout the 1970s. Once again, provincial imposition of structural reforms was the primary factor behind the creation of regional governments in many of Canada's largest urban centres. Of the twelve largest metropolitan areas, only Edmonton, Calgary, and Winnipeg do not have regional forms of government. The two Alberta cities have expanded through annexation without the existence of a two-tier regional structure; Winnipeg municipalities were consolidated, through provincial legislation, in 1971.

Regional structures were the answer to the problems created by the very rapid urbanization of the post-war period. Industrialization, immigration, and economic prosperity combined to produce massive growth in the major Canadian cities, not only in numbers but in geographical size. The pent-up demand for housing, originating in the Depression and the war years and accelerated by the policies of the newly established Central (now Canada) Mortgage and Housing Corporation (CMHC) of the federal government, resulted in the suburban development of the 1950s and 1960s.

The ensuing mismatch between the socio-economic unity of metropolitan centres and their political fragmentation was widely seen as

*Table 2:*
*Summary of local government revenue and expenditure on a financial-management basis, for the year 1990, forecast*[†]

| | *NF* | *PEI* | *NS* | *NB* | *PQ* |
|---|---|---|---|---|---|
| **Revenue** | | | | | |
| Property and related taxes | 127 934 | 16 805 | 420 887 | 164 077 | 4 815 355 |
| Other taxes | 27 138 | 3 | 11 872 | - | 102 184 |
| Sales and Services | 36 830 | 9 271 | 141 258 | 73 952 | 1 068 174 |
| Other own-source revenue | 12 356 | 2 815 | 76 515 | 12 798 | 355 135 |
| Intergovernmental transfers | | | | | |
| *General purpose* | | | | | |
| From provinces | 48 371 | 3 905 | 59 881 | 136 799 | 429 732 |
| Other | 10 109 | - | 28 642 | 8 440 | 68 256 |
| *Specific purpose* | | | | | |
| From provinces | 51 131 | 99 376 | 995 174 | 27 014 | 5 717 955 |
| Other | 22 132 | 71 | 2 359 | 2 524 | 36 992 |
| Total gross revenue | 336 001 | 132 246 | 1 736 588 | 425 604 | 12 593 782 |
| **Expenditure** | | | | | |
| Education | 32 703 | 95 972 | 858 736 | - | 5 469 537 |
| Transportation & communications | 85 159 | 6 785 | 84 860 | 90 039 | 1 912 183 |
| Protection | 25 592 | 6 455 | 107 085 | 100 510 | 1 115 324 |
| Debt charges | 59 407 | 8 158 | 55 320 | 38 862 | 1 405 987 |
| Environment | 78 499 | 4 565 | 151 709 | 75 151 | 1 891 207 |
| Health | 33 | 6 | 137 411 | 3 909 | 10 727 |
| Social services | 55 | 7 | 281 296 | - | 42 904 |
| Other | 97 587 | 13 288 | 169 770 | 103 337 | 2 492 695 |
| Total gross expenditure | 379 035 | 135 236 | 1 846 187 | 411 808 | 14 340 564 |
| **Difference** | -43 034 | -2 990 | -109 599 | 13 796 | 1 746 782 |

[†] Thousands of dollars

Source: *Canadian Tax Foundation Provincial and Municipal Finances* (Toronto, 1991); Statistics Canada, CANSIM matrices 2764 to 2776 (May 1991).

| *ON* | *MN* | *SK* | *AB* | *BC* | *NWT* | *YT* | *TOTAL* |
|---|---|---|---|---|---|---|---|
| 10 997 567 | 763 940 | 833 067 | 1 996 310 | 1 238 540 | 17 957 | 8 376 | 21 400 815 |
| - | 13 104 | 27 564 | - | 14 379 | - | - | 196 244 |
| 3 288 649 | 209 262 | 227 281 | 1 090 662 | 755 622 | 39 658 | 5 338 | 6 945 957 |
| 1 200 031 | 162 747 | 125 973 | 623 948 | 399 421 | 5 906 | 2 374 | 2 980 019 |
| | | | | | | | |
| 1 156 040 | 135 094 | 122 011 | 281 657 | 168 221 | 13 454 | 5 329 | 2 560 493 |
| 218 784 | 38 939 | 21 274 | 57 527 | 44 696 | 2 044 | 1 308 | 500 019 |
| | | | | | | | |
| 8 425 646 | 979 982 | 894 586 | 3 027 194 | 2 887 624 | 55 562 | 9 824 | 23 171 068 |
| 143 107 | 11 918 | 5 383 | 17 065 | 41 405 | 391 | 51 | 283 398 |
| 25 429 824 | 2 314 986 | 2 257 139 | 7 094 363 | 5 549 908 | 134 972 | 32 600 | 58 038 013 |
| | | | | | | | |
| 10 283 224 | 966 159 | 849 959 | 2 214 827 | 2 425 990 | 20 455 | - | 23 217 562 |
| | | | | | | | |
| 2 263 035 | 229 788 | 243 908 | 883 932 | 487 170 | 20 834 | 10 425 | 6 318 118 |
| 2 096 697 | 183 276 | 142 625 | 459 389 | 575 828 | 6 233 | 3 494 | 4 822 308 |
| 622 338 | 137 454 | 70 340 | 706 682 | 586 191 | 4 152 | 802 | 3 695 693 |
| 2 166 929 | 215 740 | 170 624 | 405 304 | 561 317 | 37 262 | 6 397 | 5 764 704 |
| 1 346 763 | 182 061 | 352 282 | 1 293 364 | 133 323 | 637 | 135 | 3 460 651 |
| 2 171 546 | 61 100 | 18 466 | 71 002 | 7 637 | 2 629 | - | 2 656 642 |
| 3 964 642 | 428 925 | 325 109 | 1 224 306 | 871 100 | 48 958 | 12 804 | 9 752 521 |
| | | | | | | | |
| 24 915 174 | 2 404 503 | 2 173 313 | 7 258 806 | 5 648 356 | 141 160 | 34 057 | 59 688 199 |
| | | | | | | | |
| 514 650 | -89 517 | 83 826 | -164 443 | -98 448 | -6 088 | -1 457 | -1 650 186 |

a problem of governance that, among other things, was slowing down urban development. When the creation of Metropolitan Toronto was followed by massive economic development in the region, many concluded that one regional political structure covering as much as possible of the built-up urban area was the route to growth and prosperity. The Ontario model was again promoted across the country as the appropriate municipal structure for the maximizing of economic growth and, once more, this model depended on provincial imposition of a solution that was not all that popular with the local population. In the case of regional government, it was particularly the residents of suburban areas who protested, fearing additional taxes and the requirement to share in the financing of services that they felt were not needed. Urban/suburban tensions and mutual prejudices fuelled these feelings of resentment, with the suburban population believing that their tranquillity was being menaced and the urban population no less convinced that the suburbs were selfishly refusing to provide social services needed by the metropolitan area as a whole.

The results of these regional reforms have been to strengthen the efficiency and effectiveness of urban services, but not to strengthen the democratic character of local government or to increase the channels of participation by the local population. Regional governments tend to be more insulated from the population than are lower-tier municipal ones, although the indirect nature of election has recently been changed in the case of Toronto and is being discussed in other places.

## *Back to Finances?*

The final phase in the evolution of provincial activity may be a return to administrative and financial tools, but this time out of a desire to clarify and simplify provincial-municipal relations. As has been shown, the earlier period of financial and administrative controls was motivated by provincial policy concerns and led to an increasingly complex system of provincial-municipal arrangements. Responsibility, accountability, financing, implementing, and control all became intermeshed and interdependent. Current provincial intentions appear to run counter to this trend; the idea now is to clarify processes of accountability and responsibility. Governments that are responsible for services should finance them; electorates should know who is accountable for what.

The reasons behind these current concerns are multiple. Provincial governments' fiscal constraints are a major factor; the clarification of provincial-municipal relations is often seen as a way to transfer more costs to the municipal level. But ideology also plays a role: clarification appeals both to the notion that local governments are the ones "closest to the people" and to the neo-liberal demand that governments be made more accountable to the taxpayers. Also underlying the current quest for disentanglement are administrative visions of greater flexibility in the development and implementation of policy.

The most concrete manifestation of this current phase has been the Quebec government's decision of 1990 to shift the financial responsibility for a number of services, including public transit and the maintenance of local roads, back to the municipalities. This action provoked a major crisis between the municipalities and the Quebec government, but the province persisted with its plan.

## *Summary of the Historical Legacy*

The overriding conclusion that can be drawn from the history of provincial-municipal relations in Canada concerns the importance of provincial initiative. For the most part, it has been provincial governments that have defined the municipal system and introduced the most important changes to it.

Yet this does not mean that the provinces exert effective leadership in relation to their municipalities. As Dupré indicates, the structure of provincial governments and the strength of the major line departments means that policy direction to municipalities comes simultaneously from a large number of sources and may not be consistent or even compatible.

In addition, provincial governments are not likely to accord high priority to elaborating and implementing a clear municipal government system. Provincial policy goals are generally seen as more important than a consistent vision of provincial-municipal relations and, as well, objectives at the provincial level often take priority over the ideal of clarity in intergovernmental relations.

CAROLINE ANDREW

# *Looking to the Future—But What Future?*

Rather than describe in detail the current functioning of provincial-municipal relations, it seems more useful to examine the facts that are likely to affect their future evolution. In this regard, the major question is whether municipal autonomy will increase, or, on the contrary, whether provincial dominance will continue and perhaps even become greater. There is support for both positions in the existing Canadian literature; Warren Magnusson takes the first view, Andrew Sancton the second.

Magnusson sees the local as the best link to the global. His argument is that globalization is putting into question the nation-state and indeed all forms of politics that are fixed, closed, and contained. Social movements and localities are the politics of the future for him and this fact offers possibilities for municipalities. "As the organization at the juncture of the local and the global, the municipality is crucial, but its liberation is properly conceived in outward, rather than inward looking terms . . . Its real promise is as an organizational node in the flow of critical and creative social movements."[5]

Andrew Sancton's argument addresses a somewhat different question in that it deals with policy making for urban areas rather than the political dynamics of these areas. His claim is that provincial involvement will increase: "Increasing provincial involvement in local decision-making is of much more long-term significance than provincial efforts to find new ways to make municipal governments cover the costs of various local programs and activities."[6] He argues that this trend does not eliminate the need for municipal governments but that their role is finding the right local mix of provincial policies, not autonomous decision making: "A given province cannot fine-tune and coordinate its policies in such a way that they can be appropriately delivered in each and every settlement in its jurisdiction. That is why we need municipal government."[7]

In order to explore further these points of view and to reflect in greater detail on the future of provincial-municipal relations, we will look at four different factors: globalization, fiscal constraints, urbanization and urban sprawl, and, finally, social heterogeneity.

## *Globalization and the Local*

Much has been written on the subject of globalization of the economy and the resulting changes in our lives. Here we will limit our discussion to the likely effect of these changes on the direction of provincial-city relations.

Some authors (for example, Anthony D. King[8]) argue that the globalized economy can be understood most clearly as a network of world cities which specialize in banking, financial services, cultural institutions, and head-office activities of various sorts and which are linked together through a broad range of information flows. Other cities, important but not of world-class status, may be linked in turn to one of these world-class cities, but the general thrust of globalization is to increase the polarization between rich and poor. The less urbanized, more peripheral parts of the globe will fall farther behind and the wealthy urban centres that can develop their head-office, financial, high-technology activities will be favoured.

Two sets of questions arise, one more empirical and one more theoretical. What kind of evidence exists in Canada to suggest that globalization exists and that it is affecting the behaviour of Canadian municipalities? Secondly, if globalization is indeed a force impinging on Canadian cities, what is the link between increasing globalization and provincial-municipal relations?

With regard to the first question, studies of the international activities of the large Canadian cities suggest that these activities are slowly, and unevenly, acquiring more importance within the global economy. Canadian municipal-international relationships play an important role in the promotion of trade but also include cultural and political dimensions (for instance, the twinning of cities).[9]

Should such activities be seen as the beginning of a major shift towards greater municipal autonomy? Perhaps, but this is certainly not the only explanation. First of all, senior governments, particularly the federal government, have been involved in some of these initiatives, and so it is too simplistic to interpret them as an indication of increased municipal autonomy. For instance, the international-development projects of cities have been initiated mainly by the Canadian International Development Agency (CIDA); municipalities have been happy participants in such ventures but have not been the moving force behind them.

Secondly, municipal-international links do not appear to have become firmly institutionalized within municipal government structures. Indeed, the level of international involvement has diminished in several municipalities during the current era of budget-cutting. Politically, international activities are very vulnerable in that municipal electorates almost invariably see them as examples of local politicians' insatiable desire to spend money and to travel to exotic places. Nevertheless, Canadian cities continue to maintain a presence on the world stage and in so doing offer tangible evidence of the impact of globalization on municipal government.

This link can also be detected in the ongoing operations of citizen groups or social movements which are in contact with similar groups and movements across the world and which pressure municipal governments to raise their international profile. Carolyn Whitzman notes this phenomenon in her analysis of violence-against-women initiatives in Toronto and argues that, in this instance, the London-Toronto links have been crucial to the spread of new ideas and to the exertion of pressure on local governments.[10] In addition to women's groups, environmental groups are also seen as important players in maintaining and fostering a close relationship between Canadian cities and the international community.

Globalization, then, is a fact of life in Canadian cities. What impact will this have on provincial-local relations? If the basic thrust of globalization is to reduce the importance of the nation-state, will this trend decrease or increase the importance of the provincial governments? If their importance is diminished, will that of local government be increased?

Globalization brings with it the idea of maximizing the strategic involvement of firms or groups of firms in the world economy. This idea in turn demands a tough-minded strategy which favours the unequal allocation of resources and the backing of winners at all costs. Of course, such a strategy runs counter to the principle that provinces have an obligation to create and maintain equality of services across their territories—a principle which, as was argued earlier, was one of the major factors underpinning increasing provincial control over municipal government. One could therefore argue that globalization will call for policy directions in which province-wide action is less appropriate. Whether this will result in greater municipal autonomy or just less efficient provincial direction is an open question; the outcome will depend in part on local political elites.

In conclusion, it is not easy to see exactly how globalization will affect provincial-local relations. In general, a strengthening of local activity seems likely but little empirical research has been done on this subject in Canada. Globalization would seem to be a reality but one whose political, and intergovernmental, implications are not yet clear.

## *Fiscal Constraints*

One of the major pressures facing all governments today is that of reducing expenditures; municipalities as well as provinces are trying to cut their budgets in ways that are politically palatable, or the least harmful politically. Strategies are relatively limited; it is possible to cut services and simply argue that they are not needed, but it is obviously more attractive politically to argue that the services will be assumed by someone else. This "someone else" can be the private sector or another level of government.

Is it possible or likely, therefore, that provincial governments will want to, and be able to, move expenditures and/or responsibilities to the municipal governments? And, similarly, is it possible or likely that the municipal governments will also try to shift expenditures and responsibilities elsewhere? Given the disparity in power between the levels of government, the more likely scenario is that the provincial governments will impose new expenditures and/or new responsibilities on their municipal counterparts.

As mentioned earlier, the Quebec government's decision to transfer the financing of several services, particularly public transit and the maintenance of local roads, back onto the municipal level has been the most dramatic example of provincial-municipal reallocation in the recent past.[11] The Quebec municipalities protested with vigour and relations between the Quebec government and the municipal associations— Union des municipalités du Québec (UMQ) and Union des municipalités régionales de comtés du Québec (UMRCQ)—were very strained. The associations brought all the pressure they could on the provincial government (including publishing a public-opinion survey indicating that the population supported the municipalities and disagreed with the provincial initiatives), but the Quebec minister of municipal affairs, Claude Ryan, refused to be swayed and the measures were adopted with only minor changes.

Yet the dilemma for provincial governments is that, in placing complete responsibility for a service (including financing) on the municipal level, the province itself loses the power to influence the nature and quality of the service. Provincial governments may be actively trying to cut their budgets, but, at the same time, they are reluctant to allow municipalities exclusive responsibility for crucial policy areas. Besides, even if the provinces were less jealous of their powers, they could not ignore the fact that local decisions affect provincial policy and provincial expenditures. Provinces that are trying to be increasingly efficient and fiscally conservative are only too aware that, in many cases, the transfer of responsibility to another level of government results in higher costs.

So, while provincial governments are naturally attracted to the idea of devolving services to municipal governments, the link between spending, responsibility, and influence on policy direction makes this unlikely. Fiscal pressure will undoubtedly reduce government activity but its impact on provincial-municipal relations may be relatively limited.

## *Urbanization and Urban Sprawl*

As we saw earlier, the rapid urbanization of the post-war period provides the general context for the provinces' creation of regional governments at the local level. In the 1950s and 1960s the multiplicity of municipal governments encouraged unplanned urban growth and ever-increasing demands for provincial expenditures on infrastructure. Concluding that the financial costs of the existing fiscal arrangements were too great, the provinces decided to rationalize the system by grouping separate municipalities under the umbrella of regional governments. It was this sort of dynamic, for example, that led to the creation of Metropolitan Toronto in 1954.[12]

Today, rates of urbanization are higher than they were in the 1970s, and urban development has clearly outgrown the boundaries of the regional governments. In Toronto, the Greater Toronto Area (GTA) covers not only Metropolitan Toronto but the regional municipalities of Halton, Peel, York, and Durham, an area that encompasses more than 40 per cent of the Ontario population.[13] In Quebec a government working group pointed out that the Montreal region has a population of 3 233 000. Of this population, only 1 775 900 fall under the regional government, la Communauté urbaine de Montréal, and only 1 017 700, less than one-third of the total, lives in the City of Montreal.[14] Crucial decisions about urban development are being taken by a large number of municipal governments, many of them relatively small and poorly equipped, in bureaucratic and political resources, to think in terms of urban-growth management. Sancton discusses three key policy areas—public transit, water supply, and garbage removal—and concludes that in each case the provincial governments are increasingly the major players.[15] The questions are too important politically, the scope of co-ordination needed too large, and the finances involved too considerable to allow municipal discretion.

The development of housing would also seem to lead in the same direction. Low-density development in suburban and urban municipalities imposes financial and other pressures on provincial governments in terms of servicing and transportation costs, the loss of agricultural land, and so on. In these circumstances, it is clear that provincial governments will continue to encourage higher-density development. It is also clear that, from the standpoint of the provinces, the expense of municipal government remains excessive and needs to be curtailed.

## *Social Diversity*

One of the most marked characteristics of large Canadian cities in the recent past has been their rapidly increasing ethnic and racial diversity. Some indication of this can be seen in Table 3, which lists those Canadian metropolitan areas with more than 20 per cent of their population foreign-born in 1986. Toronto tops the list, followed by Vancouver, and five of the eight cities are in Ontario.

*Table 3:*
*Canadian metropolitan areas with more than 20 per cent population foreign-born in 1986*

| | |
|---|---|
| Toronto | 36.0 |
| Vancouver | 28.4 |
| Hamilton | 24.1 |
| Kitchener | 20.7 |
| Victoria | 20.7 |
| Calgary | 20.6 |
| St Catharines | 20.4 |
| Windsor | 20.0 |

Source: David Ley and Larry S. Bourne, "Introduction," *The Changing Social Geography of Canadian Cities* (Montreal: McGill-Queen's University Press, 1983), 10.

Not only are there a high number of foreign-born in some of the major Canadian cities but, as Table 4 shows, this immigration increasingly comes from non-white countries. The comparison between 1956 and 1986, in terms of the ten countries sending the most immigrants to Canada in each of those years, is striking.

*Table 4:*
*Immigrant arrivals ranked by country of former residence*

| *1956* | *1986* |
|---|---|
| United Kingdom | United States |
| Italy | India |
| Germany | Vietnam |
| United States | Hong Kong |
| Netherlands | Poland |
| Greece | United Kingdom |
| France | Jamaica |
| Portugal | Philippines |
| China | Guyana |
| Switzerland | El Salvador |

Of the major countries of immigration in 1956, only the United States and the United Kingdom remain on the list in 1986. And they, along with Poland, are the only countries of white immigration on the 1986 list. What these figures do not make clear is that the changing face of Canada is largely an urban phenomenon. The large Canadian cities are becoming more and more racially diverse, but this is much less true for the country as a whole.

The impact of immigration is only beginning to be felt in terms of urban services. For example, there have been a series of confrontations in Montreal and Toronto in the 1990s over police treatment of racial minorities. Services have been set up specifically for immigrant and visible-minority populations, or for specific subsets of these populations.

What has all of this to do with provincial-municipal relations? Immigration is a shared federal-provincial responsibility, as are most of the services relating to the integration of immigrants. Yet the reality of racial and ethnic diversity is urban and the fiscal constraints on provincial governments are likely to mean that the gap between existing and needed services will grow. As this occurs, will not the pressure for municipal action increase? If so, it will likely come about from the combined actions of citizen groups, particularly those composed of members of the visible-minority and immigrant population, and municipal officials interested in adapting municipal services, programs, and structures to the new, more diverse, environment. Race relations and civil-liberties issues will affect the nature of policing in the urban community: here, too, the traditional public agenda will be seriously challenged. This may not be an immediate prospect but it would seem to be a possibility for the not too distant future. The material base for an increasingly active municipal role in areas relating to racial and ethnic diversity already exists; it is in the large cities that these questions will arise, and, politically, it is likely to be the large cities that will most feel the urgency to act. Nothing is inevitable, of course; municipalities may opt for inaction or provincial governments for greater action. Still, one can easily imagine a scenario in which municipalities take the lead in responding to the challenges of an increasingly multicultural society.

## *Conclusion*

Looking into the future is always a risky business. The four factors we have identified—globalization, fiscal constraints, urbanization and urban sprawl, and social heterogeneity—are not necessarily those that will have the greatest impact on provincial-municipal relations; they necessarily reflect the vision of today rather than one twenty years from now. Yet they do at least remind us that provincial-municipal relations operate in a broad context, where political, cultural, demographic, and economic forces all interact.

So, at the risk of being wrong, let us develop the most likely scenario for the evolution of provincial-municipal relations. The impact of the global economy will increase and, as a consequence, provincial governments (and, of course, the federal government) will become even more preoccupied with the insertion of the most dynamic sectors of the Canadian economy onto the world market. This will lead to less interest in equality as a policy goal and more interest in effectiveness and in supporting strength, and such a reorientation will be accelerated by provincial fiscal pressures and resulting budget cuts. Municipalities will receive less resources overall; certain municipalities in areas seen to be dynamic will receive more.

These resources will continue to be made available in terms of provincial policy goals. Dynamic municipalities will increasingly initiate projects destined to fit into provincial policy goals and therefore to be eligible for provincial support and financial assistance. Projects may include such areas as marketing urban services at the international level, with municipalities proposing projects and hoping to get support from provincial and federal sources. All projects will depend on the presence of dynamic politicians and/or bureaucrats at the municipal level.

These urban-growth coalitions will allow certain municipalities, likely the largest and wealthiest, to exercise greater activity. Those metropolitan areas with greater capacity to act collectively (which may or may not relate to the existence of formal structures of coordination or joint decision making) will be particularly well positioned to benefit from these changes. However, municipal activity will be in areas that correspond to provincial policy goals. Does this correspond to greater local autonomy? That is not clear. An alternate interpretation would be to see increased municipal activity as increased provincial control through the mechanism of municipalities anticipating greater provincial financial support for certain activities.

On the other hand, urban-growth coalitions will have to offer benefits to a wider group of the urban electorate than simply two or three particularly dynamic businesses. Increasing pressure will be felt from the racially and ethnically heterogeneous parts of the population, which will argue for better and more culturally sensitive services. A likely coalition strategy will be to combine support to the most dynamic sectors of the business community with support for making urban services more available and more accessible to the increasingly heterogeneous electorate. This combination of activities will be all the more likely in that the parameters of action in policy areas relating to patterns of urban growth will be increasingly limited at the local level because of greater provincial direction and control.

Local political pressure for urban services will grow as provincial government cut-backs in service and in support to community groups continue and as equality-seeking groups look more and more to the municipal level. Here again we will witness increased local activity, but only in some cities.

Our most likely scenario represents, therefore, a shift in provincial-municipal relations. Most municipalities, particularly the smaller ones, will be more controlled by their provincial governments even as they receive less provincial support for the equalization of services. Some larger municipalities will develop more dynamic strategies designed to gain support from senior governments in order to pursue policies destined to improve their place in the global economy. In order to have support for these policies, they will also develop policies aimed at improving municipal performance in areas of concern to an increasingly socially diverse population.

Our conclusions in fact come back to the title of this chapter: they represent hyper-fractionalized quasi-subordination revisited. Provincial governments do dominate provincial-municipal relations today, but it has become a very qualified domination indeed.

## Notes

1. J. Stefan Dupré, *Intergovernmental Finance in Ontario, a Provincial-Level Perspective* (Toronto: Government of Ontario, 1968; prepared for the Ontario Commission on Taxation).
2. Donald J.H. Higgins, *Local and Urban Politics in Canada* (Toronto: Gage, 1986); C.R. Tindal and S. Nobes Tindal, *Local Government in Canada*, 3rd. ed. (Toronto: McGraw Hill Ryerson, 1990).
3. Paul-André Linteau, *Maisonneuve* (Montreal: Boreal Express, 1981); Ronald Rudin, "Boosting the French Canadian Town," *Urban History Review*, vol. 11, no. 1 (1982), 1–40; Leo Johnson, *The History of Guelph* (Guelph: Guelph Historical Association, 1977); Alan F.J. Artibise, "Boosterism and the Development of Prairie Cities, 1817–1913," in *Town and City Aspects of Western Canadian Urtban Development,* Alan F.J. Artibise, ed. (Regina: Canadian Plains Research Center, University of Regina, 1981), 209–36.
4. John Taylor, "Urban Autonomy in Canada: Its Evolution and Decline," in *The Canadian City*, Gilbert Stelter and Alan F.J. Artibise, eds. (Ottawa: Carleton University Press, 1984), 478–500.
5. Warren Magnusson, "The Constitution of Movements As the Constitution of the State: Rediscovering the Local As a Site for Global Politics," in *Political Arrangements: Power and the City*, Henri Lustiger-Thaler, ed. (Montreal: Black Rose Books, 1992), 84.
6. Andrew Sancton, "The Municipal Role in the Governance of Canadian Cities," in *Canadian Cities in Transition*, Trudi Bunting and Pierre Filion, eds. (Toronto: Oxford University Press, 1991), 292.
7. Ibid., 298.
8. Anthony D. King, "Cultural Hegemony and Capital Cities," in *Capital Cities: International Perspectives*, John Taylor, Jean G. Lengellé, and Caroline Andrew, eds. (Ottawa: Carleton University Press, 1993), 251–70.
9. P.J. Smith, "The Making of a Global City: The Case of Vancouver 1943–1992," *Canadian Journal of Urban Research*, vol. 1, no. 1 (1992), 90–112; Micheline Plasse, "La politique d'internationalisation de Montreal: Une politique en devenir," *Politique*, vol. 19 (1991), 37–66; A.L. Stevenson, "The City of Toronto—International Programs," conference presentation, Institute of Public Administration of Canada, 1991, 1–14.

10. Carolyn Whitzman, "Taking Back Planning: Promoting Women's Safety in Public Places—The Toronto Experience," *Journal of Architectural and Planning Research*, vol. 9, no. 2 (1992), 169–79.
11. Caroline Andrew, "La vie municipale et régionale," in *L'Année politique au Québec 1991* (Montreal: *Le Devoir*–Québec Amérique), 131–7.
12. Timothy Colton, *Big Daddy: Frederick Gardiner and the Building of Metropolitan Toronto* (Toronto: University of Toronto Press, 1980).
13. Frances Frisken, "Planning and Servicing the Greater Toronto Area," York University Urban Studies, working paper no. 12 (1990); Andrew Sancton, "Canada As a Highly Urbanized Nation: New Implications for Government," *Canadian Public Administration*, vol. 35, no. 3 (1992), especially 292–6.
14. Groupe de travail sur Montreal et sa region, *Rapport d'etape* (Montreal 1993).
15. Sancton, "Canada As a Highly Urbanized Nation."

## *Selected Sources*

Artibise, Alan F.J. "Boosterism and the Development of Prairie Cities, 1871–1913," in *Town and City: Aspects of Western Canadian Urban Development*, Alan F.J. Artibise, ed. (Regina: Canadian Plains Research Center, University of Regina, 1981), 209–36.

Bunting, Trudi and Pierre Filion, eds. *Canadian Cities in Transition* (Toronto: Oxford University Press, 1991).

Dupré, J. Stefan. *Intergovernmental Finance in Ontario: A Provincial-level Perspective* (Toronto: Ontario Commission on Taxation, Government of Ontario, 1968).

Frisken, Frances, "Planning and Servicing the Greater Toronto Area" (Toronto: York University Urban Studies, working paper no. 12, 1990).

King, Anthony D. "Cultural Hegemony and Capital Cities," in *Capital Cities: International Perspectives*, John Taylor, Jean G. Lengellé, and Caroline Andrew, eds. (Ottawa: Carleton University Press, 1993).

Linteau, Paul-André. *Maisonneuve* (Montreal: Boréal Express, 1981).

Magnusson, Warren. "The Constitution of Movements As the Constitution of the State: Rediscovering the Local As a Site for Global Politics," in *Political Arrangements: Power and City*, Henri Lustiger-Thaler, ed. (Montreal: Black Rose Books, 1992).

Perry, J. Harvey. *A Fiscal History of Canada: The Post War Years* (Toronto: Canadian Tax Foundation, Canadian Tax Paper no. 85, 1989).

Sancton, Andrew. "Canada As a Highly Urbanized Nation: New Implications for Government." *Canadian Public Administration*, vol. 35, no. 3 (autumn 1992), 281–98.

Smith, P.J. and P.W. Moore. "Cities As a Social Responsibility: Planning and Urban Form," in *The Changing Social Geography of Canadian Cities*, Larry S. Bourne and David F. Ley, eds. (Montreal: McGill-Queen's University Press, 1993).

# 7

## *Governing Metropolitan Change: Public Policy and Governance in Canada's City Regions*

Patrick J. Smith

GROWTH MANAGEMENT AND GOVERNANCE ISSUES for the major urbanized city-regions of Canada in the last decade of the twentieth century represent what in Chinese folklore is termed "dangerous opportunities." Among most people who ponder these issues, there is clear agreement that what is at stake is the very "livability" of the most populous regions of the country. Uncontrolled growth is increasingly perceived as a threat to the sustainability of both local economies and environments.

Central to finding solutions to the policy dilemmas posed by urban growth is resolution of related questions regarding the governance of Canada's major cities and the planning for growth-management within these metropolitan settings: questions about representation and accountability, structure and capacity, leadership and function, and appropriate role(s) for senior governmental, local, and metropolitan/regional jurisdictions are at the heart of the debate about the future of our urban centres.

Canada is now a highly urbanized country. That our constitutional framework still largely reflects the Canada of the 1860s—when over three-quarters of our population was rural-agricultural—is only one of the challenges for those seeking to direct metropolitan change in Canada. Fiscal cracks in the system, with attendant preoccupations on the part of senior jurisdictions with deficits and accumulated debt, present more immediate challenges. Environmental exigencies in cities further complicate the situation.

This chapter examines the state of metropolitan governance in Canada and the prospects for reform. To date, questions about the governance of our major urban centres have focussed on the capacity of existing institutional arrangements to cope with a broad range of policy issues—from service delivery, efficiency, and preservation of urban livability to accessibility and accountability. Some, such as Andrew Sancton, have concluded that "the simple truth is that urban areas in Canada, as elsewhere, have become too big to be governed by metropolitan authorities of the type introduced in Canada from the 1950's to the 1970's. Their time is past." More important, in terms of governing metropolitan change, Sancton has concluded that "the era of *traditional* metropolitan and regional reform is over."[1]

Yet, at the same time, more Canadians live in major metropolitan areas—more than six in ten of us (61 per cent of the population, according to the 1991 census) reside in one of the twenty-five Census Metropolitan Areas (CMAs) with 100 000-plus populations, compared with just over one-quarter (26.7 per cent in the 1941 census) fifty years ago. As a result, problems with reorganizing service provision, livability, local/regional governance, intergovernmental relations, and so on have become increasingly obvious and pressing. An agenda for change to respond to the current metropolitan crisis in Canada will involve a rethinking of the involvement of senior governments (particularly the provinces) in city government. It will entail a review of current intergovernmental (including fiscal) arrangements; here, constitutional changes will *not* be required. It will necessitate a recognition of the impact of supra-national global forces with which Canadian cities deal on an almost daily basis. And it will require, on the part of both local-urban and metropolitan-regional authorities, greater flexibility and a willingness to test the outer limits of their powers and capacities. As Frances Frisken has argued, "Whether local (and metropolitan regional) governments will test the outer limits of their powers or use those limits as an excuse for inaction" will go a considerable way to determining the outcome of this reassessment.[2]

The prospects for success in meeting the new challenges of governing metropolitan change in Canada are at least partially a product of our metropolitan past. That past includes significant accomplishments, especially in the realm of public services, but also problems associated with an outgrowing of initial institutional capacity.

This is certainly apparent in the patterns of changing metropolitan form and function. Jurisdictional responses, whether in British Columbia, Quebec, Manitoba, or New Brunswick, provide important lessons on the determinants of, and challenges to, managing metropolitan change in Canada. The first "conclusion" from the comparative analysis of metropolitan governance, planning, and inter-governmental relations is that there is no agreed model for the unfolding metropolitical future.

In terms of intergovernmental dimensions (in England and Wales), John Griffith made this point almost three decades ago: he described local-senior governmental relations as "formal, informal, statutory, non-statutory, legal, extra-legal, financial, official, personal, political, functional, tragical-comical-historical-pastoral . . . Any generalization evokes shouts of protest. Every example can be shown in some way to be unrepresentative and ill-chosen."[3] This is equally the case in the United States as well: Bill Barnes, of the National League of Cities, has stated that "there is no model of state-local relations in the USA. It all depends on the state."[4]

In Canada, Frisken has recently argued that "existing differences both within and among Canada's metropolitan areas will become more rather than less pronounced."[5] Such a judgment means, not that nothing can be learned from comparative analysis, but rather that no paradigm of metropolitan governance is likely. What Griffith proposes as a "way out" of this comparative dilemma is the knowledge that "some aspects [of metropolitan governance] . . . are more important and more universal than others."[6] As with Griffith, it is those aspects of more general validity that we will emphasize. Specifically, we will examine issues of regional governance, growth-management and planning, and intergovernmental relations in Canadian metropolitan regions to determine which elements are "“more important and universal." A central theme is the compatibility or incompatibility of democratic problem-solving (through directly elected representatives) with efficient regional management.

Ontario has a long experience with urban government, stretching from the (1849) Baldwin Act "model" for municipal frameworks elsewhere in the country, through its pioneering Metropolitan Toronto experiment (in the early 1950s), to its attempts at "meta-metropolitan governing" with the Greater Toronto Area (GTA) since 1988. Consequently, this province offers a harbinger of our metropolitan futures, in terms both of failures and of successes. Its attempts to wrestle with the current, changing nature of the policy/administrative dilemma of efficiency and accountability mirror similar struggles in metropolitan settings throughout the country. It is here that this analysis of governing metropolitan change will begin.

## *Canadian Metropolitan Lessons: A Retrospective*

Upper Canada/Ontario has been in the forefront of municipal development and reform in Canada since the 1840s. Lord Durham's famous report at the beginning of the decade, following the Rebellions of 1837–38 in Upper and Lower Canada, concluded that "the utter want of municipal institutions giving the people any control over their local affairs may indeed be considered as one of the main causes of the failure of representative government and of bad administration in the country."[7] Durham recommended that the development of municipal institutions was of "vital importance" and "the people should . . . [be] entrusted with the complete control over their own local affairs, and . . . trained for taking their part in the concerns of the Province, by their experience in the management of that local business which is most interesting and most easily intelligible to them."[8]

In 1841 the new united legislature of the Canadas passed the District Councils Act, which provided for the election of district councils in Upper Canada. In 1849, the year after Durham's recommendation of responsible government was implemented in the Canadas, an act establishing a comprehensive system of municipal government for the province was passed.[9] The Municipal Corporations Act, known informally as the "Baldwin Act," served as a model for most subsequent general municipal legislation in other provinces and, as K. Grant Crawford has argued, "sustained the strains of a rapidly changing economy for over one hundred years without substantial alteration to its basic features."[10] Indeed, as C.R. Tindal and S.N. Tindal have noted, the durability of these early reforms continue into the present: "Even the reformed [that is, regional] structures introduced in the past couple of decades are essentially modified county systems."[11]

Despite the era of reform introduced with the creation of Metropolitan Toronto in 1954, basic features of the Baldwin Act continued to define much of the provincial-municipal relationship, such as the fact that municipal institutions, including metropolitan authorities, are "*creatures of the provincial legislature* and subject to its sovereign authority."[12] Since the Depression of the 1930s, when many local authorities defaulted financially, the province has taken an increasingly interventionist approach: for example, in 1932 the province created the Ontario Municipal Board (OMB), which had a quasi-judicial role in such matters as appeals on municipal zoning laws, assessments, annexations, and amalgamations. The OMB exercised its powers with considerable freedom from legislative—or executive—oversight: "Except where a matter has been declared of provincial interest, the OMB has the final say in all community planning decisions in Ontario, which have been appealed or referred to it."[13] In the 1990s the OMB (like other provincial variants such as those in Manitoba or Alberta) remains "an independent administrative tribunal . . . responsible for hearing applications and appeals concerning municipal and planning matters."[14] The final report of the Sewell Commission on Planning and Development Reform in Ontario, issued in June 1993, contained recommendations to clarify and strengthen this provision.[15] In 1935 Ontario also established a department of municipal affairs with "general responsibility for overseeing municipalities."[16] Both the OMB and the provincial ministry were crucial in resolving intermunicipal disputes and in creating Ontario's—and Canada's—first metropolitan authority, Metro Toronto.

Rapid urbanization in Canada following the Second World War[17] created growth-management pressures that demonstrated the inadequacy of local government systems. This was initially most apparent in Ontario, particularly in the Toronto-centred region. Basic service-delivery problems in the areas of water supply and sewage treatment, transportation and transit, social services and schools—areas that previously had been adequately managed by single- or multi-purpose special agencies[18]—demonstrated the incapacity of local governments to provide basic local services with any degree of efficiency; many smaller municipalities around Toronto, for example, were simply unable to cope with the pace of change. Within a decade the same kind of policy problems had begun to put equivalent pressures on other metropolitan areas of the country as well.

In Ontario, traditional solutions such as amalgamations and annexations were proposed, debated, and opposed, usually before the Ontario Municipal Board, depending on the location and size of the municipalities involved within the region. By the early 1950s, the Toronto-centred region was simply in crisis. Like many other Canadian urban/metropolitan regions, it suffered from four basic "inadequacies"[19]:

- *structural limitations:* In the Toronto area, in 1950, there were thirteen municipalities of greatly varied size, population, and wealth, as well as a large number of special-purpose (for example, school board, utility, sewerage) authorities.[20] As the Tindals have concluded, "With such a fragmented structure, concerted action to deal with urban problems was both difficult and unlikely."[21] The situation was similar in Montreal. There, the central area grew by 1.77 per cent between 1951 and 1956, versus 6.46 per cent on the rest of Montreal Island and 7.74 per cent in the other suburbs; the result was a highly fragmented metropolitan governmental system, one that has continued to bedevil local and provincial authorities into the mid 1990s.[22] More appropriate municipal boundaries and fewer, more equitable, units were called for in both cities. Bigger did seem better—at least to meet the service-delivery challenges of the 1950s.
- *functional fragmentation:* Whether as the "outgrowing" of local responsibilities—for example, in social services—or as the "reverse trend" of senior governments delegating program delivery to jurisdictions, "the combined result was that the operations of local government became increasingly

intertwined with those of senior governments."[23] The ensuing erosion of municipal powers served neither local nor senior jurisdictions well.

- *financial constraints:* Throughout Canada, property taxes proved inadequate to meet the service challenges of the post-Second World War urbanization boom. They fell from 80 per cent of municipal revenue in 1930 to just over half (53 per cent) by 1953,[24] 47 per cent by 1963, and below 40 per cent by the mid 1970s.[25] In the Toronto area, as elsewhere, individual municipalities "sought capital funds on their own credit."[26] This proved difficult and inefficient; and senior, usually provincial, government grants (whether conditional or unconditional) led to "a rapidly diminishing relationship between the taxes paid to any one level of government and the services rendered by it."[27] The increasing local dependence on revenue provided by senior governments created a new set of problems in urban governance—particularly around principles of responsibility and accountability. In 1976 the Canadian Federation of Mayors and Municipalities produced its response to a tri-level task force on public finance in Canada. Its title—*Puppets on a Shoestring: The Effects on Municipal Government of Canada's System of Public Finance*—summed up the pessimism of local governments at the time. The subsequent Federation of Canadian Municipalities (FCM) brief to the Macdonald royal commission in 1983 continued some of this lament on funding and on the lack of attention paid by senior jurisdictions to municipal expertise. The persistent lack of consideration to local/metropolitan concerns in the late-1980s and early-1990s constitutional discussions further highlighted the plight of local governments. Even production of a local government bill of rights (initially by Vancouver and then by the FCM) was little more than a plea to be taken seriously.[28]
- *unfulfilled political role:* Defenders of the "non-partisan" tradition of local government—a tradition that, as James Lightbody notes in his introductory chapter, dates to the early twentieth century—fail to recognize that the real roles and functions of this first order of government involve *politics* in

> its clearest definitional sense. Most of the policy matters now confronting urban governments in Canada concern "conflict" over public-policy choices and attempts to resolve that conflict[29]—that is, politics. One result of the "apolitical" municipal tradition was "municipal governing bodies that were ineffective in providing leadership, coordination and a clear focus of accountability and responsibility."[30] In our city regions, the idea that the only thing wrong with their governance is politics no longer holds, though that is not to say that continuing attempts to *utilize* this tradition do not exist. In Greater Vancouver, for example, there are three non-partisan associations operating as civic political parties—in Vancouver, Richmond, and (recently) Burnaby.[31]

In Canada, as indicated, problems of urban governance first became apparent in the Toronto region. Today, they are also evident in metropolitan cities such as Edmonton, Vancouver, Winnipeg, and Montreal.[32] In Winnipeg, these problems resulted in reforms to the city's initial metropolitan structure, the Metropolitan Corporation of Winnipeg, created by the province in 1961. In 1971 a second metropolitan bill amalgamated the City of Winnipeg and its twelve area municipalities in a new unified metropolitan-city government. Yet, despite such innovations as residents' advisory groups (RAGs), problems of responsiveness, representation, public understanding, authority, and political accountability continued, producing public inquiries in 1976 and 1984–85. The latter body offered recommendations to clarify lines of authority and enhance responsiveness and accountability.[33] In the Toronto area, it was similar "cracks in the foundation" that reform sought to remedy.

The first lesson from both the Manitoba and the Ontario experience is the need to itemize the "cracks" in the regional-governance system that need fixing. Certainly the capacity to manage—and plan for—rapid growth and change is important; but, as David R. Godschalk and David J. Brower contend, governance issues are at the centre of growth-management "solutions":

> One of the most troubling issues is that of governance . . . Many of the other types of issues stem from or are related to governance

> issues . . . A major governance issue concerns the lack of fit between jurisdictional boundaries and growth impact areas . . . Research is needed on the types of organizations and techniques that will work in [a] . . . fragmented . . . governance system . . . How can we rationalize the Balkanized system of governmental decision-making on development? This issue concerns the form of governance . . . It centres on the feasibility, political and legal, of broadening authority for growth decisions beyond the local government, and on the effectiveness of alternative forms of governance. At the same time, it involves dealing with the neighbourhood level, on which many growth management issues must be resolved . . . There is work to be done on governance issues. Comparative case studies of existing approaches are needed, as well as recommendations for new approaches.[34]

Douglas Porter agrees, seeing research on governance and citizen participation as the first priorities in improving understanding of the policy and practice of metropolitics: "The broader issue of governance concerns what form of government can best respond to changing urban needs; and how those entities are to be both efficient in accomplishing their objectives and responsive to a diverse citizenry . . . Traditional divisions of city, county and state governments may no longer be best suited to address these issues."[35] For Porter, whose views are shared by Andrew Sancton,[36] governance "solutions" require both understanding of and a response to the increasing complexity of urban service. That means, on the one hand, "increasingly smaller units of government to provide particular mixes of services . . . On the other hand, there is increasing evidence of regional, and even global, effects of decisions made at local levels."[37] In many of Canada's major cities, there now is a policy-making capacity focussed on the interdependent needs of a changed global setting. In Vancouver, global policy activity is now more than fifty years old.[38]

In the search for appropriate responses to the changing Canadian metropolis, Porter has called for additional research to: "a) suggest those areas where smaller units of government can effectively solve problems; b) conversely, identify issues that have impacts beyond the boundaries of existing local governments, and propose new . . . structures to address them; and c) provide models for regional and state (provincial) decision-making (and service provision) in metropolitan areas where local decisions are currently made by many fragmented governments."[39] And while citizen participation is essential, it "should be structured so it is effective in influencing decisions but does not prevent decision making."[40] Such a clear identification of problem areas is essential before appropriate action may be taken.

In the Toronto metropolitan area, initial regional-government reform in the early 1950s came as a result of a number of counter-proposals on local governance, including a 1950 application by the City of Toronto to amalgamate with its twelve closest municipal neighbours. The OMB (Cumming report) response in 1953 produced recommendations for an "upper-tier" municipality of metropolitan Toronto (the first in North America), an amalgam of the City of Toronto and the twelve surrounding municipalities with authority in such region-wide matters as borrowing, water supply and sewage treatment, and metropolitan roadways. Local governments were to remain in operation and indeed were to be the foundation of Metro government, through a system of indirect elections to the upper level.

It is arguable that the Province of Ontario, which was central to the creation of Metro Toronto, sought to resolve the most pressing service-delivery challenges and to implant the *idea* of a second-tier regional government before tackling other more politically contentious issues of governance—such as the problems posed by a number of large/small, rich/poor local units and questions of direct elections, representation, and accountability. In that respect, Metro was largely a success in its initial years: it developed "the *servicing infrastructure* needed to accommodate the growth pressures."[41] The creation of Metro also demonstrated the politically pragmatic problem-solving capacity of the OMB: the OMB agreed to the city's definition of the region's boundaries but accepted the retention of the separate, autonomous suburban municipalities.[42]

As it happened, the province was forced, initially by another City of Toronto amalgamation proposal, to "revisit" the question of Metro Toronto governance a decade later with the 1963–65 Goldenberg royal commission. In 1966, with public acceptance of the upper-tier Metro government largely in place, the province accepted Goldenberg's recommendation to deal with unit/size anomalies, cutting the number of municipalities in the region from thirteen to six.[43] The forced amalgamations generated considerable local controversies (mostly in the smaller units loosing their "identity") but the province found that the political heat was manageable and the changes were instituted on 1 January 1967. As James Lightbody has noted in chapter 1, the cause of amalgamation did not always carry the day: in St Albert's case, local political pressure on the provincial government of Alberta allowed the suburb to resist Edmonton's amalgamation plans. In Ontario, provincial management of the process of amalgamation—and of the controversy that it generated—involved increasing the size of Metro council (to thirty-two) and suburban representation (to twenty) while retaining the status quo of indirect election. Part of the conflict was also managed by the province's rejection of Goldenberg's recommendation of four, roughly equal, municipalities in favour of the existing six units: the City of Toronto and five new Boroughs (a term copied from British local government). At the same time, two additional functional reallocations (up to Metro from the lower local tier)—on waste disposal and social services—were added to region-wide services such as policing.

Yet, despite being hailed throughout North America as a model of metropolitan reform—"the only truly metropolitan government"[44]—Metropolitan Toronto was not revived by the Goldenberg reforms. Harold Kaplan, for example, has argued that it had become a relatively complacent, suburban-dominated service-delivery agent; Metro's success was in its first few years (1953-57).[45] After the mid-1960s Goldenberg review, the province was required to return again to review Metro in 1974. A royal commission chaired by former premier John Robarts recommended that the basic metro structure and its six municipal units be retained. It also recommended changes to the election of metro councillors and to some governmental responsibilities: in particular, it suggested that Metro have the the power to delegate to an executive (or other standing) committee.[46] These changes were not proceeded with by the province at that time, however. By this point, the suburbs had their basic service needs met via Metro; they dominated the revised Metro council and were not overly interested in new policy initiatives, particularly ones they saw as costly and mostly of benefit to inner-city Toronto. As in other jurisdictions, potentially conflicting interests in any metropolitan restructuring had to be balanced carefully.

Because that balance was not found, the third provincial study of Metro Toronto in its first thirty odd years was launched in the mid-1980s. In its 1986 report, a task force on representation and accountability recommended moving the governance structure toward direct elections (for the 1988 municipal elections) and allowing the six municipal mayors to hold metro council seats while providing for direct election of twenty-eight councillors in a slightly expanded metropolitan council. Only these councillors would then be eligible for election as chair.[47] For the Tindals, "These changes appear to reflect a *belated concern* by the Ontario government for the representative role of local government and its accountability and responsiveness."[48]

By then, however, the issues confronting the Toronto metropolitan region had outgrown its geographic and institutional definitions. Substantial growth in the counties and regions surrounding the original Municipality of Metro Toronto had made Metro's growth-management and governance capacity outmoded. In 1988 Ontario established the Office for the Greater Toronto Area (OGTA) to provide for more efficient handling of cross-border issues in Metro Toronto, York, Peel, Halton, and Durham and to co-ordinate provincial programming and policies in the same region.

In terms of coping with more recent development pressures, many of these adjacent regions have had to develop broader planning capacity. In the York region, for example, growth-management has been curtailed by the availability of infrastructure to handle new demands. While the region "is in the process of developing a regional official plan," this "is being done with the participation and involvement of the OGTA." Most provincial-regional contact is through the GTA co-ordinating committee of regional chief administrative officers (CAOs), an unelected body. There is also a formal system of contacts between regional and local planners as well as engineering staff. Since the region's population is expected to double again in thirty years, York, like some of its neighbours, has determined the need for a regional official plan which will focus growth around urbanized nodes, with employment having a higher priority than residential development. In February 1993 the region began to collect the public's ideas through a local participatory process for a Vision of York in 2021. This process was to be the basis for a draft regional strategic plan scheduled to be unveiled in 1994.[49]

In its 1993 reflections on the role of the regional government, under the theme "less government is better," York called for the following:

- *A rationalization of government roles:* to eliminate duplication, ensure the region provides services for the whole region and economically; and a review of local/regional boundaries to ensure these "respect people's sense of community." Plus co-operation between York/other regions on economic development, waste management, and transportation.
- *Accountability:* Here, the main focus is on the electoral system, which "should be examined with a view to analyzing and adopting direct elections. Direct elections may serve to resolve the problem of . . . municipal councillor first, regional second. Regional issues need to be tackled as a priority, not after . . . municipal responsibilities have been met." Plus the need to involve the public in "major expenditure issues."
- *Communication:* The need for more public information on the region/regional government. "There is a sense that the public simply does not know enough about regional issues, other than when one heats up."[50]

The fact that York Region waited until 1993 to start a process to establish an official regional plan, to tackle the issues of regional visibility and accountability, and to determine "measures of success" for such ventures indicates that it has been late in recognizing "the piecemeal planning of the past" and the need for "a higher quality relationship between [regional] politicians and those they serve."[51] Finally, however, York, appears to have joined the local democratic reformers of the 1990s. The issues of representation and accountability, so central to the debate currently under way in York, suggests some of what has been lacking in metropolitics to date.

In Metropolitan Toronto and the Greater Toronto Area, concerns around the themes of leadership, accountability, and governability have recently been paramount.[52] Metropolitan Toronto met its initial service-delivery crisis with regional solutions in the 1950s and 1960s. It also went some way to developing a highly visible regional identity.

Yet, as Kaplan and others have argued, it then got "bogged down" in the cozy phase that followed the 1974–77 Robarts royal commission. As noted, it was not until 1986 that the task force on representation and accountability presented a report calling for direct elections to the Metropolitan Council. Bill 29, passed by David Peterson's Liberal government in 1988, provided for a council of thirty-four with twenty-eight directly elected plus the six Metro mayors. Metro responded with its own strategic plan in 1991. Based on public consultation, this plan set as its goals a vital economy, environmentally sustainable urban development, social equity, and accountable governance. Among the "key objectives" on accountable governance were provisions for Metro to "take a leadership role" and to "assert the Metropolitan Toronto Government's autonomy to determine the nature and scope of its services, programs and policies."[53]

As a result of this "more aggressive" Metro stance, however, the region's local mayors and councils began to react more negatively. With Metro making more comments and exercising more oversight on major developments, several councils (for example, North York and the City of Toronto) passed resolutions to place a referendum before their local voters in the November 1994 local elections asking whether they should separate from Metro. While that question does not assume an actual capacity to separate, politically it says a good deal about how well things have been going between Metro and its federated municipalities,. It also suggests some of the possible problems of the "bigger is better" school of metropolitan reform.

The expectation that a more accountable system for Metro Toronto would be the basis for similar representative reforms in other Ontario metropolitan regions, both in the Toronto-centred GTA and in other urban-regions such as Hamilton-Wentworth and Niagara, was not realized. Ottawa-Carleton has been the exception. Outside Metropolitan Toronto, the very first regional government to be established in Ontario during the five years (1969–74) of municipal restructuring under premiers Robarts and William Davis was Ottawa-Carleton. Created in January 1969, it had an initial population of 467 000 and covered an area of almost 2849 square kilometres; this meant that, in comparison to the regions established in the 1970s, it was the largest in population size and the second-largest in area. Previously there had been sixteen local municipalities; after regional government in 1969, there were still sixteen; however, provincially imposed amalgamations reduced this number to eleven by January 1974—during the same period that the province was creating the Halton, Peel, Durham, Hamilton Wentworth, and the Haldimand-Norfolk regions and in the process reducing significantly the number of local municipal authorities. (A total of fifty municipalities were abolished by the acts setting up these five other regional governments.)[54]

In the mid 1970s, the Regional Municipality of Ottawa Carleton (RMOC) was reviewed by Henry Mayo. Mayo's October 1976 report recommended a reduction to nine municipalities but a council enlarged from thirty-one to thirty-four and direct elections as an alternative to the indirect system used since Ottawa-Carleton had been created. Mayo concluded that "direct elections have very powerful advantages which are insufficiently recognized. These chiefly revolve around the questions of perspective, or how regional councillors perceive their role, and of conflicting loyalties."[55] He also cautioned against regional "at large" elections, which were "difficult and too expensive" and had the potential to shut out small communities; in this regard, he cited "the failure of . . . Metropolitan government in Winnipeg," where "overlapping and crosscutting of regional and local boundaries may well have been a contributing factor" in unsuccessful reform efforts. Despite the extent of the Mayo report's recommendations (and of similar reviews in the last part of the 1970s in Niagara, Hamilton-Wentworth, and Waterloo), "only minor changes were introduced, notably the creation of the City of Kanata and the elevation of Nepean to city status."[56]

Another review of the Ottawa-Carleton region was undertaken by the Peterson government in the late 1980s. This review ultimately took the form of three studies: an initial study in RMOC under David Bartlett during 1987–88 focussing on regional roles and the allocation of responsibilities and on accountability and representation questions; a study of regional electoral boundaries by a commission under chair Katherine Graham in 1988–90; and a study, conducted by Graeme Kirby in May–November 1992, that consulted "the municipalities and the public on issues arising from previous reviews of regional government in Ottawa-Carleton."

In the first study, Bartlett, like Mayo a decade earlier, concluded that there was an appropriate functional distinction between local and regional government.[57] To resolve the questions "What is local? What is regional?" Bartlett added the following guidelines:

> —unless there are good reasons to the contrary, the regional municipality should be responsible for those municipal policies which are important throughout all, or a large part of the region. The lower tier should deal with matters which do not have substantial ramifications beyond each individual municipality.
>
> —unless there are good reasons to the contrary, one should try to achieve economies of scale.
>
> —unless there are good reasons to the contrary, regional administration is appropriate where it is essential to apply uniform policy and practice across the region.[58]

In a November 1992 follow-up review under the NDP government of Bob Rae, Commissioner Graeme Kirby, drawing on the 1967 Smith committee, added two additional criteria: "unless there are good reasons to the contrary, matters affecting the long-term well-being of the region . . . should be dealt with at the regional level. Local municipalities should be responsible for more day-to-day matters; and unless there are good reasons to the contrary, the structure of the region should be such as to provide each resident with the sense of being a participant in the decisions of local government.[59]

Bartlett's other central recommendation was that RMOC move to a system of directly electing the majority of regional councillors, "who are exclusively responsible to and accountable for the region . . . so that the Region may carry out its full political role as well as its service functions." This was because "in broad economic, social, cultural and functional terms, *the metropolis operates as an organic whole.*"[60]

The Graham commission was appointed in July 1988 "to establish electoral boundaries for the Regional Municipality of Ottawa Carleton and its local municipalities"[61] without increasing the total number of local politicians in the region. Graham concluded that there "was a sense of frustration with the current system overall and with the lack of political accountability of the regional government in its present form."[62] Graham's other conclusion—which is of comparative use—is that while there was generalized public support for regionalized solutions, the RMOC was "prevented from doing this effectively because regional council is characterized by excessive political parochialism." The parochialism was generally perceived as a product of representative structure: "Observers see this parochialism as stemming from the tendency of regional councillors to vote on proposals . . . through the prism of what they might mean to their local municipality."[63] This was a theme raised in each of the recent Ontario reviews of regional governments. Graham's solution, reported at the end of November 1990, was the "creation of a system of regional wards which will make the regional government as accountable as possible." To do that, Graham recommended the maximum number of direct-election regional seats—eighteen.[64] Representation of geographically defined communities of interest was also considered important to ensure "some potential for political efficacy in the regional government of Ottawa Carleton." Finally, the Graham report endorsed "the principle of having one representative per ward . . . because it enhances political accountability by lessening the chance of public confusion about 'who is responsible for what' and potential 'buck passing' among elected representatives who might share the same ward."[65]

In comparative terms Graham's conclusions on mayoral representation at the regional level are also useful; Graham echoed Bartlett's view that "the function of local mayors on regional council is to bridge municipal interests with regional concerns, whereas directly elected regional councillors are to take the region as their primary focus."[66] Graham did recommend eighteen rather than fourteen regional representatives, however, so the eleven mayors would have a strong presence without being the dominant force on the regional council. Graham's concluding recommendation was for the reforms to be put in place for the 1991 municipal elections to ensure "a regional council that combines a sense of direction for the region as a whole with sensitivity to the needs . . . of communities of interest."[67] Yet, as it turned out, a provincial election and change of government intervened.

In the fall of 1991, shortly after the coming to power of the NDP, an in-house review of most regional governments was begun in Ontario. This continued into the winter and spring of 1992, but then its focus shifted to Ottawa-Carleton alone. On 15 May 1992 the Kirby commission was appointed to study the government of the Ottawa region, and the rest of the general review process was quietly dropped by the then minister of municipal affairs. Indications are that Ottawa-area minister Evelyn Gigantes, who favoured one-tier government for the region, insisted that Ottawa-Carleton be pulled from the package for more immediate attention. The other reason for action on Ottawa-Carleton alone was the view that Ottawa, as the only major population centre in eastern Ontario, was an anomaly that required separate consideration. It was thought that there were too many administrative links and too great a variation in the levels of service in the region. The prospect of cost savings and a stronger capacity to plan—both strong indicators of efficiency—was yet another motivating factor behind the new approach.

The Kirby study's interim report in September 1992 caused considerable reaction, particularly in Ottawa's suburbs. Kirby outlined two governance options: a reduction of the eleven municipalities to five, with the upper tier remaining; and a one-tier government for all urban taxpayers. Kirby also called for regional policing, streamlining hydro commissions and libraries, and a direct vote for regional councillors. The smaller communities reacted with outrage, calling the report a "shotgun marriage," "something that someone dreamed up," and the like.[68]

After additional discussion, Kirby produced a final report in November 1992. Though recommending the preservation of the two-tier structure, the report supported amalgamations in Ottawa-Vanier, Kanata/Goulbourn, and Gloucester/Cumberland if these were approved in referenda. It also emphasized the need to move several responsibilities to the upper-regional tier, such as economic development.[69] In the wake of the 1991 change to an "at-large'"election of the regional chair, Kirby called for the direct election of regional councillors. He supported Graham's call for eighteen regional councillors, with her recommended wards; he proposed reducing the number of mayors by one—eliminating Rockcliffe Park. As with the interim report, the municipalities surrounding Ottawa were not very positive. The City of Nepean funded its own study to counteract Kirby. This was forwarded to the minister of municipal affairs in January 1993. Other municipalities (for example, Ottawa) also responded to the minister.

Most commentators assumed that difficulties over the social contract in the summer of 1993 in Ontario had sapped the province's energy to press ahead with changes in Ottawa-Carleton, but, to everyone's surprise, the government introduced a bill on 22 July 1993 to amend the Regional Municipality of Ottawa Carleton Act. Bill 77 regionalized policing, waste collection, sewers, home-care, and economic development; it also reduced the number of local councillors and included direct elections for all regional councillors. (Education was left alone for the time being, but a separate report on this subject was to follow.) Bill 77 was soon withdrawn but then resurfaced in amended form as Bill 143, which became law on 2 May 1994.

The 1994 legislation certainly represents the most significant shift in regional government in Ontario in several years. Whether this stands as an aberrant case or as the model of Ontario's new response to the problems of representation and accountability that have plagued its regional governments remains an open question. There is considerable indication that the RMOC changes will not be repeated in Ontario in the short term. In any event, the issue of direct versus indirect election of regional councils has dominated much of the recent discussion of metropolitan reform in Ontario, with the trend pointing increasingly to direct election. That has not been the universal response. In both Vancouver and Montreal, recent (1993–94) reviews have concluded otherwise.

In an ongoing review of regional government in British Columbia, that province's Ministry of Municipal Affairs has suggested that major growth areas such as the Victoria/Capital Region or the Greater Vancouver Regional District (GVRD) may require separate consideration. The Vancouver-centred region is the fourth-fastest growing metropolitan area in North America.[70] The combination of a major metropolitan region with most of the best arable land in British Columbia—in the lower mainland—creates significant potential for policy conflict. The resultant dilemmas—for example, on land-use planning, transportation, and green space—stand out as illustrative of the necessity of devising regional solutions and highlight the implications of such solutions for governance in metropolitan Vancouver. The premise argued here is that metropolitan governance has emerged in place of metropolitan government in the Vancouver region: that is, metropolitan-wide services are managed regionally in the absence of metropolitan government.[71] As the inheritor of the

Lower Mainland Regional Planning Board's (1966) official regional plan, the GVRD undertook its own process of developing a planning strategy in the late 1960s and early 1970s.

In 1975 the GVRD adopted a planning process, entitled the Livable Regional Programme (LRP). The LRP sought to create guidelines, based on forecasts, citizen preferences, and economic conditions, for the future development of the lower mainland. Distinct from the Official Regional Plan, the LRP was intended to be dynamic enough to respond to changes. It centred upon five strategies that would manage growth within the GVRD: establishing "job targets" for the various core areas; establishing "regional town centres" as growth poles ; allocating residential growth consistent with services and jobs; preserving farmland, parkland, and significant views; and establishing a system of light rapid transit as the key to achievement of the other four strategies.

The LRP, which had been based on an extensive citizen participation process, enjoyed the widespread support of the metropolitan community. It had a lasting impact on regional development decisions between 1976 and 1983, particularly the introduction of strategically located regional town centres throughout the GVRD. The legacy of the LRP for regional urban development in metropolitan Vancouver was demonstrated in continuing GVRD support for the preservation of farm land in the region. It was also shown in the continuing capacity to plan regionally, even after the 1983 loss of regional planning authority when it was taken away by the province over a land-use dispute.

During the rest of the 1980s, the consensus achieved throughout the LRP process "helped shape the region and focus action." By 1989 the GVRD had developed the outline for a major update of the LRP. Initiated as a region-wide consultative process—under the title *Choosing Our Future*—the GVRD's review highlighted seven broad "livability goals" (on the natural environment, the economy, accessibility, health and safety, diversity, equity, and efficiency). After a year of discussion and consultation, the 1990 blueprint *Creating Our Future* set out fifty-four steps to ensuring a "livable region" for the Vancouver metropolis. Afterwards, the GVRD undertook a series of working exercises which aimed at the implementation of these regional planning goals, including a series of public forums in 1993 on air and water quality, liquid and solid-waste management, land-use, transportation planning, parks, and hospitals.

That the GVRD achieved such policy consensus without formal planning authority attests to the conclusion that planning regionally has become an accepted staple of governance in the Vancouver region. Intergovernmental "defeats" for the regional district have not substantially altered that regional "accord." At present, the provincial government is engaged in a series of policy discussions revolving around the return of regional planning authority to the regional districts. Legislation is anticipated during the term of the current NDP government. Indications are that the province will "enhance" regional planning powers but not return full planning authority to its regional districts. Instead, the province will put in place a "step-by-step mediation process" via "provincial referees" as a "way out" for any issues that might become or remain too contentious for local-regional resolution.[72] At the same time, planning exercises are going on at alternative levels both below and above the Greater Vancouver region: in Vancouver, for example, a *City Plan* exercise under way throughout 1993 produced a series of initiatives and meetings that will lead to a report by year's end. Much of this work has emphasized "neighbourhoods."[73]

How Greater Vancouver manages metropolitan change represents a particular dilemma for the provincial authority. With the Vancouver Census Metropolitan Area containing 51 per cent of British Columbia's population, the province is cautious in its dealings with the region. There also seems to be a tendency on the part of the province to prefer the benefits of maintaining a system of indirect election to the regional district rather than direct elections because of the benefits of regional solutions emerging with high degrees of local governmental "buy-in."

In Quebec, the provincially appointed task force on greater Montreal, in its December 1993 report *Montreal: A City-Region*, took the same approach. In recognizing the need for better co-ordination of regional actions through the creation of a new "Montreal Metropolitan Region" with responsibilities in regional planning and development, economic development, the environment, culture and the arts, transportation, and public safety, the task force rejected the idea of direct elections. Instead, it called for a metropolitan council to be "made up exclusively of municipal councillors." Its decision was "based on the need to achieve the best possible harmony between regional and local issues."[74]

## *Conclusion*

The initial pressures for reform of local governing structures in Canada's city-regions were efficiency-driven. The failure of the post-Second World War municipal framework to provide basic services in an era of rapid growth and change produced increased provincial intervention and metropolitan governmental reforms, initially in Toronto and subsequently in such city regions as Montreal, Vancouver, and Winnipeg. These metropolitan authorities met the service-delivery challenges of the 1940s, 1950s, and 1960s. By the 1970s, however, cracks had begun to appear in the new metropolitan framework. The pressures impinging on metropolitan governments included a continuing shortage of revenue which was exacerbated by senior-governmental "downloading" of responsibilities, geographic/boundary fragmentation, and increased interdependency/global factors. Metropolitan authorities also had to contend with a range of concerns about representation, accessibility, and accountability.

The solutions reached in metropolitan regions in Canada and by their provincial political masters suggests a multiplicity of responses. Two observers of the metropolitan experience in Canada have expressed fairly gloomy projections of the capacity for managing metropolitan change, though for different reasons. Andrew Sancton has concluded that "it is time to reconceptualize provincial governments as institutions primarily concerned with the major issues of urban life. Local governments . . . [will] have a crucial role in delivering services and expressing local opinion. The role, *if any*, for existing top-tier metropolitan and regional authorities is much more difficult to envisage."[75] Frances Frisken feels that senior governments are virtually incapable of solving the metropolitan challenges: "The federal government [is] generally indifferent to the nature and needs of metropolitan Canada," and the future of Canadian cities is going to be drawn largely by themselves because provinces are "ambivalent" and incapable of coping with and comprehending the needs of large urban places.[76] Sancton calls for "getting on with the job rather than engage in constant structural tinkering," with an emphasis on enhanced provincial and local roles, while Frisken sees "little evidence that a pro-urban value system motivates federal or provincial governments either to help cities adjust to disruptions associated with global economic restructuring or to counteract the processes promoting decentralization and dispersal within individual metropolitan areas."

One response to these conclusions is that Sancton and Frisken may simply reflect a current pessimism about the Ontario metropolitan experience. The experience of Ontario suggests a sometimes fumbling reformist hand, with interminable investigations, reports with substantially undifferentiated recommendations, and subsequent governmental inertia. On top of all this, reform efforts have generally sought to appease irreconcilably opposed institutional actors. Still, it is possible to be hopeful. If Canada's metropolitan regions are in flux, most are not in crisis. Metropolitan policy making and agenda setting in Canada take a variety of forms; no one template fits all of them. In Unicity Winnipeg, for instance, a commitment to direct democracy allowed the province to bypass the roadblock presented by various forces. The examples of Ottawa-Carleton (and Metro Toronto) suggest that these lessons have not been entirely overlooked in Ontario either.

In terms of who will take responsibility for a new metropolitan agenda, the picture is not entirely clear. There is broad agreement that, in Canada, it will not be the federal government, even with the mid-1990s $6-billion urban infrastructure initiative of Jean Chrétien's Liberal administration. What remains to be resolved are the future roles of the provincial, local, and metropolitan/regional governments.

For Sancton, provincial authorities will be the key players in reconceptualizing metropolitan governance; for Frisken, provincial governments are at best "ambivalent" about urban matters. The reality, however, is that provinces will be more involved, less ambivalent, and an important—if not the key—actor in the setting of a new metropolitan agenda.

Local governments, as Sancton suggests, will remain significant vehicles for democratic access and involvement. Indeed, as H.P. Oberlander and P.J. Smith conclude, "in some instances, local governments are the essential (though not exclusive) decision makers."[77] In some settings what will be required will be amalgamations to create units of more equitable size, and on this front the provinces will be important actors.

Metropolitan/regional governments will remain significant, too. What is at question is the form, or forms, such governments may take in the future. Sancton has been the most pessimistic about the role of metropolitan government in resolving the urban crisis. Contrary to Sancton, however, not all metropolitan regions face the dilemmas of the Greater Toronto Area or the San Françisco Bay region. In settings such as metropolitan Vancouver, Oberlander and Smith argue persuasively that "it is entirely possible to talk of regional governance as a viable alternative to more traditional forms of regional government."[78]

Provincial responses exist and are varied. Ontario's response to the accountability-efficiency dilemma is far from clear. As was shown, there is some indication, for example, through representative and functional reforms in Metropolitan Toronto and Ottawa-Carleton, that the province sees more significant, and directly elected, regional authorities as the solution. Yet it does not take the same view with regard to Niagara or many of the other regional governments in Ontario.

Direct elections for regional authorities is also not the only option. In Greater Vancouver and likely in the other British Columbia metropolitan regions too (Victoria/Capital, Nanaimo/Mid-Island, and Okanagan), the model of metropolitan *governance* rather than *government* has recently been re-enforced. The GVRD, which since 1983 has lacked formal planning authority, has spent almost five years (through its highly consultative *Creating Our Future* process) developing plans for a doubling of the region's population over three decades and the "sharing" of that growth by member local municipalities in (and immediately beyond) the regional district. While a variety of local-regional problems remain—for example, the linking of rapid transit and other transportation improvements to particular municipalities—a considerable degree of local consensus has emerged in the metropolitan region without the presence of formal regional authority and with a system of indirect representation.

The major conclusion of this chapter is that *all* levels of government—federal, provincial, regional, and local—will continue to be important components in setting metropolitan agendas and in solving the policy dilemmas of our urban regions in Canada.

One key factor, as Sancton has noted, will be the emergence of a metropolitan governing structure which is "flexible and adaptable."[79] Sancton's conclusion—that a GVRD with restored and expanded planning powers would be the appropriate model—goes too far. An enhanced regional district system as in British Columbia, with provincial arbitration only when local-regional systems cannot reach decisions, would appear to be a more sensible approach.

Finally, Frisken offers a second key. She notes that "much of the onus for meeting [the] challenges [of global economic restructuring, urban growth, decentralization, and dispersal] is falling on municipal authorities; whether they test the outer limits of their powers or use those limits as excuses for inaction; whether they cooperate or compete with each other; and whether they persist in traditional land-use practices or undertake to modify them, their activities will have a considerable influence on the future form of metropolitan areas and the distribution of advantages and disadvantages within them."[80]

Frisken is uncertain "whether or not Canadian local governments [will] acquire the capacity or willingness for purposeful action."[81] Yet there is considerable evidence that many local and regional governments in Canada have the willingness. Frisken's comment about "testing the outer limits of their powers" is the clue to how they will find the capacity. It will not be straight-line progress. Senior provincial authorities will at times find such "testing" difficult, but it is already occurring. Having encouraged the local "hens" to come out of their jurisdictional henhouses—through such "pushes" as "down-loading" and encouragement of global activism—senior provincial governments will need to recognize Judge Dillon's warning of "the folly" of failing to distinguish between authority and power. Frisken is certain that the responses of city regions "to the demands and expectations arising from economic change and social complexity are likely to become increasingly important to the development of Canada's metropolitan areas and the well-being of their populations."[81] Much of the new metropolitan agenda will be set by—and within—the city regions themselves.

## *Notes*

1. Andrew Sancton, "Canada As a Highly Urbanized Nation: New Implications For Government," *Canadian Public Administration*, vol. 35, no. 3 (autumn, 1992), 292, 298. Author's emphasis.

2. Frances Frisken, "Metropolitan Change and the Challenge to Public Policy," introduction to *The Changing Canadian Metropolis*, Frances Frisken, ed. (Berkeley, Calif.: Institute of Governmental Studies Press, University of California, 1994), 1–35.
3. J.A.G. Griffith, *Central Departments and Local Authorities* (London: George Allen and Unwin, 1966), 17.
4. Bill Barnes, "Notes," in Richard Gilbert and Don Stevenson, *Disentangling Local Government Responsibilities: International Comparisons* (Toronto: Canadian Urban Institute, January 1993), 143.
5. Frisken, "Metropolitan Change and the Challenge to Public Policy."
6. Griffith, *Central Departments and Local Authority.*
7. *Lord Durham's Report*, Gerald Craig, ed. (Toronto: McClelland and Stewart, 1963), 67.
8. Ibid.
9. This Municipal Act was actually introduced in 1843, just after the passage of the District Councils Act, but was not passed "because of a rupture with the Governor General" until 1849. See C.R. Tindal and S.N. Tindal, *Local Government in Canada,* 3rd. ed. (Toronto: McGraw-Hill Ryerson, 1990), 22.
10. K. Grant Crawford, *Canadian Municipal Government* (Toronto: University of Toronto Press, 1954), 32.
11. Tindal and Tindal, *Local Government in Canada.*
12. Warren Magnusson, "Introduction: The Development of Canadian Urban Government," in W. Magnusson and A. Sancton, *City Politics in Canada* (Toronto: University of Toronto Press, 1983), 6. Italics added. See also P.J. Smith, "Local Governance: First Order or Third Level?" in *The Puzzles of Power: An Introduction to Political Science,* Michael Howlett and David Laycock, eds. (Toronto: Copp Clark Longman, 1994), 485–92.
13. Ministry of Municipal Affairs, Province of Ontario, *Ontario Municipal Board: A Citizen's Guide* (Toronto: Queen's Printer, 1993), no. 6:2.
14. George G. Bell and Andrew D. Pascoe, *The Ontario Government: Structure and Functions* (Toronto: Wall and Thompson, 1988), "Ministry of the Attorney General," 196. In its deliberations, the OMB takes into account environmental, social, and economic considerations; provincial interests; the rights of individual citizens; and the best interests of the community as a whole. Apart from the Ontario Municipal Board Act, the OMB derives its jurisdiction and authority from over seventy other statutes and over one hundred private acts for individual municipalities.

15. *New Planning for Ontario, Final Report of the Commission on Planning and Development Reform in Ontario*, John Sewell, Chair (Toronto: Queen's Printer, June 1993).
16. Bell and Pascoe, *The Ontario Government*, "Ministry of Municipal Affairs," 129–42. The department assumed responsibility for standardizing municipal accounting, compiling statistical data, conducting special investigations, and advising municipalities. Later, policy and planning functions were added.
17. Between 1945 and 1975 Canada had the fastest pace of urban growth among Western industrial nations. See Len Gertler and Donald Crowley, *Changing Canadian Cities: The Next 25 Years* (Toronto: McClelland and Stewart, 1977), 40ff.
18. See, for example, Fred F. Schindler, *Responsible Government in Ontario* (Toronto: University of Toronto Press, 1969).
19. These are identified in any number of reviews of local government reform; the list is from Tindal and Tindal, *Local Government in Canada*, 67–76.
20. See Marie-Odile Trepanier, "Metropolitan Government in the Montreal Area," in *Metropolitan Governance: American/Canadian Intergovernmental Perspectives*, Don Rothblatt and Andrew Sancton, eds. (Berkeley, Calif.: Institute of Governmental Studies Press, University of California, 1993), 111–52. See also Province of Quebec, Task Force on Greater Montreal, *Montreal: A City Region* (December 1993).
21. See, for example, Dominic DelGuidice and Steven M. Zacks, "The 101 Government of Metro Toronto," in *Politics and Government of Urban Canada*, 1st. ed., L. Feldman and M. Goldrick, eds. (Toronto: Methuen, 1969), 219–29.
22. Tindal and Tindal, *Local Government in Canada*, 68.
23. Ibid., 69.
24. See, for example, Carl Goldenberg, "Municipal Finance and Taxation: Problems and Prospects," in *Forecast of Urban Growth Problems and Requirements, 1956–1980* (Montreal: Canadian Federation of Mayors and Municipalities, 1955).
25. See *Policies, Programs and Finance*, report of the tri-level task force on public finance (Ottawa, 1976).
26. Tindal and Tindal, *Local Government in Canada*, 79.
27. Ontario Economic Council, *Government Reform in Ontario* (Toronto: Queen's Printer, 1969), viii. The council concluded that the major disadvantage of senior-government assistance was "accountability": "The

public never knows who is responsible for what or how much the services provided really cost" (19).

28. See *Toward New Generation of Government: Making Government Work for You* (Vancouver: City Council, September 1991).
29. J.D.B. Miller, in *The Nature of Politics* (London: Gerald Duckworth, 1962), defines politics as "conflict." For Harold Lasswell, politics is simply, "who gets what, when, how." See Lasswell's *Politics: Who Gets What, When, How* (New York: McGraw-Hill, 1936).
30. Tindal and Tindal, *Local Government in Canada*, 76.
31. See P.J. Smith, "1993 Municipal Elections in Metropolitan Vancouver: Left? Right? Indifferent?" Canadian Political Science Association paper (Calgary, June 1994) for a discussion of this point.
32. See the following papers in *Metropolitan Governance*, Rothblatt and Sancton, eds.: Ted Thomas, "Edmonton: Planning in the Metropolitan Region," 283–328; Peter Oberlander and Patrick Smith, "Governing Metropolitan Vancouver: Regional Intergovernmental Relations in British Columbia," 375–432; Trepanier, "Metropolitan Government in the Montreal Area," 111–52; and Frances Frisken, "Planning and Servicing the Greater Toronto Area: The Interplay of Provincial and Municipal Interests," 205–44. On Winnipeg, see, for example, Harold Kaplan, *Reform, Planning, and City Politics: Montreal: Winnipeg, and Toronto* (Toronto: University of Toronto Press, 1982); and Meyer Brownstone and T.J. Plunkett, *Metropolitan Winnipeg: Politics and Reform of Local Government* (Berkeley, Calif. University of California Press, 1983).
33. See *Our City in Review: The City of Winnipeg Act Review*, 1984–85: *Issues Paper* (Winnipeg, 1984); and *Report: Summary of Sections and Recommendations* (1985).
34. David R. Godschalk and David J. Brower, "A Coordinated Growth Management Research Strategy," in *Understanding Growth Management: Critical Issues and a Research Agenda*, David J. Brower, David R. Godschalk, and Douglas R. Porter, eds. (Washington, D.C.: The Urban Land Institute, 1989), 163–65. In the United States, given "traditions of limiting government intervention into market decisions, granting local governments autonomy over development decisions within their borders, and protecting individual property rights, growth managers find their powers constrained by law, custom and politics" (163).
35. Douglas R. Porter, "Significant Research Needs in the Policy and Practice of Growth Management," in *Understanding Growth Management*, Brower, Godschalk, and Porter, eds., 181.

36. See Andrew Sancton, "Governing Canada's City Regions," *Policy Options,* vol. 15, no. 4 (May 1994), 12–15.
37. Ibid.
38. On global features and local policy making in the Vancouver region, see P.J. Smith, "The Making of a Global City: Fifty Years of Constituent Diplomacy—The Case Of Vancouver," *Canadian Journal of Urban Research,* vol. 1, no. 1 (July 1992), 90–112.
39, Porter, "Significant Research Needs."
40. Ibid., 183.
41. Albert Rose, *Governing Metropolitan Toronto: A Social and Political Analysis, 1953–1971* (Berkeley, Calif.: University of California Press, 1972), 80. Italics added.
42. See ibid. for one of the most extensive reviews of the early Metro Toronto experience.
43. *Report of the [Goldenberg] Royal Commission on Metropolitan Toronto,* (Toronto: Queen's Printer, 1965).
44. Stanley Scott and Victor Jones, "Foreword," in A. Rose, *Governing Metropolitan Toronto,* vii.
45. See, for example, Harold Kaplan, *Reform, Planning, and City Politics,* 683–739.
46. *Report of the [Robarts] Royal Commission on Metropolitan Toronto* (Toronto: Queen's Printer, 1977).
47. *Analysis and Options for the Government of Metropolitan Toronto,* report of the task force on representation and accountability in Metropolitan Toronto (Toronto, November 1986).
48. Tindal and Tindal, *Local Government in Canada,* 83. Italics added.
49. See *Planscape,* no.1 (York Region: February 1993), appendix I.
50. *York Region 2021: Draft Vision Document,* 25 May 1993, "Role of Regional Government," 19–20.
51. Ibid., 21, "Conclusions."
52. See *Governing Metropolitan Toronto* and Kaplan, *Reform, Planning, and City Politics.*
53. Municipality of Metropolitan Toronto, *Metropolitan Toronto Government Strategic Plan,* executive summary, May 1991, 7.
54. For a detailed discussion of regional governance in Ontario, see P.J. Smith, *Regional Governance in Ontario: Leadership, Accountability and Governability* (B.C. Ministry of Municipal Affairs, 1993).
55. Henry B. Mayo, commissioner, *Report of the Ottawa-Carleton Review Commission* (Toronto: Queen's Printer, 1976), 111.
56. Tindal and Tindal, *Local Government in Canada,* ch. 4, "Local Government Reform," 85.

57. Mayo *Report*: "Matters of purely local concern should be left to the lower tier, and matters of region-wide concern should be handled by the upper tier" (120–1).
58. *Report of the Ottawa-Carleton Regional Review, Phase II*, David Bartlett, commissioner (1988).
59. Ottawa Carleton Regional Review Commission, *Final Report*, Graeme Kirby, commissioner (November 1992), 14.
60. Ottawa Carleton Regional Review, *Accountability and Representation, Phase One Report*, David Bartlett, commissioner (December 1987), 9. (Bartlett's emphasis). Information for this Ottawa-Carleton discussion is also drawn from the *Report of the Ottawa Carleton Electoral Boundaries Commission*, Katherine A. Graham, commissioner (November 1990); André Bernard, Jacques Leveille, and Guy Lord, *Profile: Ottawa-Hull: The Political and Administrative Structures of the Metropolitan Region of Ottawa-Hull* (Ottawa: Ministry of State for Urban Affairs, 1974); RMOC Economic Development Task Force, *Partners for the Future: A Strategic Economic Vision for Ottawa Carleton* (March 1992); various "Responses" by area municipalities to the Kirby reports—for example, RMOC's (March 1993) and Nepean's (January 1993); the 1993 RMOC Statute Law Amendment Act; and various press commentaries. As well, interviews were conducted with Katherine Graham, director, School of Public Administration, Carleton University, Caroline Andrew, University of Ottawa; David Siegel, Brock University; Engin Isin, York University; Andrew Sancton, University of Western Ontario; David Root, municipal adviser, Field Management Branch, Ottawa Regional Office, Ministry of Municipal Affairs, Ontario; Chris Bradshaw, community relations officer, RMOC; Luce Lavoie, manager, Corporate Communications, RMOC; Les Hedgie, director of planning, City of Gloucester; David Eyre, president, Rockcliffe Park Conservation Association; Mare Brown, Boundaries Branch, Ministry of Municipal Affairs; David Shtern, manager, Local Government Policy Branch, Ministry of Municipal Affairs; and Sue Lott, assistant to Evelyn Gigantes, minister of housing, Ontario.
61. *Report* of the (Graham) Ottawa Carleton Electoral Boundaries Commission (November 1990), 2.
62. Ibid., 5.
63. Ibid., 6.
64. Interview with Katherine Graham, and *Report* of the Graham commission, "Principles For Designing Wards," 7.
65. *Report* of the Graham commission, 11.

66. Ibid.
67. Ibid., 55.
68. *Ottawa Citizen* and various rural/suburban region newspapers.
69. This was called for in *Partners for the Future.*
70. Between 1986 and 1990, population in the Greater Vancouver metropolitan area grew by 12 per cent, which tied the region with Seattle-Tacoma. Only Orlando, Sacramento, and San Diego experienced more rapid growth in North America. See *Sustainability in the Georgia Basin/Puget Sound Region*, discussion paper for the British Columbia Round Table on the Environment and the Economy (December 1992).
71. For a more detailed discussion that includes case studies of policy making in the Vancouver region, see Oberlander and Smith, "Governing Metropolitan Vancouver"; see also Patrick J. Smith, "Globalization and Fragmentation: Governance and the Changing Public Policy Agenda in Greater Vancouver," *Urban Policy and Research: An Australian Guide to Urban Affairs*, vol. 11 (spring 1994).
72. Statement, Hon. Darlene Marzari, minister of municipal affairs, Ministry-GVRD Strategic Planning Committee meeting, Burnaby, 22 May 1994.
73 See *City of Vancouver, City Plan: Tool Kit, Parts 1–15*, on process, existing policies, environment, housing, governance, economy, transportation, infrastructure, green space, finances, and so on.
74. *Montreal: A City-Region*, 17.
75. Sancton, "Canada As a Highly Urbanized Nation."
76. Frisken, "Metropolitan Change and the Challenge to Public Policy."
77. Oberlander and Smith, "Governing Metropolitan Vancouver, 368.
78. Ibid.
79. Andrew Sancton, "Governing Canada's City Regions," 12–15.
80. Frances Frisken, *The Changing Canadian Metropolis*, vol. 1: 32.
81. Ibid.

## *Selected Sources*

Bunting, Trudi and Pierre Filion, eds. *Canadian Cities in Transition* (Toronto: Oxford University Press, 1991).

Cullingworth, Barry. *Urban and Regional Planning in Canada* (New Brunswick, N.J.: Transaction Books, 1987).

Frisken, Frances, ed. *The Changing Canadian Metropolis*, 2 vols. (Berkeley, Calif.: Institute of Governmental Studies Press, University of California, 1994).

Fry, Earl, Lee Radebaugh, and Panayotis Soldatos, eds. *The New International Cities Era: The Global Activities of North American Municipal Governments* (Provo, Utah: Brigham Young University Press, 1989).

Goldberg Michael A. and J. Mercer. *The Myth of the North American City: Continentalism Challenged* (Vancouver: University of British Columbia Press, 1986).

Jacobs, Jane. *Cities and the Wealth of Nations: Principles of Economic Life* (New York: Random House, 1983).

Magnusson, Warren and Andrew Sancton, eds. *City Politics in Canada* (Toronto: University of Toronto Press, 1983).

Rothblatt Donald and Andrew Sancton, eds. *Metropolitan Governance: American/Canadian Intergovernmental Perspectives* (Berkeley, Calif.: Institute of Governmental Studies Press, University of California, 1993).

Tinda, C. Richard and Susan N. Tindal. *Local Government in Canada*, 3rd. ed. (Toronto: McGraw-Hill Ryerson, 1990).

Yeates, Maurice. *The North American City* (New York: Harper and Row, 1990).

# 8

## *Council-Administration Relations in City Governments*

Trevor Price

CANADIAN LOCAL government emerged almost painfully and, in some regions, reluctantly from the efforts of pioneer settlers to adapt the institutions of democracy to a new land and unique economic circumstances. The founding influences were British, American, and, in Quebec, French and Catholic. Yet, as William Bennett Munro, an American observer of our system of local government, pointed out in the 1920s: "Of all branches of Government in Canada the government of the cities has proved the most susceptible to American influence."[1] Munro was mainly referring to the institutions and devices of American municipal reform which newly emergent Canadian cities adopted in an effort to cope with the enormous burdens of rapid growth in the forty years from 1890 to 1930.

### *Background*

Ontario's earliest institutions of local administration were a direct copy of those that existed in English rural society and were transplanted to some of the American colonies. These were the courts of quarter sessions administered by justices of the peace. The JPs, appointed by the lieutenant governor and his Executive Council, were drawn from the local elites who enjoyed a patron-client relationship with the small oligarchy which ran the colony of Upper Canada (now Ontario). Their privileged position and wide powers made them a focus of criticism by reformers such as Robert Gourlay and William Lyon Mackenzie, who argued that the over-centralization of decision making and the relative powerlessness of the elected House of Assembly were hindering the development of the country. The Rebellions of 1837–38 in Upper and Lower Canada stimulated the famous Durham report, written by a liberal aristocrat from England who had been sent out to avert what some Britons feared might be another American war of independence. As a municipal reformer himself, Lord Durham strongly supported the yearnings for local self-government and, owing largely to his report, it was not long in coming. During the 1840s reformers led by Robert Baldwin established a pattern of two-tier local government which has persisted as the basic framework in Ontario from 1849 to the present day. This pattern proved to be the influential model both for developments in the Maritime provinces in the 1870s and during the western expansion that followed Canada's annexation of the Hudson's Bay Company's territories in 1870.[2]

The basic structure of democratically elected councils with chief officials variously named reeves, mayors, and wardens was a complex mixture of British terminology, American democratic sentiments, and a basic Canadian conservatism which rejected the more populist, liberal habits of American direct democracy. While Canada preceded Great Britain in its adoption of local self-government, it did not embrace those institutions of direct democratic control spawned by American Jacksonian democracy (which ensured the accountability of government through the direct election of a wide range of officials carrying out specific functions). Interestingly, however, Canadian local government did include the practice of direct election of mayors, rather than the British method—still in effect today—of having mayors elected by their councils. Only upper-tier units have retained in-house election of their heads of council, now known as wardens or, in regional governments, chairpersons.

The elected council as the central instrument of Canadian local government had thus emerged by the late nineteenth century. Its interpretation of the democratic roles of its players owed more to Edmund Burke than to populism. That is, although the council members, including the mayor, believed that they were elected to carry out the wishes of their constituents, they did not feel the need to be at the direct beck and call of the people at all times. In other words, the councils reflected the more deferential political culture of this country, which, as noted by Seymour Martin Lipset among others, results in our still being encumbered with an unrepresentative, non-elected, Senate whose members must satisfy a property ownership requirement.[3]

In the early stages of these developments the council expected to be involved in all the specific details of municipal administration, a task apparently made possible by the generally restricted scope of all governments of this period. To handle its duties more effectively, the council was broken down into a small number of standing committees for such matters as public works, finance, and other functions as were gradually added (the administration of a public cemetery, the provision of potable water, and so on).

The tradition of amateur administration and a close involvement between the few paid public servants and business entities contracted to undertake civic works was the characteristic style of early local government.[4] It is still the *modus operandi* of the many thousands of small and rural municipalities across the country. The real crunch for administrative effectiveness, service-provision, and political leadership arose in the early years of the twentieth century, when urbanization became more rapid and intense. Local public administration had to be invented and the amateur politicians who held municipal office embarked on organizational experiments aimed at managing the rapidly growing burdens on administration. Herein lay the fascination of civic politicians and local business elites with "reform" ideas in the United States which, they claimed, could revitalize civic life. Unfortunately, their efforts produced a continuing problem for local government administration: how could unfettered expertise be reconciled with general political control and direction?

## The Reform Influences

A whole array of influences began to play on the Canadian city scene between 1900 and 1910. In these influences, emanating mainly from Britain and the United States, we can recognize the incipient organizational changes that began to shape the administrative and political structure of the twentieth-century Canadian city.

Reform ideas for modernizing and making more efficient the municipal mechanism had become widespread in many regions of the United States in the last quarter of the nineteenth century. The Progressive movement directed its fire largely at the patronage-ridden and corrupt practices of the political machines and their urban bosses, who had cannily used the opportunities of open democracy to assume control of major American cities, focussing especially on the municipal budget and the jobs it could provide for the machine's supporters.[5] The Progressives, for their part, were ostensibly in favour of introducing merit and professionalism into municipal administration. They saw municipal-service provision as just another form of business enterprise. Efficient cities should emulate the organization and methods of the well-run business corporation and the self-interest of political factions should be rooted out. Like a corporate board of directors, the council should devise policy which would subsequently be implemented by a professional team of highly skilled managers.

Although partisan political machines were not a phenomenon of Canadian city politics, there was a strong feeling that Canadian cities needed to introduce organizational improvements and more professionalism if urban problems were to be tackled effectively. In many Canadian cities, the Board of Trade, or the Chamber of Commerce as it is now named, believed that community progress was being hindered by the bumbling amateurism of many councillors who interested themselves in all of the petty details of administration but could not as readily establish policy priorities or introduce new concepts of financial management, land-use planning, and objective personnel-selection. Large councils based on wards were thought to be vying to ensure that each got their share of the local government pie, oblivious to the needs of the community as a whole.

Business elites were in close contact with their opposite numbers in the United States through such organizations as the Masons. They also promoted reform through the Canadian Union of Municipalities, a Canadian version of the National Municipal League of the United States, which had published its reform position, *A Municipal Program*, in 1900. Strong leadership came from such bastions of WASP business elites as the municipality of Westmount within the greater Montreal area. Westmount was subsequently the first city in Canada to adopt the council-manager form of government. The innovations urged by Canadian municipal reformers included the election at large of smaller councils, elected executive committees called boards of control, "commission government," and, finally, the council-manager system. All of these proposals were resisted by ethnic and working-class voters, who correctly viewed them as detrimental to their interests. From their perspective, the business elites, while promoting the changes for the sake of "good government" and efficiency, would demonstrably benefit politically if they were enacted. Small councils elected at large would make it difficult for those with limited funds and mainly neighbourhood support to stage a campaign. Candidates who commanded a broader community profile, and possibly the support of the local newspaper, could more easily dominate a small council.[6]

Although it would not be true to say that urban reforms swept Canada in the period from 1910 to 1930, they certainly took deep root. Saint John, New Brunswick, many cities in Quebec, and several smaller towns in Ontario appointed managers, and a version of this reform called the board-of-commissioners system became dominant in larger western Canadian cities. The idea of council-manager government essentially rested on two assumptions. First, a small council elected at large would act as a board of directors establishing broad policies. Secondly, the administration would be headed by a professional city manager directly responsible to council. This individual would act as policy adviser, determine budget priorities, shape and direct personnel policies, and supervise administration on a day-to-day basis. In the purest form of city management, standing committees were abolished and all matters were filtered through the manager, who acted as gatekeeper to a council sitting as committee of the whole. Finally, in the United States, to maintain the solidarity of council and to prevent a single political figure from possibly offering competition to the manager, the mayor was elected by council. In

Canada, as noted earlier, the popular election of the mayor had become so well established by the early twentieth century that almost nowhere has the practice of indirect election been followed, although it was initially suggested (and quickly abandoned) as part of the Winnipeg Unicity reforms of 1971.[7]

If these changes had been implemented in Canada, their effect would have been to enhance drastically the power and influence of the administration in relation to the elected council. The administration under the leadership of a strong and experienced manager would have presented a united front, and, since the manager was to have the predominant influence over budgets and the selection, promotion, and dismissal of heads of municipal departments, his power would essentially have been unchallenged. The abolition of standing committees would have eliminated the close personal contact and dialogue which in the past had occasionally made councillors experts in certain fields and effective proponents of specific policies. In the view of reform purists, the council would not need to adopt a strong political role. Administrative advice on policy would be developed on the basis of professional expertise, which was thought to be objective, rational, and free from partisan favouritism. Council, as a sort of cabinet, would be free to discuss broad policy questions and quite properly leave the minutiae of administration to the administrators.

This ideal of non-political administration was never completely accepted in Canada, except in the small, affluent, suburban enclaves where the intangible values of such a system were widely shared by fairly homogeneous electorates. In the larger cities of Canada, political mechanisms that reflected social heterogeneity and political cleavages were retained. As T.J. Plunkett has shown, we have devised a uniquely Canadian adaptation of the American reforms.[8] Still, Canadian cities with populations smaller than 100 000 have turned overwhelmingly to some type of council manager, or chief administrative officer (CAO), form; by the late 1980s, thirty-three of the thirty-five cities in this category had done so. Of the two dozen larger cities, sixteen had also adopted this organizational structure; of the others, the most prevalent administrative format remains the commission board. But in many of the larger urban centres of Canada three features in particular of the earlier arrangements have survived: ward elections, standing committees, and some form of political executive committee.

The small council and at-large elections retained a strong place in many communities, and such cities as Vancouver and Chatam, Ontario, have resolutely refused to move to a ward system.[9] Fierce political debates along predictable lines ensue. When a city such as Windsor, Ontario, abolished the at-large election system, slightly expanded its council, and created five, two-member wards in the early 1960s, there was a noticeable politicization of council. Decisions were not as easily reached through "common agreement" as they once were. After a 1965 annexation, the city's diversity and size was no longer accurately represented by a council which was overwhelmingly representative of certain geographic and class elements of the city at the expense of other equally legitimate groups and areas.[10]

At approximately the same time during the first years of this century that the council-manager format was being introduced, mainly in eastern and central Canada, a variant of this form in which administrative co-ordination would be shared by three or four commissioners was becoming established in western Canada. This commissioner system offered some hope of better co-ordination of policy areas by having a particular commissioner responsible for a group of compatible departments such as urban development, planning, and social services. A standing committee of council would keep councillors apprised of work in each policy area. The mayor would also be a member of the board of commissioners, thus theoretically providing a crucial linchpin between politics and administration. This system appeared to have many attractions before the Second World War, but recently (in 1984) Edmonton moved in the direction of a single CAO and both it and Winnipeg (1971) have introduced an executive committee of council to offer policy co-ordination and leadership on the political side.

In Ontario, the provincial government came to the realization that councils advising only through standing committees were having a difficult time developing coherent policy co-ordination and leadership. It responded by requiring that, in cities with populations greater than 100 000, the council would be elected by wards to represent the diversity of the community. But these cities would also have a directly elected political executive to be known as the Board of Control. The Board of Control, consisting normally of four members plus the mayor (ex officio), would represent city-wide interests and be given control over the key functions of budget, personnel and labour relations, and major policy initiatives. Board members were also full members of council; the latter, to overturn a board decision, was required to do so by a two-thirds vote.[11]

Where this system existed, the appointment of a chief executive officer on the administrative side was deferred and control over the permanent administration rested in the hands of politicians. In the case of those cities that adopted the manager form of government (such as Windsor in 1959), the province exempted them from the requirement to establish a board of control.

Boards of Control remained in existence for a long period in the larger Ontario cities, becoming defunct with provincial acquiescence only during the past twenty or so years. The different electoral bases of councillors and the boards led to frequent clashes, with the former often describing themselves as "second-class." Mayors, too, frequently felt threatened by the boards of control, for controllers were also elected at large and sometimes they used their special status as a springboard to achieve the top office. In no way was the typical Board of Control the equivalent of a federal or provincial government cabinet. Under such conditions as these, the task of providing coherent policy direction for the administration of cities often proved impossible.

## *Bureaucratic Accountability*

The burst of urban growth in the years from 1900 to 1930 led to increased spending and the expansion of administrative staff at the municipal level. Unfortunately, the level of training, methods of recruitment, and professional standing of municipal public servants were weak. Patronage, political connections, and nepotism were often the way to job placements and there was an easy camaraderie among elected politicians and the staff.[12] Since the ability of public servants to give honest advice on efficiency and economy in the use of public funds was limited, cities turned to outside experts.

"Town planning," as it was initially called, was an exotic art whose apostles drew up official master plans and zoning by-laws. Much engineering advice and actual project execution was done by newly created engineering firms which specialized in municipal works. To solve the pervasive problem of incompetent tax collection and financial management, the provinces created autonomous regulatory boards and departments of municipal affairs during the 1930s. Finally, in many fields of local service such as parks and recreation, libraries and cultural affairs, economic development and social services, the public was called in to constitute a plethora of *ad hoc* boards. These boards, which allowed municipal governments to draw on the business know-how and experience of lay people, were beyond direct political control; city politicians did sit on the boards and councils funded them, but the members of these agencies did not directly come under city government administration. All in all, there may have been good reasons for this fragmentation of responsibility, but it has since been termed the bane of Canadian local government in that no single elected body has clear control over the full range of activities connected with local government.

In the post-war period an even greater expansion of urban activities occurred as cities grew rapidly and provinces mandated new functions through far-reaching legislation in many fields. A real municipal public service now emerged, organized mainly along professional lines with recognized avenues of training and accreditation. Still, municipal administration in Canada has never developed as an integrated general service and certainly does not possess the degree of unity characteristic of local government in the United Kingdom, where city officials belong to a national organization. In this country, municipal administration has always been highly departmentalized, with each function vertically integrated but almost no horizontal movement among the various departments. Added to this, there has also been a fairly sharp break between the professional/managerial staff and the lower paid and less-educated clerical workers, secretaries, and manual workers.The standing-committee structure of councils and the *ad hoc* special-purpose bodies provide a measure of contact between the different levels of employees, but the overall administration remains highly fragmented.

The department of the clerk, responsible for communications, agenda making, and recording of minutes and decisions, was not a perfect vehicle for bringing about administrative co-ordination. In smaller municipalities, where the clerk was a jack-of-all-trades and essentially council's main policy adviser, it was easier to co-ordinate all administrative matters. But, in the larger city administrations, council and the mayor often proved ineffective at co-ordination of the individual efforts of diverse, highly specialized, departments, let alone the loosely connected local agencies with weak legal and financial ties to the general government.

The bureaucracy itself grew much stronger in the post-war period as training and standards became more uniform. Roads and sewerage engineers, planners, traffic engineers, recreation administrators, horticulturalists and foresters, social workers, lawyers and accountants all became the badge of professional administration. They undertook often rigorous university education and created and belonged to associations which strictly controlled admission into their professions. Such a greatly enhanced public service offered a serious challenge to council control over not only the specialized activities but also the collective corporate direction, or strategic plan, presumed necessary if the city was to succeed in a competitive global economy.

The considerable strengthening of the municipal bureaucracy and its ever-tightening links with the various provincial departments left many councils feeling somewhat overwhelmed with the complexity of the new policy world which they were facing. Closely associated with this "unlikely alliance" of municipal and provincial bureaucracies were powerful interests in the private sector. It is little wonder that by the 1960s citizens' groups in many of Canada's largest cities raised a hue and cry about the conspiracy of city hall and the development industry to produce schemes which they believed threatened their quality of life, property values, and even civil rights. Councils did not seem to be doing an adequate job of representing the average citizen, and there were widespread calls for organizational reforms which would, to paraphrase a British aphorism, make the public servant "on tap but not on top."[13]

The 1960s were a period of great ferment throughout the western democracies as youth, in particular, questioned the existing political system and demanded greater participatory democracy at all levels of government. As Tim Thomas has noted in chapter 5, the movement for participatory democracy brought forth a variety of demands for citizen consultation, or at least more open discussion, before plans were formally ratified by council. Among academics and in some political circles, the idea was advanced that councils could not be effectively accountable unless they were organized along lines similar to those of the provincial and federal legislatures.[14] Council candidates should be part of larger groups that stood for something, and run on a policy platform for which they could be held accountable. The NDP, of all the national parties, was most in favour of an organized presence at the municipal level,[15] and political groupings and factions did emerge in a number of cities.

In many cities such as Vancouver and Montreal political parties were purely municipal and lacked formal ties to provincial parties, although close examination would reveal a good deal of collusion and assistance from those parties and their workers. Where parties did arise with a majority support for a particular mayoral candidate, a completely different political situation sometimes arose in which one party, even one political leader, became a dominant influence over policy for a long time. The outstanding example is Mayor Jean Drapeau of Montreal, whose Civic Party held sway for more than twenty years. Whether such developments provided greater democratic accountability is a moot point; Drapeau, in tandem with the bureaucracy and powerful private interests, certainly did *not* usher in an era of greater citizen participation. Drapeau viewed municipal elections as plebiscites on his popularity, and he interpreted each of his victories as a new carte blanche for his great schemes of "grandeur" for Montreal.

Political unrest died down by the later 1970s and partisan politics did not become widely entrenched as a mechanism of accountability in Canadian urban politics. Instead, a more gradual evolution occurred which brought in more effective policy making by councils, more effective means of central control, and an acceptance of more openness in the decision-making process. These phenomena have been collectively described as "corporate management."

## *Corporate Management*

Many commentators on municipal administration have criticized the lack of long-term planning, ineffective co-ordination of various branches of administration, and the preoccupation with petty details at the expense of major policy issues. In the 1960s attempts were made to induce municipalities to adopt a corporate-management approach together with its corollary in strategic planning. The goal was to have each city administration work together towards a set of politically determined unifying goals. While professionalism had increased technical expertise, the specialization that came with it hindered organizational synthesis for each department saw itself engaged in a battle for resources and attention.

Cities were not alone in their awareness of the need for more centralized policy making; similar views were being expressed at the provincial and federal levels, and over time such strong institutions as the Prime Minister's (or Premier's) Office, cabinet, Treasury Board, and Privy Council Office underwent further reform in the expectation that better policy making and more accountability and coordination would develop. It would not be accurate to say that large municipal administrations emulated these changes which formed so much of the dialogue of public administration at the time. Still, there was almost universal agreement that cities needed a strong administrative head whose main duty would be to review municipal operations and work closely with council on the key issues of finance, personnel, and policy determination. Traditional texts on local government in Canada tend to refer to a range of different structures of which the council-manager type was one among many. A recent study by T.J. Plunkett (using data developed by T. Price and R. Krause), however, shows that the creation of a particularly Canadian version of the office of chief administrative officer has now become the most common strucutre among larger municipalities. The title may vary from place to place but the role has nevertheless been recognized as essential.[16]

The one potential problem with the creation of a powerful and experienced professional head of administration is that such an office may not be balanced on the political side by equally effective political mechanisms. There is simply no equivalent of the prime minister in local government. Mayors, reeves, wardens, and the like usually have few special powers to make appointments or to initiate action. Usually, they have no disciplined party caucus behind them. Neither do they possess the staff and resources to give them a powerful political voice. The chairs of standing committees can be potentially influential, but here again we are faced with part-time, amateur politicians with no independent staff to rely on; through no shortcomings of their own they may well be susceptible to the persuasive arguments of permanent, professional department heads. The Board of Control, chaired by the mayor, was Ontario's way of maintaining council's control over city administration. Yet, as we have seen, there often was antipathy between boards of control and councils; the latter naturally responded more to popular pressures than did the controllers, whose votes were collected at large.

In moving to adopt a council-manager format, many cities abolished the board of control and reduced the size of council (which was then to be elected at large). In this way it was hoped that council itself, served by a chief administrator, would become an executive body with a corporate, administration-wide perspective. For the very largest cities this proved to be a change which depopularized council and made it too much a captive of the administration. Sensitivity to neighbourhoods and citizen groups was thought by opponents to be better served by a larger council and ward elections. Some cities, such as Toronto in 1969, devised a political counterpart to the CAO's office by replacing the Board of Control with an executive committee drawn from and elected by council. This would ensure a body not likely to be at odds with council, one that was able to take on additional responsibilities of scrutinizing the broad implications of expenditure plans, personnel issues, and major new policy initiatives.

The burdens of such extra duties really called for full-time municipal politicians whose executive responsibilities would be recognized by more pay and greater staff support. The largest cities have reluctantly moved in this direction, but medium-sized cities have rejected the idea of full-time professional municipal politicians. The 1990s are a time during which the rhetoric of "government down-sizing" across Canada is sufficiently engrained that only the most courageous, or foolhardy, of councillors are likely to advocate personal pay raises sufficient to attract careerist councillors.

Organizational change will not establish corporate management. This theoretically requires a close working relationship between the administrative and political sides. Ideally, the CAO and department heads will work together closely as a policy team providing the organizational and strategic proposals for political approval. Council will exercise its powers through detailed work in distinct policy areas and close dialogue with administration on standing committees. All policy initiatives will be passed to the executive committee, or its equivalent, for consideration before final approval by the entire council.

An example of an attempt to bring together the entire range of policy issues, both those under the direct control of administrative departments and those under the jurisdiction of *ad hoc* bodies, is displayed in the organization of Metro Toronto's government. There, instead of a single executive committee, there are two committees. One develops policy and priorities which integrate the input of the standing committees, while the other considers the personnel and financial implications of policy choices. This organization somewhat approximates that of the federal cabinet and its committees.

The galvanizing instrument for the entire corporate operation is said to be a strategic plan.[17] This plan's mission statement establishes broad future goals and then reduces these into quite specific tasks for each department, division, and individual. Ideally, each person is guided by his or her general, as well as specific, mission and not simply by strict adherence to a set of rules. Personnel management and budgetary planning are to be guided by the strategic plan which, in turn, is constantly being re-evaluated according to resources available and careful assessments of the rates of failure as well as success. Clearly, there is much more to strategic planning and corporate management in the 1990s than there ever was to the general municipal plans they have superseded.

## *Reinventing Government: Modern Challenges*

The last two decades have been a difficult time for councils, city employees, and those who are being served by municipalities. In this respect cities are not alone, for roughly similar problems have arisen at all levels of government. These problems have challenged not only the existing organization of government but also the way services are paid for, and the thread running through all of them is the need to maintain and improve performance with fewer financial and human resources.[18]

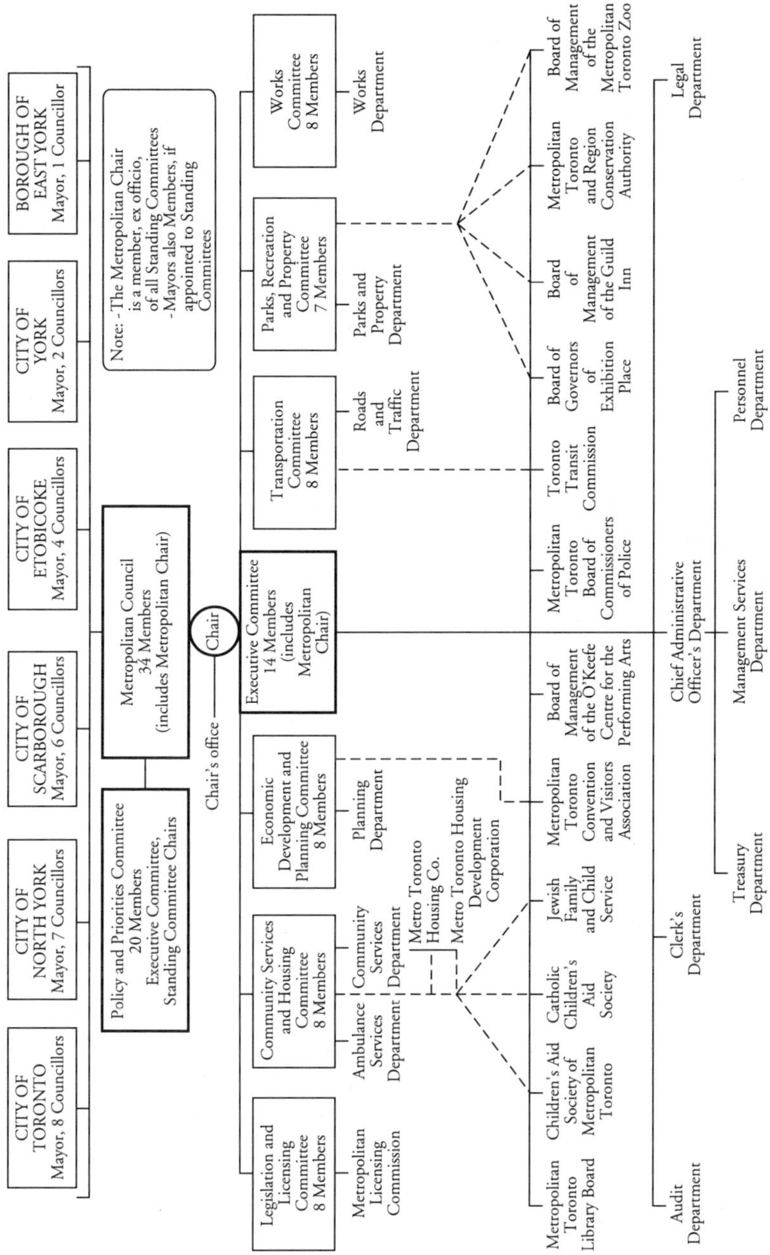


*Figure 1: Governmental organization, Metropolitan Toronto, November 1988*

Recession, mounting government debt, and high rates of unemployment have helped to make government revenue growth sluggish at best. This has forced senior governments to look closely at the levels of transfer payments to their municipal governments. Complicating the already grim financial picture is the active resistance of citizens to any significant increase in the rate of property taxation as they feel doubly squeezed by increasing provincial tax rates and, in the 1980s, the introduction of a highly visible and unpopular federal sales tax (the GST).

In response, municipal departments and their employees have felt the pressure of cuts, roll-backs, and less certain job security. All this has followed after approximately twenty-five years of growing union strength in larger cities, with resulting higher salaries and generous fringe-benefit packages. Until the 1980s, Canadian local government had not felt the savage bludgeoning which was the lot of American and British cities during the Reagan and Thatcher periods; for this good fortune, Canadian cities could thank their country's constitution, which does not give the federal government the kind of centralized authority accorded the national governments of the United States and Great Britain. But by the 1990s, even in Ontario under a social democratic government, wage concessions were demanded in return for a measure of job security. In all these instances, local councils found themselves virtually helpless bystanders since it was desperate provincial governments which wielded the economy axe as their own debts spiralled beyond control.

The term "re-inventing government" is the current face of public-choice theory. While this idea is not as popular in Canada as it is in Britain and the United States, it has definitely begun to win advocates here. The central claim of its proponents in the media and among certain special interest groups is that there is a desperate need to oust the twin ogres of irresponsibility and incompetence from public service. Public-choice theorists once again want to model the provision of local government services on their perceptions of the competitive, free-market methods of private industry. They argue for decentralization, privatization of certain activities, competitive bidding for such services as garbage collection, street cleaning, and snow removal, and, whenever possible, charging the consumer the full cost of public goods whether it be for parking, recreation, or sanitation. "Free service" is seen to promote wasteful consumption, and so charging consumers "real costs" presumably would make them more discriminating in the amount and types of service demanded.

The new public-choice school is a direct threat to the city work force (particularly its labour unions) and to the power and resources of municipal government departments. It also implies hostility to centralized metropolitan reorganization through its policies of decentralization of functions to small independent agencies. These agencies will theoretically work according to set objectives while being free to innovate and to try new methods outside the red tape of large and complex organizations whose emphasis is control rather than service-efficiency.

As David Osbourne and Ted Gaebler have argued in their influential writings, the problem is not to eliminate or decrease the role of the state, particularly municipal and city governments. Rather, it is "to steer not row" by revolutionizing management, budgeting, and personnel systems. These principles are hardly unfamiliar to any good student of the literature on public administration over the last twenty-five years.[19] Their basic concept is that, instead of being controlled by elaborate rules and directives and immersed in petty administrative minutiae, public servants and managers should be allowed to exercise more discretion in how they go about their jobs. The main criterion for performance is the achievement of the goals set out in mission statements, and this is more possible now because the effective use of computers can provide constantly updated information while monitoring management performance. Costly external reports should not be required if information gathering, storage, and retrieval is built into the administrative process.

While the discerning student might choose to differ, Osbourne and Gaebler do not think that this "revolution" implies a callous disregard for the rights of public servants through the ever-present threat of dismissal or realignment of responsibilities. Nor do they seem to believe that their shrivelled public infrastructure favours a wealthier public clientele than the one served by the existing standard of equal treatment for all citizens according to their requirements. They seem to subscribe to the virtues of a civic culture in which the politicians, public servants, media, and citizens' groups have a wider sense of shared values. So, as always, the need is for a political leadership capable of reaching out to the pluralistic elements of the community and carrying out major policies after frank, full, and open discussions. Other chapters in this book query whether such an effective city leadership is likely to evolve quickly in Canada.

## *Conclusion*

The largest cities of Canada have emerged as major engines of economic growth in an economy that is becoming both continentally integrated and globally challenged. In response, the structures of government at the local level have had to be dragged into growing, and adapting, at a prodigious pace.

Municipal government first emerged with the idea of having democratically elected, representative, *local* councils make choices within clear traditions of independence and self-reliance. Administrative and service structures of the early city were shaped with little outside support or direction from the provinces. Structures and disciplines were borrowed eclectically from Britain, the United States, or wherever else valuable ideas could be identified. Local businessmen were both community leaders and the elected political representatives. Bureaucratic expertise was scarce, to be borrowed from the same local businesses that led the community.

The depression of the 1930s imposed a severe shock on this urban system and led directly to the gradual imposition of detailed provincial financial, legislative, and administrative controls over even the smallest aspects of local government. The rise of new professional bureaucratic classes in provincial and municipal administrations, both of which grew particularly rapidly after the Second World War, created new sources of power and influence based upon expertise. City politicians appeared to be little more than ciphers rubber-stamping the grand designs of the professionals.

The counterpoise evolved partly out of the citizens' revolts of the late 1960s, and partly through the emergence of centralized instruments of budgeting and personnel management as well as strategic policy designs forged by an administrative team led by council-appointed CAOs. Supplemented by such support mechanisms, the political leadership role of mayors and councils grew as they increasingly worked full time and were able to reach out into the community for alliances and support among voluntary associations and non-governmental agencies.

This has also meant that in the 1990s, as provinces have seen their financial powers lessen relative to those of their cities, provincial control over municipalities has begun to erode. The new language of province-city relations now speaks in terms of decentralization and "disentanglement." Such newly emergent lines of clear policy authority, coupled with more functional independence for cities and the new electronic capacities to evaluate the impact of policy implementation very quickly, suggest that services may be more responsively attuned to the expectations of local electorates than they have ever been before.

One can hope that this may lead to a new age of community revival, one in which citizens, public servants, and elected representatives in each major city can together set the stamp of a unique identity and coherent mission on their own community. As they should.

## *Notes*

1. William Bennett Munro, *American Influences on Canadian Government* (Toronto: Macmillan, 1929), 99.
2. Although many historical works deal with this period in great detail, note especially the three basic texts on local government in Canada: K.G. Crawford, *Canadian Municipal Government* (Toronto: University of Toronto Press, 1954); D.J.H. Higgins, *Local and Urban Politics in Canada* (Toronto: Gage, 1986); and C.R. Tindal and S.N. Tindal, *Local Government in Canada*, 3rd. ed. (Toronto: McGraw-Hill Ryerson, 1990). See also Engin Isin's chapter 3 in this book.
3. "Revolution and Counter-revolution: Canada and the United States," in *The Canadian Political Process*, O. Kruhlak *et al.*, eds. (Toronto: Holt, Rinehart and Winston, 1970), 13–38.
4. Much of my insight into this matter was gained from a detailed examination of the late-nineteenth-century history of Windsor's administration. See Trevor Price and Larry Kulisek, *Windsor, 1892–1992: A Centennial Celebration* (Windsor: Chamber Publications, 1992).

5. Many historical works discuss the origins and impact of American machine politics, but for a discussion of the social-class structure involved see Edward C. Banfield and James Q. Wilson, *City Politics* (Cambridge: Harvard University Press, 1963). This work still ranks as one of the best studies of the Progressive era.
6. Crawford, *Canadian Municipal Government*, 84–5.
7. Meyer Brownstone and T.J. Plunkett, in *Politics and Reform in Local Government* (Berkeley, Calif.: University of California Press, 1983), recount, as participant-observors, some of the reforms they suggested. Had they been implemented, those reforms would have constituted a radical departure from established traditions.
8. T.J. Plunkett, *Urban Canada and Its Government* (Toronto: Macmillan, 1968); T.J. Plunkett, *City Management in Canada: The Role of the Chief Administrative Officer* (Toronto: Institute of Public Administration of Canada, 1992).
9. Consult, for example, D.J.H. Higgins's detailed discussion of the long and spirited struggle for a ward system in Vancouver in his *Local and Urban Politics in Canada*, 325–31.
10. My own familiarity with council government has owed much to a close examination of its development and operation in Windsor where these issues have been debated since the 1920s. See Trevor Price, "City Manager Government in Windsor" (PhD thesis, Queen's University, 1975).
11. Paul Hickey undertook an exhaustive study of structures and their implications in a study commissioned by the Ontario government in the heyday of post-war reform. See his *Decision-Making Process in Ontario's Local Government* (Toronto: Ministry of Treasury, Economics and Intergovernmental Affairs, 1973).
12. C.R. Tindal and S.N. Tindal discuss this growth of expertise and new concepts of municipal service. *See Local Government in Canada*, especially 43–76.
13. There was much writing during this period on the topic of the tactics and influence of the development industry at city hall. See especially James Lorimer, *A Citizen's Guide to City Politics* (Toronto: James, Lewis and Samuel, 1972), and also his *The Developers* (Toronto: Lorimer, 1978).
14. See, for example, the essays on this theme in *Emerging Party Politics in Urban Canada*, Jack Masson and James D. Anderson, eds. (Toronto: McClelland and Stewart, 1972).
15. A strong case for the development of party politics in major cities has been made by James Lightbody in "The Rise of Party Politics in

Canadian Local Elections," *Journal of Canadian Studies*, vol. 6 (February 1971), 39–44.

16. T.J. Plunkett, *City Management in Canada.*
17. One very fine example of a major city's strategic plan is that of the City of Calgary, produced in 1990. It identifies, and "sets the context for," five crucial issue-areas. For each of these it provides a handful of more general goals and identifies about a dozen specific strategies to be pursued by particular managers or agencies. Even so, the mission statement struggles through the hilarious—"to [boldly] go where few councils have gone before"—to reach the banal: "City Council's mandate is to govern; our mission is to serve Calgarians, provide leadership and direction, and ensure a vibrant, participatory and healthy city, now and for the future." See *Council's Strategic Plan: Charting Calgary's Future* (Calgary: 1990), 2, 4.
18. For a comparative analysis of "what works, where, and why" see *Urban Innovation: Creative Strategies for Turbulent Times*, Terry Nichols, ed. (Thousand Oaks, Calif.: Sage, 1994) and *Urban Innovation and Autonomy: Political Implications of Policy Change*, Susan E. Clarke, ed., (Newbury Park, Conn.: Sage, 1989).
19. David Osbourne and Ted Gaebler, *Re-inventing Government: How the Entrepreneurial Spirit Is Transforming the Public Sector* (New York: Plume Books, Penguin USA, 1993).

## *Selected Sources*

Bingham, Richard *et al. Managing Local Government: Public Administration in Practice* (Newbury Park, Conn.: Sage, 1991).

Clark, Terry Nichols, ed. *Urban Innovation: Creative Strategies for Turbulent Times* (Thousand Oaks, Calif.: Sage, 1994).

Crawford, Kenneth G. *Canadian Municipal Government* (Toronto: University of Toronto Press, 1954).

Higgins, D.J.H. *Local and Urban Politics in Canada* (Toronto: Gage, 1986).

Jackson, Ian, ed. *The Future of Cities in Britain and Canada* (Ottawa: Institute for Research on Public Policy, 1991).

Masson, J.K. and J.D. Anderson, ed. *Emerging Party Politics in Urban Canada* (Toronto: McClelland and Stewart, 1972).

Osbourne, David and Ted Gaebler. *Reinventing Government: How the Entrepreneurial Spirit Is Transforming the Public Sector* (New York: Plume Books, Penguin USA, 1993).

Plunkett, T.J. *City Management in Canada: The Role of the Chief Administrative Officer* (Toronto: Institute of Public Administration of Canada, 1992).

Plunkett, T.J. and G.M. Betts. *The Management of Canadian Urban Government* (Kingston: Institute of Local Government, Queen's University, 1978).

Tindal, R. and S. Nobes Tindal. *Local Government in Canada*, 3rd. ed. (Toronto: McGraw-Hill Ryerson, 1990).

# 9

## *Urban-Planning Systems for Metropolitan Canada*

P.J. Smith

As an intellectual discipline and a way of thinking about the city, urban planning has traditionally seen itself as commanding an extremely broad terrain. Its scope embraces the whole of the urban environment, natural as well as built, in both two-dimensional and three-dimensional form, and at all levels of detail, from the overall structure of large urbanizing regions to the specific settings of individual buildings. In practice, however, as an area of public decision and action, urban planning is much more narrowly focussed. In the legal or statutory form in which it has become institutionalized in Canada, urban planning has been primarily a mechanism for regulating land use and the land-development process.[1] Its most powerful tools, and the tools that account for most of the contact that the general public has with their local planning systems, are those known as "zoning" and "subdivision control." In planners' minds they do not come into play until late in the planning process, as detailed technical instruments by which planning policies are implemented at the scale of the individual property. But the larger public neither knows much about the chain of decisions that lies behind every application of these regulations, nor can appreciate the connection between a highly generalized plan for an entire metropolitan area and the bureaucratic decision that is made about a particular development application.

This puts urban planning in an oddly ambiguous position. On the one hand, issues concerning the urban environment make up a large part of the business of a modern urban municipality, and they are often among the most difficult and controversial matters that local governments have to confront. On the other, the planning process is poorly understood, certainly by the general public and all too often by its elected representatives. In the popular perception, planning tends to be identified with the enforcement of highly restrictive regulations, while the fundamental decisions, the real *planning* decisions, are too far abstracted from day-to-day realities. The manner in which municipal councils respond to urban development issues may therefore owe more to their need to cope with immediate political pressures than to the farsighted, integrative viewpoint that urban planning is supposed to stand for. Indeed, the political decisions may—and often do—go directly against the expert advice of professional planners. This does not necessarily mean that the decisions are wrong or that they will have bad outcomes, but it does underline the confusion and uncertainty that attends the planning function of urban government. In the abstract, planning seems such a logical and reasonable thing to do. It so obviously makes sense to think ahead, to set long-term goals, to have a carefully thought-out plan of action. The overall aspirations of urban planning look equally sound. It is so clearly desirable to want to improve the quality of the urban environment and hence, by extension, the quality of urban life. That, in broadest terms, is what urban planning sets out to do. Yet the reality seems to fall far short. Public decisions are taken, as inevitably they must be, but it is so difficult to make genuine *planning* decisions, forward-looking decisions that can truly be said to be moving Canadian cities towards a better future.[2]

The explanation for these difficulties rests largely in the way that urban planning is conceived as a function of government. With that in mind, the main purpose of this chapter is to explain how urban planning systems are normally constituted in Canada. The review will focus on two broad questions: What, in general, are planning systems empowered to do? And in whom are these powers usually vested? By and large, the answers to these questions are quite straightforward, but they also serve to raise more demanding philosophical ones that cut to the very essence of contemporary urban governance—questions about personal rights and freedoms, for example, especially with respect to the institution of property, and about the democratic rights of individuals and communities to decide upon their own futures. The essay will try to show how such fundamental concerns are normally regarded in Canadian planning systems. Wherever appropriate, as well, the discussion will be related to the special context of metropolitan government and the procedures that have been adopted to try to overcome the obstacles that fragmented jurisdictions put in the way of effective urban planning.

## *System Elements*

Two general points must be made by way of introduction:. First, the term "planning system" refers to those systems of public administration that are created to deliver land-use planning services to urban and rural communities. For purposes of this chapter, urban communities will be the primary concern, but the enabling legislation for planning does not normally differentiate. One immediate implication is that surviving rural municipalities within metropolitan areas will generally operate under exactly the same statutory requirements as their urban neighbours.

Secondly, every province and both territories in Canada have their own individual planning systems. This relates to the constitutional separation of powers between the Government of Canada and the provinces. Specifically, it derives from section 92(13) of the British North America Act, 1867, as continued by the Constitution Act, 1982, which grants provincial legislatures the exclusive right to make laws with respect to matters affecting property. The whole elaborate apparatus of Canadian planning systems rests on this one subclause and the authority it gives provincial governments to make laws respecting the use of property—meaning, in this context, "real" property, or land and improvements to land, especially the "improvements" that result from preparing land for development and building on it. Here is the constitutional explanation for the central place that land-use planning is given in the design of Canadian planning systems.

The fact that the right to make laws about property falls under provincial jurisdiction has another implication as well. It is left at the discretion of each provincial government to decide how to structure its planning system, and even whether to have one at all. Canadian planning systems therefore differ, not in their broad outlines perhaps, but certainly in the detailed powers and procedures that are so vital to local planning practice. For this reason, it is uncomfortably difficult to generalize about Canadian planning systems, and all generalizations must be treated with caution.[3]

As illustrated in Figure 1, all planning systems are built around the same few essential elements. It is the purpose of provincial planning statutes, as the enabling legislation for planning, to give specific form to these elements. This chiefly means three things: deciding upon the particular powers and responsibilities that will be delegated to the planning system, and then allocating those powers and responsibilities to particular agents or agencies; specifying the different kinds of plans and regulations that together make up the set of planning tools that the planning authorities have to work with; and determining the rules and procedures that the authorities must follow if their decisions are to be legally binding and enforceable. Each of these elements will be reviewed in turn.

*Figure 1: Basic elements of a planning system*

A. Planning agencies and authorities

1. General-purpose agencies (e.g., city councils)
2. Special-purpose agencies (i.e., planning boards and commissions)

B. Machinery of planning administration

1. Planning tools (i.e., types of plans and regulations that planning agencies are authorized to employ)
2. Administrative procedures (i.e., procedures that give legal effect to planning decisions)

## *Planning Authorities*

Planning-system design always entails the creation of a number of *ad hoc* or special-purpose authorities—that is, boards and commissions of various kinds, each responsible for some aspect of the planning service. Thus, area-wide planning at a metropolitan scale may be placed in the hands of a special commission, while boards or tribunals with quasi-judicial powers are created to hear appeals against certain kinds of planning decisions. The most important responsibilities, however, along with the greatest power, tend to be vested in the conventional institutions of government—in city and county councils, for example, or in provincial ministers. In these cases, certain urban-planning responsibilities are added to their more general duties.

It follows from these characteristics that planning systems have complex, fragmented structures in which powers are highly divided. In general, too, Canadian planning systems are strongly decentralized. This rests on the belief—a long and widely held belief—that urban planning is most properly a task of local communities. Indeed, planning is generally regarded as one of the most vital ways in which communities manifest their individuality and independence, at once a mark of their sense of place, of their own uniqueness, and an expression of their rights of self-determination and autonomy. As a consequence, to quote one Canadian authority, "Local government structures provide the primary institutional context for planning by a community."[4] Yet this does not mean that all power will be delegated to the local level. Every Canadian planning system includes some central agencies, and the precise division of powers and responsibilities between the provincial and municipal levels is one of the chief sources of variation across the country.

Two issues are involved here. The first issue concerns the prevailing attitude towards municipal government in general, and the degree to which particular provincial governments are prepared to devolve planning authority onto their municipalities in the name of local autonomy. This is an old tune in Canada, but, although recent planning reforms have commonly been motivated by a stated desire to enhance municipal autonomy, no provincial government has ever completely surrendered its authority over urban planning matters. In the second place, and quite apart from the ideological imperatives that may be driving particular provincial governments at particular times, there are factors inherent in the operation of planning systems that are pulling in opposite directions—that is, pulling simultaneously towards centralization and towards autonomy (Figure 2). Planning systems must always accommodate these opposing tendencies and find an acceptable balance between them—a *locally* acceptable balance.

*Figure 2: Pressures for centralization in a planning system*

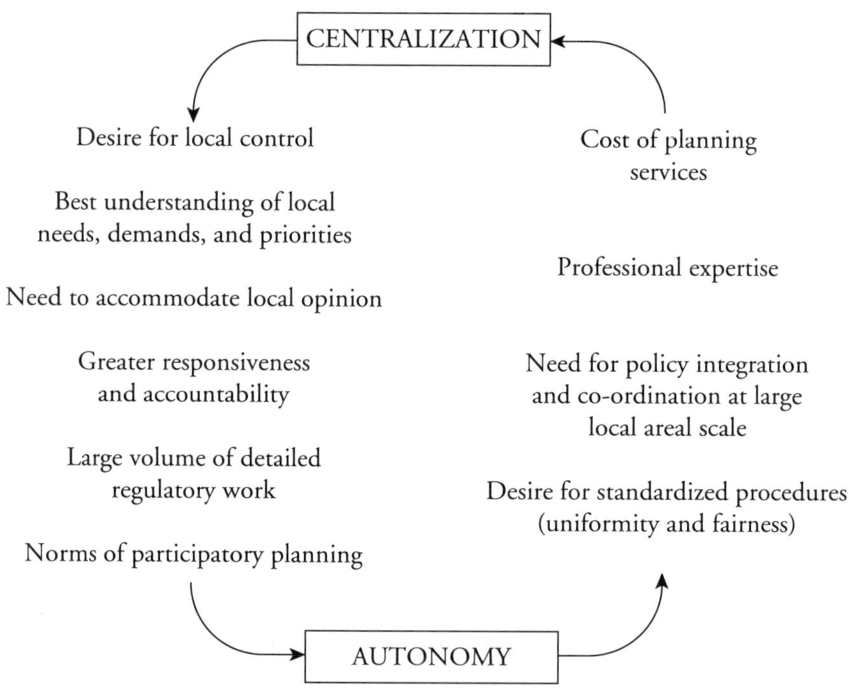


Source*:* P.J. Smith and Patricia E. Bayne, "The Issue of Local Autonomy in Edmonton's Regional Plan Process," in *The Changing Canadian Metropolis*, Francis Frisken, ed. (Berkeley, Calif.: Institute of Government Studies Press. University of California, 1994), 729.

## *Planning Tools*

With respect to the tools of their trade, planners have definite theoretical expectations to guide system design (Figure 3). These expectations may not always be realized, but at the very least there are three tools that are regarded as indispensable and are always provided for. They are the municipal or general plan, the zoning or land-use bylaw, and the subdivision-control system. The latter two are the conventional tools by which private development is regulated, under the general guidance of the municipal plan.

The nature of the plan, and the key concepts that it embodies, are well described in T.J. Kent's definition: "The general plan is the official statement of a municipal legislative body which sets forth its major policies concerning desirable future physical development; the published general-plan document must include a single, unified general physical design for the community, and it must attempt to clarify the relationships between physical-development policies and social and economic goals."[5] This is an American definition, but it captures the reality of Canadian practice all the same. Thus, Edmonton's General Municipal Plan (to give it its full technical title) is explicitly concerned to itemize a large set of physical development policies, some 130 of them in total. It is also made clear, however, that these policies have been adopted in support of economic and social goals, which together aim at ensuring the long-term health and vitality of Edmonton and at enhancing its attractiveness as a place to live, work, raise families, do business, and so on. These policies are also given summary expression in the "development concept" that Figure 4 illustrates. This is the Edmonton version of a "unified general physical design for the community," the community in this instance being the entire city.

In normal circumstances, such a plan will not be used directly for regulatory purposes. Rather, it can be likened to a constitution, a statement of the goals and principles that constitute the rationale, both social and technical, for the detailed regulations that then follow. At the same time, there are many situations in which the plan itself should be referred to, again in its role as a policy guide. No regulatory code can—or should—be expected to anticipate every conceivable development demand or opportunity. Zoning, in particular, is frequently changed,

*Figure 3: Organization of planning tools in a conventional planning system*

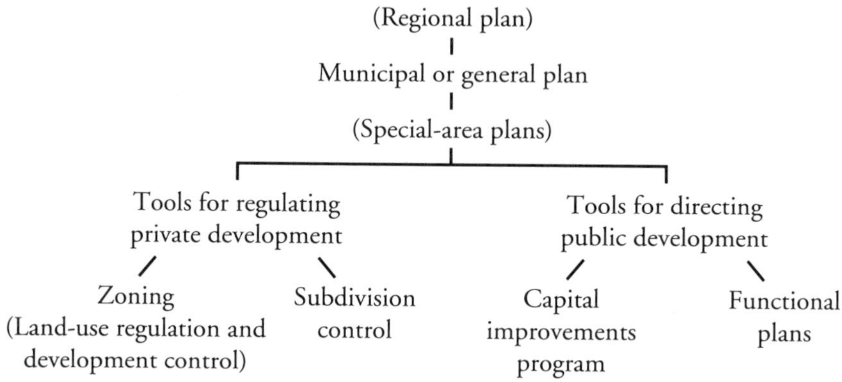


but the plan should always be referred to first, as the comprehensive framework against which the desirability of specific changes can be assessed. Without that grounding, zoning changes will be made in an *ad hoc*, disjointed fashion, with no thought to their cumulative effects.

In theory, then, the two conventional forms of planning regulation, zoning and subdivision control, are tools that planners use to *implement* policies laid down in the general plan. They are also highly interdependent, although they serve distinctly different purposes and are usually administered separately. Zoning, or "districting" as it is sometimes known, is a procedure by which a municipality (and the procedure is just as applicable to rural municipalities as it is to cities) is divided into precisely delimited land-use districts, based on the planning concept of compatibility. That is, certain land uses are kept separate from one another because they are regarded as incompatible—factories in residential areas, for example, or apartment towers in single-family suburban neighbourhoods. Incompatibility, in its turn, is judged primarily in terms of negative externalities or "nuisance" effects, a concept that derived originally from common law. Simply put, common law established that the rights of property ownership are not absolute; they do not convey a right to use property in ways that may be harmful to others, particularly in the sense of creating a nuisance for nearby owners whose ability to use and enjoy their properties is diminished in consequence. The fundamental legal ration-

*Figure 4: The "development concept" or general land-use plan for Edmonton*

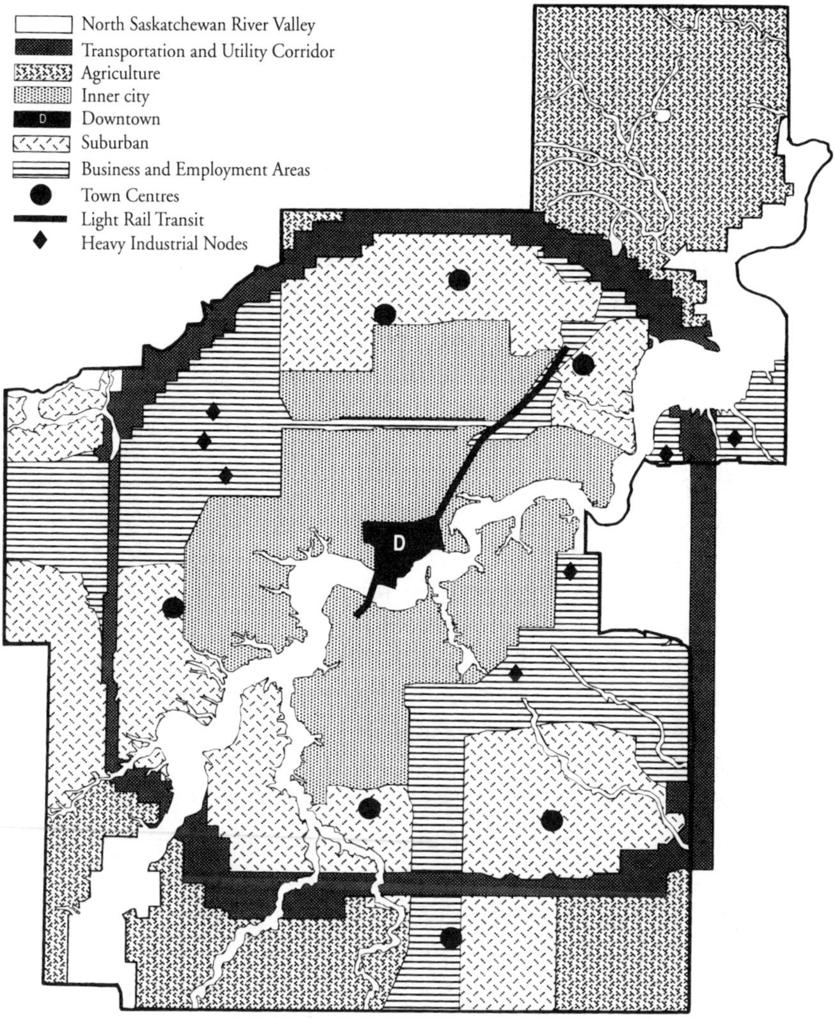


Source: Edmonton's General Municipal Plan, adopted 1990.

ale for zoning is that it aims to prevent effects of this kind by sorting out an acceptable arrangement of land use in fine detail. In the process, larger planning intentions will be served as well. Thus, the zoning system is used to achieve the desired pattern of land use for a whole city or for a whole metropolitan area. It is here that the connection between a general plan and a zoning by-law is most direct. The plan determines where certain kinds of land uses and service facilities should be located and how much land should be allocated to them to meet forecast needs; the by-law amplifies those general patterns and translates them into legally enforceable rules by specifying the forms of development that will be permitted in each land-use district. The actual use of land and buildings is the first concern, of course, but it is not the only aspect of development that is regulated. The intensity of development, the availability of ancillary facilities such as parking, even the appearance of buildings and the materials from which they are constructed, these are all characteristics that can affect the "use and enjoyment" of property and so fall within the normal scope of zoning regulations.

By contrast, the scope of subdivision control is considerably narrower, though it serves an equally vital role in the planning system. Subdivision refers to the process of breaking parcels of land down into smaller parcels or "lots," which can then be sold for development purposes. To establish the legal basis for the transfer of title or ownership, there has to be an approved subdivision plan—approved by the appropriate planning authority and registered in one of the province's land-titles offices. The subdivision-control procedure is concerned with deciding whether or not to approve a proposed plan. Many technical considerations come into play here, but two are most important from an urban-planning standpoint: that the area be laid out in a form that is appropriate to its planned uses; and that the land be needed for the intended development in the reasonably near future. To turn those points around, the subdivision should not be premature and it should conform with both the municipal plan and the zoning by-law. The municipal plan will help the approval authority judge whether the proposed subdivision is both timely and appropriately located; the zoning by-law will specify the development regulations that the subdivision must be designed to fit. A plan for an industrial park, for instance, takes a completely different form from a plan for a new housing project, and it would be foolish to submit an industrial subdivision plan for an area that is intended and zoned for eventual residential development. In fact, the subdivision-control system is a critically important tool for regulating the expansion of cities into their rural fringes. Since it is the subdivision plan that determines the detailed land-use configuration of each prospective development site, and since detailed zoning cannot be applied until *after* a plan has been finalized, it is the subdivision-control system that determines which land will be approved for development in what order and for what specific purposes.

In addition to the tools for regulating private development, all planning systems should incorporate a set of tools that relate to the public or community aspects of urban development (see Figure 3). These will not normally be formal requirements under the planning legislation, since they fall within the regular scope of local government duties, but they are nonetheless vital if planning is to be both well balanced and effective. All urban development places demands on public services—indeed, depends on their being available when and where they are needed. It is therefore imperative that the two sides of the development equation, the public and the private, be fully integrated to ensure that the provision of public services is closely co-ordinated with privately initiated construction.

Two main kinds of tools are required to give effective direction to public development. First there are "functional plans," meaning the long-range plans that every line-agency of civic or metropolitan administration should be expected to have for its particular service function. These would include plans for the management and construction of school facilities, parks and recreation facilities, sewer and water-distribution networks, and so on. But by far the most important functional plan from an urban-planning standpoint is the transportation plan. This is a comprehensive plan for the long-term development of transportation facilities of all kinds, which are woven together into a single, unified transportation system for the whole city or the whole metropolitan area. Effective transportation planning is vitally important in its own right, of course, but it is equally vital that it be thoroughly co-ordinated with land-use planning. Land use and transportation are functionally inseparable, and so it is illogical to attempt to plan them separately. On the one hand, transportation demand is a direct function of land use, and determining the future land-use pattern is fundamental to the successful planning of future transportation facilities. On the other, no part of any urban area—no residential district, no house even, and no school, no shopping centre, no service facility of any kind—can exist without access to other areas and other service facilities. To a very large extent, therefore, the effective functioning of any city as a highly connected system of human activities is dependent on the supply of transportation facilities. Ideally, these two features, land use and transportation, should be planned together as complementary aspects of a unified entity, the city. That was standard procedure in an earlier generation of city plans, but today there are more likely to be two separate plans: a land-use plan, such as the one in Figure 4, prepared by urban planners under the authority of the planning legislation, and a transportation plan prepared by traffic engineers as part of their responsibility as a key line-agency of local government. The division, to put it bluntly, is about professional "turf"—the division of responsibility between urban planners and engineers, staff agencies and line-agencies.

These divisions of responsibility extend to other service areas as well, and give rise to large difficulties of co-ordination within local administrations. In response, a "corporate planning" office is sometimes established, meaning a central agency that is responsible for the long-range planning of the municipal corporation's own development activities. Unfortunately, this can lead to further confusion about the urban-planning function. In theory, corporate planning should be part of the urban-planning system, but in practice, as long as urban-planning responsibilities are focussed on land use and the regulation of private land development, they tend to operate separately. Whatever administrative approach is taken, however, there is one planning tool that can be used as a powerful aid to co-ordination. This is the capital-improvements program. It usually takes the form of a five-year budget, rolling forward year by year, in which public funds are allocated to the specific projects that best serve the city's overall development policies as set by the municipal plan. The connection between the capital-improvements program and the municipal plan is really a two-way one. Not only is it important to ensure that community costs are factored into every decision to permit (or not to permit) private development, but a well-thought-out, politically acceptable plan of capital projects is the most effective tool that any municipal government has for directing urban growth. Deciding to build a new trunk sewer, for example, or not to build a new highway, have long-lasting effects on the development potential of land. Similarly, deciding to provide subsidized housing projects for low-income families or to upgrade rundown parks can be invaluable steps in the revitalization of deteriorating inner-city communities.

Another planning tool that can be used to co-ordinate the public and private aspects of urban development, and one that has become fairly standard in recent years, is the special-area plan. There are two general types: plans (variously known as structure plans or outline plans) for the initial development of suburban land, and plans for the protection or revitalization of already developed districts, mostly in the inner city. Plans for downtown districts fall into the latter category as well, and historically the downtown was regarded as the one area of such special importance in any city that it should have its own plan. By the 1960s that idea was being applied to other parts of the city as well. The primary motive was the wish to build more effective bridges between highly generalized municipal plans and highly specific regulatory codes. The special-area plans are seen as filling this gap. By limiting their focus to smaller areas, they can also give stronger guidance to the particular application of zoning and subdivision control. Thus, the Alberta Planning Act provides for area-structure plans which are intended to set the "framework for subsequent subdivision and development." This "framework" includes the future land-use pattern of the district, the sequence of development within it, its intended population density (and hence its population capacity), and "the general location of major transportation routes and public utilities." Typically, too, such plans are used to determine what service facilities the future population will need—how many schools of various kinds, how many shopping centres, how many parks, and their distribution in relation to the intended housing areas.

Finally, just as modern planning systems will commonly provide for a level of plan below the municipal plan, so too they will often provide for plans at an even larger areal scale. For want of a better name, these are usually referred to as regional plans, though that term takes in a considerable variety of planning situations.[6] Still, there is one usage that stands out as being most pertinent in the present context, the regional plan as a mechanism for co-ordinating urban development over whole metropolitan areas. If the metropolitan area is consolidated under the jurisdiction of a single governing body, Winnipeg being the obvious case in point, the city plan is automatically the metropolitan plan and only one local planning organization is required. But where a metropolitan area extends over several municipalities, as most do, a two-tier planning system is often established, with the upper-tier jurisdiction being responsible for the "regional" plan.

The precise structural arrangements differ, depending on the form of metropolitan government that has been adopted, but in general there are two possible approaches. The first, which is best represented by Ontario, is to have a two-tier system of municipal government. Each level will then have its assigned responsibilities within the local planning system, and all the normal powers of municipal government to back them up. The precise division of powers and responsibilities is a matter for provincial determination, but the recent report of the Commission on Planning and Development Reform in Ontario presents a good review of the factors that should be considered in organizing such a two-tier system.[7] The second approach, which is typified by Alberta, is for the metropolitan level of planning to be superimposed on a uni-level pattern of municipal government in the form of special-purpose planning authorities. In Alberta, they are known as regional planning commissions, and their one essential duty is to prepare regional plans and keep them up to date. Since the commissions are not themselves municipal governments, however, quite different administrative procedures are required than for municipal planning, which tends to leave regional planning in an ambiguous and weak position.[8] Although special-purpose authorities can be powerful within their specific jurisdictions, this is not normally the case with regional planning bodies. Urban-planning responsibilities cut close to the heart of municipal government, and having to surrender some of that authority to an *ad hoc* agency can readily be interpreted as an attack on municipal autonomy. In practice, then, in all planning jurisdictions in Canada, the regional plan is a less important tool than the municipal plan.

## *Administrative Procedures*

Administrative rules and procedures comprise the final basic element that all planning systems must incorporate. Precision is an essential requirement here, because it is through its administrative procedures that a planning system has its most immediate and forceful impact on the people it is designed to serve, the residents, property owners, entrepreneurs, and organizations that make up the urban community. The procedural rules provide two-way protection: they protect those who administer the planning system, both elected and appointed officials, by setting clear limits to their legal authority; and they also, and more important, protect those who are directly affected by planning decisions. With respect to the latter, two main kinds of procedures are normally provided. There are, first, procedures to ensure that there will be opportunities for the public to be involved in decision-making processes; and second, procedures to guarantee rights of hearing and appeal to those residents whose interests have been or may be harmed by a particular planning decision. "Protection," in this situation, does not mean that interested parties necessarily obtain the decisions they want; that would be impossible, since opposing interests are engaged. But at least, to borrow an American term, the decisions are made with regard to "due process," in the sense that the procedural rules are laid down in advance and apply equally to everyone. From a legal perspective (as distinct from a planning one) the most important requirement of any planning legislation is that it should protect individuals and communities from arbitrary acts, whether taken by other individuals or communities or by public officials. This is the fundamental justification for the elaborate procedural superstructure that all planning systems need, and that takes up the greater part of a typical planning statute.

## *Types of Planning Decisions*

Another way of approaching urban-planning systems so as to understand their role in metropolitan government is to consider the variety of decisions they are obliged to make. For descriptive convenience, these decisions will be grouped into four types: administrative, quasi-judicial, technical, and legislative.

### *Administrative Decisions*

Administrative decisions are those that are taken by some appointed authority, whether an individual official or one of the various planning boards or commissions. The decisions they are authorized to make can be divided into two categories: those that allow some discretion to the responsible authority and those that do not. The latter case entails the application of cut-and-dried rules and usually forms part of the routine duties of a planning bureaucracy. Discretionary decisions, by contrast, require the exercise of planning judgment, and so the responsibility for making them is normally shared.

Non-discretionary or routine administrative decisions are best exemplified by development-permit procedures under a zoning by-law. At bottom, all zoning regulations have one purpose: to spell out the precise conditions that have to be satisfied before a development permit can be issued—and the by-law, of course, will make it illegal for any development to proceed without a permit. When a development application is received, the approving officer has only one question to consider: Does this application conform in every respect with the relevant regulations? If it does, a permit *must* be issued; if it does not, the application *must* be refused. The officer has no choice.

Discretionary administrative decisions are much more interesting for planners, and much more challenging. They also have a high likelihood of being controversial, which is why they are not normally left to an individual planner or bureaucrat. The most common cases, once again, relate to the regulatory aspects of the planning system, including the zoning by-law. It is standard practice, for instance, to schedule for each land-use district (or "zone") a list of permitted uses and another list of discretionary uses. The permitted uses are those for which permits must be issued "as of right," whereas the discretionary uses carry no such guarantee. For example, a home-operated business *may* be permitted in a residential district, but only if the approving authority concludes that it would not have undesirable effects on neighbouring residences or on the overall quality of the area. That is a matter of judgment—a judgment that everyone may not agree with.

Discretionary decisions are required to an even greater degree in the subdivision-control process. Although there are some features of subdivision plans that can be regulated exactly—minimum road widths, for example, or lot dimensions—there are others that cannot. Indeed, if the evaluation of subdivision plans was reduced to mechanical rules, the quality of subdivision design would be hopelessly compromised. It is precisely because good subdivision planning requires original design that administrative discretion is necessary. Deciding whether a particular road layout is safe and attractive, or whether a proposed school site is well related to the area that it will serve—these are matters of judgment, preferably professional judgment of the kind that is best learned through practical experience. This does not mean that planners are the only ones who should be involved in these sorts of decisions, but the advice of competent planners is certainly required.

## *Quasi-Judicial Decisions*

To ensure that the power of administrative decision is not exercised arbitrarily in those situations where discretion is permitted, any planning system must provide mechanisms that act as checks against possible abuses and unreasonable hardship. It is also imperative, in the interests of fairness, that these mechanisms be completely outside the influence of the authorities charged with the responsibility of making the original decision. This means that separate appeal authorities are required. In some instances, the regular judicial system will meet this need, as it does in the United States, but the more common practice in Canada, following British tradition, is to vest the requisite authority in administrative tribunals which are granted quasi-judicial powers. That is, they are empowered to act like courts, especially in the sense that their decisions are legally binding, without having to adhere to all the formalities that court appearances require. These agencies are the final resorts in the planning system, the last seat of judgment on certain planning matters. Sometimes they are constituted at a provincial level, sometimes at a municipal level, and sometimes at both. In Alberta, for example, subdivision appeals are decided upon by a provincial agency, the Alberta Planning Board, whereas development appeals (meaning appeals under a zoning by-law) are dealt with by local boards that every municipality is required to organize.

Another general situation in which quasi-judicial powers are called for involves disputes between planning authorities that cannot be resolved through conventional mechanisms of local government. The potential for conflict is especially high in the tight confines of metropolitan space, where actions taken (or not taken) by one municipality may well have detrimental effects ("negative externalities," again) on one or more of its neighbours. Individual municipalities may also find themselves in dispute with their metropolitan planning authority. It may be, for example, that a suburban municipality, desperate for industrial development to strengthen its property tax base, wishes to rezone a block of farm land to provide a site for a new industrial park. But the metropolitan plan designates the site as part of a permanent conservation zone for the protection of prime agricultural land, and neither the regional planning authority nor the neighbouring municipalities are prepared to allow the plan to be amended. So should that be the end of the matter, even if the opposing municipalities are motivated more by their own self-interest than by any sense of metropolitan altruism? They may be anxious to prevent competition for their own industrial parks, for example, or they may see threats to some other development aspirations that they hold. Whose interests should prevail? There is no easy answer to this question, and the most that any planning system can offer is that there will be procedures to ensure that all parties will receive a fair and disinterested hearing. It must also be clear which agency has the authority to make the final, binding decision. It may be the upper-tier municipal government, in which case the decision will be made through the normal legislative process. But if the upper-tier government does not have explicit authority to make decisions that are binding on the lower-tier municipalities, or if there is no upper-tier government at all, the right to refer the matter to some neutral arbiter is generally admitted. Without it, there would be no effective way of resolving disputes; and that, in turn, could cause the metropolitan planning system to collapse in disarray, as Winnipeg learned in the late 1960s.[9]

## *Technical Decisions*

Technical decisions are those made by professional planners in their role as advisers to their employers or clients. They are the least visible and the least understood of all planning decisions, but although they do not have legal force they can exercise great influence. That, after all, is what professional advice is about. And to the extent that the advice is accepted and becomes the basis for subsequent action, planners must be viewed as powerful agents in any planning system. In making decisions, they will also follow their own criteria, under the general rubric of "sound" planning principles. These principles come from their professional knowledge and experience and represent the special skills—the technical skills—that they "sell" to the decision-making authorities.

To understand this relationship it is necessary to realize that the enabling legislation rarely, if ever, grants direct decision-making responsibilities to professional planners. On the contrary, the legislation is normally at pains to establish that the real responsibility rests with elected bodies, either directly or indirectly (through their control over the membership of appointed boards and commissions, for example). Hiring planners is really a matter of administrative convenience. Given the volume of work that most planning systems generate, and the often complex technical considerations that are involved in most planning decisions, no planning organization of any size could operate without professional staff. All the major cities in Canada have their own planning departments, and so too do many suburban municipalities in metropolitan areas. However, if a municipality is too small to warrant having its own permanent planning establishment, it may look to some central agency to provide it with planning services (see Figure 2). This has always been an important factor in the creation of regional planning organizations in Canada.[10] Alternatively, municipalities may prefer to hire private planning consultants, especially if they wish to maintain an independent voice against the regional point of view that staff planners from a metropolitan agency may be thought to favour.

In one way or another, a stream of technical decisions underlies virtually every official decision taken by a public planning authority. Yet there is something of a paradox here. Planners are always quick to disclaim any suggestion of power, on the grounds that they merely advise those who have legal authority to act on behalf of the communities they represent. Planners may even express frustration at their lack of power, especially when their advice is rejected or they find themselves the target of blame for unpopular decisions. From an outside perspective, however, what planners seem to lack is not power but responsibility. It is not the planners who are directly accountable to the communities they serve, but the politicians who employ them. That gives the appearance of an open planning system, yet the significant decisions—the decisions that have lasting effect—may have been made at some remove from the public arena.

### *Legislative Decisions*

The final kinds of decisions are those that are the particular responsibility of some legislative body, normally a municipal council. Many of these decisions will be legislative in the most literal sense, since councils are the only agencies empowered to adopt planning by-laws—and many planning tools require by-laws to give them legal effect. More generally, however, as in other aspects of local government, the council is expected to be the policy-making authority in planning matters; and the ultimate expression of planning policy in any municipality, harking back to T.J. Kent's definition, is its general plan. The actual plan document will be written by planners, and it is their ideas, their technical decisions, that give it its form and substance. Nonetheless, for the plan to become official, and to have legal force, it has to be adopted by the council, though not in a blind, rubber-stamping way. The policies laid down in the plan, and the goals they are directed at achieving, have to be embraced by the council as *its* policies and *its* goals. Nor are planners the only people who should be consulted during the plan-making exercise, a principle that is now well accepted in Canadian planning practice.[11] Ideally, any plan should be a *community* plan, not just a planners' plan or a council's plan. It should capture the community's real needs and aspirations as expressed by community members themselves in a democratic forum. It is commonplace these days to describe urban planning as a political process, but that does not diminish the reality one whit. If politics is defined as the activity by which the members of any group attempt to resolve their conflicts, then the most important planning decisions, the decisions that relate to entire communities, must be political decisions in the purest sense of the word.

## *Planning and Conflict: The Substance of Planning Decisions*

To this point, the discussion has focussed chiefly on the procedural aspects of urban and metropolitan planning. But procedures alone, no matter how carefully prescribed, cannot guarantee that planning decisions will be reasonable and responsible or that no one will be harmed by them. On the contrary, in situations of conflict—and the great majority of planning decisions entail conflict of some kind—the standard procedures are framed so as to produce clear winners and clear losers. It is pretty much a zero-sum game: one party's gain is another party's loss.

There is an underlying ethical problem here, and it rests in the fact that the crux of any conflict is not procedural but substantive. And on the substance of planning decisions, planning statutes are virtually silent. If they give any direction at all it is couched in such bland language as to be practically useless. For example, the Alberta Planning Act, which goes farther than most in stating the purpose of the planning system, refers sweepingly to "the orderly, economical and beneficial development and use of land and patterns of human settlement." As fundamental principles of good urban planning these are unexceptionable, but, as operational criteria for the many different kinds of decisions that the planning system is empowered to make, they are of little help. It is left to the respective planning authorities, whoever they may be, to decide what the terms mean in particular contexts. The critical issue, and hence the ethical dilemma, is that they can simultaneously mean different things to different people. They will be rated differently as well; one person's saving is another's loss, and one vision of order is too costly for others to tolerate. Whose views should dominate? And how should that be reflected in the design of planning systems? Should some interests be valued above others—communities above individuals, perhaps, or property owners above planners? Priorities can also change, as witnessed in the growing strength of the environmental movement and its conflict with the pro-development attitudes that have long prevailed in Canadian cities.

The usual response to issues of these kinds, especially from professional planners, is to say that the planning system represents the "public interest" in urban environment and urban development. Yet even that is not terribly helpful. The difficulties of putting into practice a concept as abstract as public interest are legion; nor is it necessarily agreed that public interests should always come before private ones. The ambivalence is well expressed, once again, in the Alberta Planning Act, which declares that planning measures must be undertaken "without infringing on the rights of individuals *except* to the extent that is necessary for the greater public interest" (emphasis added). If those rights are thought of solely in procedural terms, then the Alberta statute, like all Canadian statutes, lives up to its own prescription. But on substantive grounds the situation is much cloudier; indeed, it is thoroughly ambiguous. Is it more in the public interest to permit a developer to construct a high-rise apartment project in an existing neighbourhood than it is to insist that the site continue to be used for detached houses? On one side, it can be argued that construction jobs will be created, that under-used service facilities will benefit from the influx of population, that tax revenues will be generated, and that the needs of a special segment of the housing market will be met at an appropriate location; on the other, that the established character of the neighbourhood will be irretrievably altered and that the wishes of the present residents should outweigh any other consideration. Where does the *public* interest lie in such a conflict?

In its attempt to cope with conundrums of this kind, modern planning legislation has to accommodate three fundamentally different value systems or "ideologies." Patrick McAuslan describes them as the traditional common-law view of the role of law, the orthodox public administration and planning view, and the radical or populist view.[12] The first refers to the belief that the law should be used to protect the institution of private property[13]; the third, which is much more recent, considers that the law should be used to advance the cause of public participation and popular control. As the example in the previous paragraph was intended to demonstrate, these views of planning law are potentially in conflict, both with each other and with the orthodox planning view, which endorses the public interest as its central value. Moreover, the law itself does little if anything to resolve the conflicts. As long as they are addressed only in procedural terms, the critical choices will be left to the local planning authorities.

Perhaps this is as it should be, if urban planning is truly about communities determining their own futures, but it is also attended by a high degree of doubt and confusion. The old verities are going by the board, especially the too-simple view that urban planning is just a technical arm of local government.[14] Professional planners are still needed to provide technical guidance, but this is no longer the sum of urban-planning practice, as it was once thought to be. In its modern applications, urban planning is as much a mechanism for resolving controversial issues—a mechanism that is expected to be public, open, and democratic. Planning is no longer something that only people called planners do; it is something that communities do, with the help of planners. The kind of help is changing as well. Where planners were once defined as experts on future urban forms, today it is just as important that they bring the skills of mediators, facilitators, and *animateurs* to the community-planning process.[15] That may blur the boundary between "administration" and "politics"—and, as T.J. Plunkett and G.M. Betts have pointed out, the boundary is fuzzy at the best of times[16]—but increasingly the planning process is coming to be seen as an exercise in negotiation. It is the medium through which community groups, developers, politicians, and planners, in shifting combinations, try to work out mutually acceptable solutions to urban problems. This new form of planning is still evolving in Canada, and it is not yet clear how much of the traditional structures will survive the transition, but there is much hope and promise here as well—the hope of a more effective style of urban planning which lives up to its historic promise of creating cities that are truly satisfying to live in.

## *Notes*

1. Matthew J. Kiernan, "Land-use Planning," in *Urban Policy Issues: Canadian Perspectives*, Richard A. Loretto and Trevor Price, eds. (Toronto: McClelland and Stewart, 1990), 58–85.
2. Ibid. See also William T. Perks and Walter Jamieson, "Planning and Development in Canadian Cities," in *Canadian Cities in Transition*, Trudi Bunting and Pierre Filion, eds. (Toronto: Oxford University Press, 1991), 487-518; and P.J. Smith and P.W. Moore, "Cities as a Social Responsibility: Planning and Urban Form," in *The Changing Social Geography of Canadian Cities*, Larry S. Bourne and David F. Ley, eds. (Montreal: McGill-Queen's University Press, 1993), 343-66.
3. For the fullest description and a critical interpretation of Canadian planning systems, see J. Barry Cullingworth, *Urban and Regional Planning in Canada* (New Brunswick, N.J.: Transaction Books, 1987).
4. Gerald Hodge, *Planning Canadian Communities: An Introduction to the Principles, Practice and Participants* (Scarborough, Ont.: Nelson Canada 1991), 110.

5. T.J. Kent, *The Urban General Plan* (San Francisco: Chandler Publishing, 1964), 18.
6. Ira M. Robinson and Douglas R. Webster, "Regional Planning in Canada: History, Practice, Issues and Prospects," *Journal of the American Planning Association*, vol. 51 (1985), 23-33; Gerald Hodge, "Regional Planning: The Cinderella Discipline," *Plan Canada*, July 1994, 35–49.
7 Ontario, Commission on Planning and Development Reform, *New Planning for Ontario: Final Report* (Toronto: 1993), 60-6.
8. P.J. Smith and Patricia E. Bayne, "The Issue of Local Autonomy in Edmonton's Regional Plan Process: Metropolitan Planning in a Changing Political Climate," in *The Changing Canadian Metropolis*, Francis Frisken, ed. (Berkeley, Calif.: Institute of Governmental Studies Press, University of California, 1994), 725–50.
9. Harold Kaplan, *Reform, Planning, and City Politics: Montreal, Winnipeg, Toronto* (Toronto: University of Toronto Press, 1982).
10. Hodge, "Regional Planning."
11. See, for example, Harry Lash, "Planning in a Human Way: The Public in the Process," in *Urban and Regional Planning in a Federal State: The Canadian Experience*, William T. Perks and Ira M. Robinson, eds. (Stroudsburg, Pa.: Dowden, Hutchinson and Ross, 1979), 318–29; and Brian Riera, Tom Fletcher, and Ann McAfee, "New Partnerships, New Directions: Vancouver's Cityplan," *Plan Canada*, November 1993, 16–20.
12. Patrick McAuslan, *The Ideologies of Planning Law* (Oxford, England: Pergamon Press, 1980), 1–6.
13. C.B. Macpherson, *Property: Mainstream and Critical Positions* (Toronto: University of Toronto Press, 1978), 1-12.
14. Matthew J. Kiernan, "Ideology and the Precarious Future of the Canadian Planning Profession," *Plan Canada*, vol. 22 (1982), 14–22.
15. John Forester, *Planning in the Face of Power* (Berkeley, Calif.: University of California Press, 1989).
16. T.J. Plunkett and G.M. Betts, *The Management of Canadian Urban Government* (Kingston: Institute of Local Government, Queen's University, 1978), 33–5.

## *Selected Sources*

Cullingworth, J. Barry. *Urban and Regional Planning in Canada* (New Brunswick, N.J.: Transaction Books, 1987).

Hodge, Gerald. *Planning Canadian Communities: An Introduction to the Principles, Practice and Participants* (Scarborough: Nelson Canada, 1991).

Kaplan, Harold. *Reform, Planning, and City Politics: Montreal, Winnipeg, Toronto* (Toronto: University of Toronto Press, 1982).

Kiernan, Matthew J. "Land-use Planning," in *Urban Policy Issues: Canadian Perspectives,* Richard A. Loreto and Trevor Price, eds. (Toronto: McClelland and Stewart, 1990), 58–85.

Lash, Harry. "Planning in a Human Way: The Public in the Process," in *Urban and Regional Planning in a Federal State: The Canadian Experience,* William T. Perks and Ira M. Robinson, eds. (Stroudsburg, P.A.: Dowden, Hutchison and Ross, 1979), 318–29.

Macpherson, C.B. *Property: Mainstream and Critical Positions* (Toronto: University of Toronto Press, 1978).

McAusland, Patrick. *The Ideologies of Planning Law* (Oxford, England: Pergamon Press, 1980).

Perks, William T. and Walter Jamieson. "Planning and Development in Canadian Cities," in *Canadian Cities in Transition,* Trudi Bunting and Pierre Filion, eds. (Toronto: Oxford University Press, 1991).

Riera, Brian, Tom Fletcher, and Ann McAffee. "New Partnerships, New Directions: Vancouver's Cityplan," *Plan Canada,* November 1993, 16–20.

Smith, P.J. and P.W. Moore. "Cities As a Social Responsibility: Planning and Urban Form," in *The Changing Social Geography of Canadian Cities,* Larry S. Bourne and David F. Ley, eds. (Montreal: McGill-Queen's University Press, 1993), 343–66.

Smith, P.J. and Patricia E. Bayne. "The Issue of Local Autonomy in Edmonton's Regional Plan Process: Metropolitan Planning in a Changing Political Climate," in *The Changing Canadian Metropolis,* Frances Frisken, ed. (Berkeley, Calif.: Institute of Governmental Studies Press, University of California, 1994), 725–50.

# 10

## *Governing Education: The Myth of Local Control*

Robert Carney

Frank Peters

THIS CHAPTER addresses questions related to local public schooling in Canada: who is "in the game" of education politics, who participates in the development of decisions, who generally prevails in such matters, and why they do. While the present discussion concerns that particular form of education known as public schooling, it must be noted that schools have not been the only, or perhaps even the primary, institutions of education in Canada. Families, peer groups, religious and community organizations, libraries, museums, print media, and, most recently, television and computer systems have shared significantly in educating Canadians. What is of interest here, however, is how citizens participate in the governance of public schooling at the local, territorial, and provincial level, how they have sought or been encouraged to play a role in this aspect of public life, and how their participation has been aided or limited by such centralizing agencies as regional and provincial school authorities. The following analysis traces the historical development of public schooling in Canada from its inception to the present with reference to the political structure and administration of public schools.

## *Historical Development*

School districts governed by locally elected boards of trustees have been an aspect of public schooling in this country since the early nineteenth century. Legislation passed in Upper Canada (Ontario) in 1816 establishing common school districts, and based in part on values inherited from the United States, set a pattern of school governance which, in one form or another, has prevailed to the present in much of Canada. There have always been concerns, however, about the powers of these districts, especially in relation to the control exercised over them by colonial, territorial, and provincial governments. In 1976, for example, an Organization for Economic Co-operation and Development (OECD) review of education in Canada summarized historical developments in the area of school governance. It noted that provincial affirmations of local participation in education have an "insincere tone" given the predominant power of ministries of education in educational policy making and administration.[1]

Three major phases of school governance will be examined. The first encompasses the period of the establishment and expansion of school districts from the mid-1800s to the 1930s. A principal outcome of this phase was that most settled areas of the country had obtained a considerable degree of local involvement in the establishment, maintenance, and administration of publicly funded schools by the onset of the Second World War. The second phase occurred from the 1930s to the 1960s, when the affairs of school districts became subject to forms of consolidation and regionalization. The third phase, from the 1970s to the present, has been characterized by further regionalization and greater provincial control of schools.

Elizabeth Graham's analysis of the development of public education in the United States, which indicates how certain expectations or priorities have changed the objectives of American schooling,[2] can be generally applied to the Canadian experience. She outlines three major expectations which have been largely replicated in this country in terms both of periodization and of orientation. The first concerns the efforts of public-school promoters in the nineteenth and early twentieth centuries to increase school attendance through such measures as free, universal, and compulsory education. The second expectation, which became common by the 1920s, involved increasing access to schools for those who had not attended for such reasons as poverty, location, and ethnicity, or whose attendance was short-lived because of lack of appropriate programs. The third expectation, that of academic achievement, began to take hold in the late 1970s. By this time, the expectations of attendance and access had been generally attained, but they were no longer deemed to be sufficient in that both rested on the belief "that academic learning was useful for some but not necessary for all."[3] Graham sums up the present-day expectation of academic achievement in these terms: "What has happened is that we have changed our expectations both for children and for schools, thus making the schools' job both immensely more difficult and immensely more important than it was in earlier decades. In addition to attendance and access for our children, we have now added a third and absolutely new goal, academic achievement for all our children. The needs of the American work force and of American society in the twenty-first century dictate that all, not just some, children must become academically proficient."[4]

School trustees and ministers of provincial departments of education have been responsible for determining and implementing the phases and expectations outlined above. Their decisions have been influenced by parent, teacher, business, linguistic, and religious interests, but, except in three instances which are pertinent to this study, none of these interests have been granted any constitutional educational privileges. The first exception concerns the guarantees accorded religious denominations in section 93 of the Constitution Act (1867), formerly known as the British North America Act; the second is specified in section 91 of the same act, which gives the Canadian parliament exclusive authority in matters concerning "Indians and Lands reserved for Indians"; and the third involves the language minority rights (English and French) specified in section 23 of the Charter of Rights and Freedoms. The provinces have otherwise maintained exclusive authority in matters of education, which is clearly affirmed in the preamble of section 93 of the Constitution Act (1867): "In and for each Province the Legislature may exclusively make Laws in relation to Education, subject and according to the following Provisions" (the denominational guarantees in subsections 1 to 4). This stipulation has not prevented the federal government from influencing provincial educational activities by making funds available for programs seen to be in the national interest. Yet, while the provinces have been open to accepting federal funding, they have never doubted that each phase of school governance and the expectations associated with it have been theirs to determine.

## *Establishment and Expansion: The Attendance Expectation*

Public funding of schools in Upper Canada began in 1807 when the colonial government passed its first educational act authorizing an annual grant of $400 apiece to the masters of Upper Canada's eight grammar schools. Located in large centres, operated under the auspices of the Church of England, and governed by appointees chosen from the colony's elite, the grammar schools charged high fees and followed an academic curriculum for small numbers of pupils at both the elementary and the secondary level. The grammar schools were not subject to any significant form of government supervision until the 1850s, nor were they governed by elected trustees until 1871. As an elite, largely urban-based type of schooling, the grammar schools set a pattern that continues to this day: urban high schools and collegiates, modelled on the old grammar schools, set a standard that rural schools have difficulty matching. This pattern is also reflected in the privileged position of high schools in the more affluent areas of cities and their suburbs vis-à-vis those schools in less prosperous areas; schools in the former category possess a greater range of programs, more staff resources, and better school facilities than those in the latter.

In 1816 control of public schooling by elected trustees was implemented in Upper Canada with the passage of the first Common (elementary) School Act. Similar legislation was adopted in Lower Canada (Quebec) in 1824 and 1829. To be eligible for a small school subsidy from the legislature, those wishing such support were required to elect three school trustees whose responsibilities for their school district or section included providing a schoolhouse, choosing a teacher, and determining the curriculum and texts to be used. Local boards of trustees were abolished in 1841 (a year after the amalgamation of the two Canadas), when responsibility for supervising the common schools was given to municipally appointed superintendents of schools. School legislation passed in 1843 restored local trustees, who were given their former duties except for teacher inspection and certification.

The 1841 legislation also provided for a unified system of common schooling for Canada West (Ontario) and Canada East (Quebec). Given their different religious and linguistic character, however, this provision proved to be unworkable. As a result, educational acts were passed for each area in 1843. Over the next half-century, the Ontario system of public schooling became highly centralized. Similar levels of centralization occurred in Quebec, but in this instance the governing authorities became the churches, Catholic and Protestant, rather than the state. The result was a dual system of schooling in which the two designated religious communities in Quebec had access to completely separate and distinct systems of formal education.

In Ontario, the first steps towards centralizing control of local schooling were taken during the tenure of Egerton Ryerson, who was appointed chief superintendent of schools for Upper Canada in 1844. Legislation passed in 1850 permitted school districts to levy taxes on the basis of property assessment. Although districts were expected to fund an increasing share of the cost of schooling from local sources, district control of local schooling matters was continually diminished. As Alison Prentice puts it, by the time Egerton Ryerson retired in 1876 responsibility for the character and operation of public schooling was largely in his hands and those of an appointed body known as the Council of Public Instruction:

> The choice of courses of study, school books, school rules and prayers, which prior to the Ryerson era had been left to the discretion of parents and local school section authorities, was by 1871 clearly in the hands of central bodies . . . as were the complex rules and regulations which increasingly governed the qualifications, hiring and behavior of teachers and other previously unheard of functionaries within the growing public school systems. Equally lost to . . . local control in many cases were the regulation of school attendance, school financing and a host of other items related to the founding and organization of schools.[5]

The Quebec model of public schooling was implemented in the prairie west following its acquisition by Canada in 1869. The government of Manitoba set up a board of education composed of Protestant and Catholic sections in 1871, and the government of the North-West Territories followed suit in 1884 with the passage of the first territorial school ordinance. In the latter case the lieutenant governor appointed to each section six members who were responsible for setting the regulations for their respective schools. These regulations included appointing school inspectors, determining curriculum and texts, and inspecting and certifying teachers. The ordinance also provided for the establishment of school districts, which were not to exceed 93 square kilometres, and for the election of school trustees. The duties of the latter, such as providing a schoolhouse, finding a teacher, and securing the funds to sustain these initiatives, were similar to those assigned their counterparts in Ontario at the time.

Manitoba's dual system of public education was dissolved in 1890 when the provincial legislature passed a new schools act. The act set up a non-sectarian, unified system of public education, which at the local level was to be administered by a board of elected trustees. Existing denominational schools could become public schools and operate within the framework of the new act, or revert to the status of a private institution without access to local rates or provincial grants. All the Protestant schools formerly operated by the board of education opted to join the new system; some of the Catholic schools did the same while others closed or became private schools. It is not possible here to trace the protracted litigation and the bitter political controversies that ensued. Suffice it to say that, other than for some short-term concessions obtained following the federal election of 1896, the autonomy enjoyed by Catholic ratepayers prior to 1890 was never restored. The single system of public schooling in Manitoba was further strengthened in 1916 when the government ended its support for bilingual schools and made school attendance compulsory for children aged five to fourteen. At this stage the character of Manitoba's system of public education became virtually identical to that in place in British Columbia when it joined confederation in 1871.

Roman Catholic schools fared somewhat better in the North-West Territories. A new school ordinance in 1892 established a unitary system governing both public and separate schools. The powers of the local trustees remained the same, but those formerly delegated to the

Protestant and Catholic sections were now assumed by the ministry. While Catholics strongly opposed the adoption of the Ontario model of public education, and sought to have the dual system re-established, their efforts were tempered by events in Manitoba. As the outcome there was much worse than what they faced in the territories, the Catholic hierarchy and its supporters eventually, albeit reluctantly, accepted the change.

This acquiescence became apparent in 1905 when Prime Minister Wilfrid Laurier introduced the autonomy bills in the federal parliament to create the provinces of Alberta and Saskatchewan. The original draft of the bills included a clause that might have led to the re-establishment of the dual system of schools provided for in the ordinance of 1884. When Clifford Sifton, who had been minister of education in Manitoba during the stormy years between 1891 and 1896, learned of the clause, he resigned as Laurier's minister of the interior. The prime minister avoided a cabinet split when he subsequently accepted in principle a draft clause proposed by Sifton which gave the two provinces unified school systems based on the Ontario, rather than the Quebec, model. Bishop Émile-Joseph Legal, archbishop of St Albert, indicated during an interview in Calgary in 1905 that he accepted the revised clause: "We are satisfied with the system of separate schools which we have. I do not say it is the best possible system for us. A system can be modified from time to time by ordinances and other measures so that you can never say that a system is the best possible. But we are getting along peacefully, and we only hope that we will be allowed to retain what we have."[6]

As the issues relating to denominational schools were being resolved in the settled areas of Ontario and the prairies, public-school promoters gave increasing attention to having every child in school. Two major tactics were used to achieve this end. The first was reflected in compulsory education legislation, and the second involved hastening the establishment of rural school districts. The first compulsory attendance law in the country was passed in Ontario in 1871. The school act of that year required children aged seven to twelve to attend school for at least four months a year. British Columbia and the North-West Territories enacted similar legislation in 1873 and 1884 respectively, making attendance compulsory in those areas where school districts were established. The enforcement of these laws was thrust upon local trustees, who found this an unenviable task and one that they pursued with great reluctance. Religious and linguistic controversies prevented Manitoba from passing attendance regulations until 1916. The Maritime provinces were equally slow in adopting measures of this kind. New Brunswick made a weak attempt to enforce attendance in 1905, and Nova Scotia left the matter to local trustees to sort out until 1915 when legislation was passed requiring attendance in all town districts. Quebec and Newfoundland, which were bastions of denominational schooling, waited until 1943 before catching up with their neighbours. Such legislative measures undoubtedly had some effect in increasing school attendance, but, as Cecil Race argues, "improvements in school attendance appeared to result more from positive forces operating in people's lives, such as the desire for schooling . . . and the voluntary and speedy erection of schools in pioneer settlements . . . than [from] compelled attendance."[7]

Ontario led the way in nineteenth- and twentieth-century Canada in extending opportunities for public schooling by establishing school districts and by using various means to strengthen the resolve of trustees to keep their school districts operating. This process began in earnest in the 1840s and continued throughout Egerton Ryerson's superintendency. Upon his retirement in 1876 there were 465 000 pupils in over 5000 publicly supported schools operated by 4900 public, separate, and high school boards.[8] Although these figures were impressive, only 45 per cent of school-age children in the province were enrolled by the mid-1870s. This low percentage combined with the sporadic attendance of many of those enrolled indicated that the goal of universal education had yet to be attained. Partly as a result, the government of the day abolished the office of chief superintendent of schools and assigned responsibility for public education to a minister of the crown, who, as a member of the cabinet, was directly responsible to the legislature. Interestingly enough, the Quebec government abolished the education portfolio in 1875 "to remove any danger of political interference."[9] The ministry was not re-established until 1964, as part of the far-reaching social and political changes associated with the "Quiet Revolution."

Statistics for 1910 show that Ontario had by then achieved its goal of having most children in school. In that year, 76 per cent of that province's six- to nine-year-olds were in school for part of the year and 84 per cent of the ten- to fourteen-year-olds were enrolled. However, in Alberta only 50 per cent and 65 per cent respectively of the same age groups were enrolled, the lowest figures in the country. The provincial government responded by reducing the size of the school districts from 64 to 41 square kilometres, thus lessening the distance children would have to travel to school. By 1921 the enrolment of seven- to fourteen-year-olds was 87 per cent in rural Alberta and 89 per cent overall, and the number of children attending school for less than twenty days dropped from 9.7 per cent of the total enrolment in 1910 to 3.9 per cent in 1922.[10]

The above figures are representative of what happened elsewhere in the country. Most children went to school for brief periods, and in the minds of many this amount of schooling was enough. What was necessary for them was an acquaintance with reading, writing, and arithmetic taught in an atmosphere infused with political loyalty, Christian morality, and the values required for a disciplined work force. After receiving two to three years of instruction, many children were seen to be ready for the unskilled jobs available in towns and rural areas. In the initial decades of the present century, however, there were increasing signs that this view was changing. Not only were children staying in school longer, but the level and range of the programs available to them were improving as well.

## *Consolidation: Increasing School Access*

While a number of provinces attempted to amalgamate or consolidate some of the small school jurisdictions in earlier years, it was not until the 1930s in Canada that any major successful ventures were undertaken in this area. The movement to consolidation, which is still a feature of Canadian education today, was driven partly by a desire to reduce costs and partly by a commitment to access and quality. Graham points out that the movement to consolidation in the United States was aimed at increasing access to school for those of diverse ethnic, religious, linguistic, and economic backgrounds who were unable to avail themselves fully of quality educational programs. While the same motivation was evident in Canada, there was considerable variation from one context to another in terms of whether ethnic, religious, linguistic, or class considerations predominated. Generally, however, ethnicity was a secondary and almost accidental feature of Canadian efforts at school-system consolidation. Small rural communities were, on occasion, made up almost exclusively of particular ethnic groups, and so the deprivations associated with the smaller rural school districts—especially the problem of access to enriched programs and to high school instruction—did have an ethnic dimension. Nevertheless, it is clear that the major thrusts to reduce the number of school systems were based on considerations of financial cost, access, and program quality.

In Alberta in 1935 there were 3812 distinct school districts educating a school population of approximately 178 000 students.[11] Each of these districts had its own school board and most were responsible for single-room schools. In Alberta, in the school year 1935–36, there were 5873 school rooms in operation in 3859 different school districts. Most of the multi-room schools were found in the cities and towns while the smaller, single-room, multi-grade schools looked after the needs of the rural pupils. Almost 65 per cent of the students enrolled in Alberta's schools in the mid-1930s lived in the rural parts of the province. By way of comparison, today there are 142 jurisdictions operating schools in Alberta, with a combined enrolment of approximately 460 000 students. Almost 70 per cent of these are enrolled in school systems in the province's eight largest cities.

Alberta was among the first of the provinces to attempt seriously to reduce the number of distinct school districts by means of the establishment of school divisions in 1936. The development of a larger unit of school governance had been a major component in the Social Credit Party's platform in the 1935 election, and upon assuming office the government promptly implemented this proposal. Consolidation was precipitated to some extent by the fact that many of the tiny rural districts were so poor that they were unable to pay their teachers' salaries and faced bankruptcy. At the same time, the choice of programs in the small rural schools was seen as less than optimal, and consolidation, as well as spreading the cost of schooling over a broader economic and resource base and thus introducing some efficiencies, was seen as a means of enhancing the quality of the programs available to students, particularly at the high school level. By the end of 1940 a total of 3346 districts had been amalgamated into 103 school divisions or consolidated districts. By 1950 there were 57 school divisions in operation and only 189 districts operating outside the divisions. By 1960 these numbers had increased somewhat to 58 and 204 respectively, and by 1968 there were 60 school divisions and counties and 169 additional jurisdictions in the province.[12]

Moves to consolidate and regionalize educational services took place in every province across the country, though at different times. In British Columbia the Cameron commission of 1945 looked into the entire matter of local administration and recommended that the province's 650 school boards be regrouped into 74 regional boards. This recommendation was implemented and currently, following a number of subsequent rearrangements, there are 75 school divisions in that province. Reorganization on a voluntary basis began in Saskatchewan as early as 1912, with the introduction of legislation permitting the amalgamation of smaller districts into "consolidated" districts. This initiative was a resounding failure, and a subsequent recommendation in 1918 whereby the province's 4075 school districts would be replaced with 300 municipal school districts was also never acted on. It was not until 1944 that the newly elected Co-operative Commonwealth Federation, acting on a campaign promise, passed the Larger School Units Act, and this legislation has continued to dictate the structure of the basic units of school jurisdiction in Saskatchewan to the present. Today there are 127 different school jurisdictions in the province. In Manitoba there are currently 57 public school systems, including one francophone board. In Quebec, when a ministry of education was re-established in 1964, there were almost 1800 local school authorities. By 1971 it was possible to propose a major reorganization and, excluding the island of Montreal, the province's school districts were regrouped into 189 school commissions. Subsequently the school districts on the island were reorganized into seven commissions. The end result of all this is that at present there are 199 distinct school jurisdictions in Quebec.

Similar amalgamations took place in Ontario where, by 1950, 536 township boards had replaced a total of 3465 small rural districts. In 1964 the province stipulated that henceforth the smallest school jurisdiction would be the township. During the next decade county boards of education were created, and further changes reduced the total number of public, separate, and francophone school boards to the current number of 172. In Prince Edward Island, a new school act in 1971 reorganized the province's 217 school districts into 5 large area boards and in May 1994 the entire island was redivided into two English school jurisdictions. In New Brunswick, the province's 433 districts were consolidated in 1967 into 33 larger units and in 1992 this number was reduced to 18, with 12 anglophone and 6 francophone districts. In Nova Scotia an initial reduction of jurisdictions took place in 1974 when the entire province was organized into 62 jurisdictions. A subsequent series of amalgamations in 1982 further reduced the number to 21 and since then one francophone jurisdiction has been added, for a total of 22. In Newfoundland a major reorganization took place in 1964 and approximately 300 districts were amalgamated into 34. This number subsequently dropped to 27 and the government is now, following a royal commission, planning to reduce the number of school jurisdictions to 10.

## *Restructuring and Reform: Academic Achievement*

The third phase identified by Graham relates to the expectation that all students will achieve a high level of academic proficiency while in school. Graham suggests that this phase became noticeable in the late 1970s, and in the United States it led to an outburst of investigations of one sort or another into the various aspects of what was perceived by many to be a crisis in education. Thomas O. Maguire states that by 1985 there had been about three dozen reports in the United States, all of which advocated fundamental educational reform.[13]

Possibly the most prominent of these reports is *A Nation at Risk*, published in 1983. This document starts out with words which have become, in practice, the rationale of the continuing campaign for school reform both in Canada and in the United States: "Our Nation is at risk, our once unchallenged preeminence in commerce, industry, science and technological innovation is being overtaken by competitors throughout the world."[14] The same viewpoint has been voiced stridently in Canada and has led to calls for changes to the manner in which education is both governed and delivered.

Concerns with academic achievement in Canadian schools have been heard more frequently and more clearly during the recent years of economic recession—a development that may be linked, in part at least, to the prominence in public discourse of what two authors have recently referred to as the politics of blame.[15] One of the criticisms of the educational system frequently advanced today is that our graduates are not equipped with the skills necessary to compete in a highly technological work environment. This charge, however, is not new; it goes back to at least the 1970s, when a successful campaign was waged to reintroduce standardized and/or departmentalized testing in those jurisdictions where these practices had been abandoned. The current demand for greater achievement is fuelled partly by the fact that, when we compare Canadian scores on tests of academic ability with results from other countries, they are lower than we would like.

The increasing anxiety about student achievement has led to the establishment by provincial ministries of education, through the Council of Ministers of Education, of a national School Achievement Indicators Program (SAIP). Launched in 1992, this project will have a stratified sample of thirteen- and sixteen-year-olds in each province tested, on a three-year cyclical basis, in reading and writing, mathematics, and science. SAIP is designed specifically to identify key areas of relative strength and weakness within the curriculum.

The results of a national public opinion poll reported by the Angus Reid Group in 1993 indicate that one-half of those surveyed felt that the quality of education was worse than it had been in 1967.[16] Three-quarters of those polled felt that high school graduates were deficient in reading and writing skills, while 60 per cent indicated that they thought high school graduates did not have an adequate understanding of mathematics and science. The results of a survey conducted in 1990 on behalf of the Canadian Education Association provided findings that were less critical of the schools in many respects. This survey did point out, however, that people with children in elementary school were more likely to provide positive comments than were parents of high school students or members of the general public, and it also found that there was an alarming level of dissatisfaction with schools in areas with populations of more than one million. "The writers suggest that the high degree of dissatisfaction felt with large American systems is increasingly being felt in Canadian metropolitan areas."[17]

In addition to the emergence of a profound unease with the level of achievement of Canada's students, another development during the 1980s has had considerable impact on the general operation of schools. Decisions in virtually all provinces that children with disabilities should be placed in the least restrictive environment possible have meant that many classes now contain students whose mental or physical abilities would previously have dictated that they should receive special attention in segregated or partially segregated settings. While the impact of this change in policy is being experienced in all school jurisdictions, it is felt most acutely in cities because urban schools act as a magnet for challenged students from rural areas.

The demands for greater accountability and more satisfying results within the educational industry are sustained and strident. Provincial governments have indicated that they intend to accede to these pressures and are producing plans and blueprints which will provide for greater competition between schools and school systems, which will allow for the establishment of "Charter" (private) schools and for much greater parental involvement at the school level, and which will compel teachers to specify clear learning outcomes and demand high-performance standards from students. It is a sign of the times that all ten provinces and both territories have, within the past five years, established either a commission or a major review both to examine the performance of their schools and to consider alternative structures whereby education could be delivered more effectively and more efficiently.

## *Present Structures*

We now turn to those aspects of education in Canada that distinguish it from education in other countries, such as our unique way of accommodating linguistic and religious differences, our manner of providing for Indian education, and our ways of organizing and funding education. It is worth repeating that there is not a Canadian educational system as such but rather twelve different systems, one for each of the provinces and territories. These systems share some features in common, but on the whole it is best to see each province and territory as having its own unique form of educational structure.

The governance of education is a distinct function in Canada, assigned to boards elected solely for that purpose. The most notable exception to this rule is the county structure in Alberta, where, in thirty of the school systems, the control of education is in the hands of a committee made up of representatives from the towns and villages elected only to that committee, along with the county councillors whose mandate includes not just education but such other functions as libraries, public works, and recreation and who are appointed by the county council to the education committee.

In urban Canada the school jurisdictions are, at times, coterminous with the cities. This is more frequently true of the larger cities though in all provinces there are cases where it also applies to smaller cities. In British Columbia the school jurisdictions in the lower mainland area are all coterminous with the municipalities, but this practice does not extend either to the rest of the mainland or to Vancouver Island. In other provinces, such as Prince Edward Island and New Brunswick, the larger cities tend to be the administrative or organizational centre of the district but the school district includes rural as well as city schools. Another model is to be found in the Winnipeg area where the city and the surrounding region is divided into a number of school districts, each including those satellite communities and rural areas outside the city which are linked geographically and historically with it. The city of Toronto provides two examples of completely different models of educational governance. In Ontario all of the separate school boards except one are Catholic, and Toronto's Catholic school district is coterminous with the entire Metropolitan Toronto area. For public schools, however, the Metro area is divided into six boards and a larger Metro board which is made up of representatives from each of the smaller boards. The areas of responsibility for the two levels of operation are clearly separated.

The table below provides a listing of the ten largest school jurisdictions in the country according to enrolment.[18] In seven of these ten districts there was an increase in enrolment over the previous year. In Toronto Separate there was a miniscule drop of seven students reported while in Edmonton there was a decline of about 160. In Montreal Catholic a decline of almost 4700 was reported, dropping that board from third- to fourth-largest in terms of enrolment.

Alongside these large jurisdictions are many smaller school systems, mainly though not exclusively in rural Canada, where the enrolment for the entire jurisdiction is well below a thousand. In Alberta alone there are approximately seventy school systems with enrolments below this number while in Saskatchewan there are approximately forty-five. Indeed, a recent report in Saskatchewan has pointed out that about three-fourths of the province's school divisions have enrolments of under 1500 and about one-fourth have enrolments of fewer than 500. The report states that most of the divisions have enrolments more in keeping with what one might expect in a school rather than in a school jurisdiction.[19]

*Table: Canada's ten largest school boards*

| *Board* | *Enrolment* |
|---|---|
| Metro Separate (Toronto) | 103 363 |
| Calgary Public | 98 398 |
| Peel (Mississauga) | 93 196 |
| Montreal Catholic | 88 197 |
| Edmonton Public | 78 871 |
| Scarborough | 78 000 |
| Toronto | 76 083 |
| York Region (Aurora, ON) | 71 543 |
| Dufferin-Peel RC (Mississauga) | 68 025 |
| North York | 62 551 |

## *Funding of Education*

In four of the provinces—Newfoundland, Prince Edward Island, New Brunswick, and British Columbia— school boards are no longer authorized to raise money by means of taxation; instead the boards receive all of their funding from the provincial government. The Alberta government recently indicated its intent to change to a centralized funding arrangement. In Nova Scotia, where school boards are permitted to levy a supplementary local tax for special programs, most boards have never exercised this right and in fact receive all of their operating grants directly from the province.

The arrangement in Ontario, Manitoba, and Saskatchewan has the province providing each school jurisdiction with a portion of its funding. In Ontario the province provides, on average, about 40 per cent of the required funds while the remainder is collected through local taxation. The proportion paid in grants, however, varies considerably depending on local fiscal capacity. For example, the York Regional Board of Education raises approximately 90 per cent of its funds through local taxation and receives only 10 per cent from provincial grants.[20] In Manitoba and in Saskatchewan, school boards receive approximately 70 per cent and 50 per cent respectively of their funds from the province. In Quebec the province provided approximately 85 per cent of funding to school boards for the 1990–91 school year while the boards raised about 10 per cent from taxes— double the amount they were required to raise the previous year. The remaining 5 per cent is obtained from other sources such as rentals and donations.

In each of these provinces the local jurisdiction sets its own mill rate based on the shortfall between its anticipated expenditures and its anticipated revenue from grants. The requisition, however, is collected by the municipality as it collects its own municipal taxes. This system has a number of benefits from the point of view of those on the education board, even if the municipality charges a fee for the service provided. The most obvious advantage is the fact that there is no need to duplicate tax-collection agencies. The municipal tax bill indicates the amount payable by the taxpayer for educational purposes; the municipality remits the requisitioned funds to the appropriate school jurisdictions and does so regardless of whether taxes are in arrears or delinquent. In this way, the school systems are assured of the required operating funds and taxpayers receive only one tax bill. If a taxpayer is in default, the municipality is responsible for collecting, and, should it become necessary to seize assets, this is the responsibility solely of the municipality.

## *Organization and Enfranchisement*

In a number of provinces the larger urban school jurisdictions are divided into wards or subdivisions for electoral purposes. This is not the case in Vancouver, where school trustees are elected at large, but

Edmonton, Calgary, Saskatoon, Regina, and Winnipeg follow the ward model. In all these cities, school trustees, like city councillors, are elected on a ward basis though school wards may not have the same boundaries as those for the city councils.[21] In New Brunswick, each school district is divided into subdistricts and one board member is elected from each.

The concerns expressed regarding city-council wards also apply to wards or subdistricts in school systems. Their biggest drawback is that they can create an inappropriate sense of responsibility for a segment of the entire jurisdiction, or for a number of schools, rather than for the welfare of the entire district. On the other hand, proponents of the ward system correctly point out that it is impractical and costly to select, from a huge number of candidates in an open election, trustees for ten or twelve positions in cities with populations of a million or more.

School board members or trustees are elected across Canada by those classified as electors within the school jurisdiction in which the election is being held. The most notable exception to this mode of operation is in Newfoundland; there, trustees are appointed by the minister of education, but, in a peculiar democratic twist, at least two-thirds of those to be appointed are selected by means of an election while the remainder are either members of the clergy or officers of the religious denomination for which the district was established. Another exception to the principle of election is found in Alberta, where county councillors are eligible to be appointed to the board of education. Generally, the basic requirement in order to be able to vote in a school board election anywhere in Canada is that one must be a Canadian citizen, eighteen years of age or over, and have resided in the particular province for at least six consecutive months immediately preceding election day. On the day of election the voter must also be a resident of the school jurisdiction. In a similar vein, the first prerequisite to having one's name stand for election is that one be eligible to vote in the particular election. If you are ineligible to vote yourself then it will not be possible to have others vote you into office either.[22]

In most provinces there is nothing to prevent a school board trustee from holding some other public office. However, in the provinces of Nova Scotia and Ontario, legislation expressly prohibits an individual from being a member of a school board and a municipal councillor at the same time. In Newfoundland, all employees of the Department of Education are prohibited from being school trustees, as are all employees of school boards except teachers, and a teacher may not be on the board which is his or her employer. This last requirement is a common one in other provinces. In Saskatchewan the only specified impediment to running for a school board appears to be the requirement that one not be under a contract of employment with the board for which one seeks nomination. A similar obstacle is present in both New Brunswick and Alberta, though the former province also prohibits employees of the minister of education from running for office. In Alberta there are a number of additional stipulated impediments, including the requirements that one not be either a judge or an undischarged bankrupt nor in arrears in tax payments to the municipality in which one is seeking office. In British Columbia a number of recent court cases dealing with questions of conflict of interest have provided rulings which appear to make it illegal for a teacher in any school system to be a school board member anywhere.

School boards vary in size across the country, from five members to well over twenty, and the number of board members is not in any way dictated by the number of students served by the board. In Alberta the school board with the largest number of trustees is Northland School Division, which serves fewer than 3000 students; however, the students are scattered through more than twenty different Native communities in northern Alberta, and the extremely large school board is an attempt to provide these communities with some voice in the education provided to their children. In New Brunswick a school board has seven, nine, or eleven members, the number being determined by the lieutenant-governor-in-council. In Newfoundland, where each school board operates under a constitution which it has itself prescribed and which has been approved by the minister, the minimum number of school board members is seven. In Saskatchewan a school board must have a minimum of five members and a maximum of ten, while Manitoba boards vary between five and eleven. In Ontario the size of school boards varies between five and twenty-six.

Approximately 40 per cent of the members of school boards in Canada are women and most members, men and women, are between forty and fifty years of age. For the vast majority, school trusteeship is a part-time job which pays a small stipend, if it pays one at all, and most trustees are willing to provide this service to their community for more than one term of office.

## *Denominational School Systems*

We have already referred to the guarantees accorded the Protestant and Roman Catholic religions in section 93 of the Constitution Act (1867), formerly known as the British North America Act. These guarantees have resulted in a dual-track educational system in Quebec, Ontario, Saskatchewan, and Alberta and a multi-track denominational system in Newfoundland where all public schools are, *de jure*, denominational schools. In the remaining five provinces, denominational schools are private or independent schools.[23] This constitutional protection is a product of simpler times and a less culturally pluralistic society. The intention was clearly to guarantee to Protestants and Catholics that both could have their own school systems and neither would be compelled to attend the schools of the other unless they wished to do so. Consequently, the religious minority was granted the right to set up its own schools and support these schools out of its own tax payments. This dual system was first recognized in law, as has been mentioned, in Canada West in 1843, and while the precise wording was modified from time to time the principle was enshrined in the constitution of 1867 and indeed it has been recognized that the confederation agreement would have been impossible had this clause not been included. A clause similar to section 93 of the 1867 act was part of all subsequent acts establishing new provinces in Canada, but they were only of significance, in terms of denominational rights, in Manitoba, Alberta, Saskatchewan, and Newfoundland. As noted, changes to legislation in Manitoba in 1890 effectively abolished the denominational school system and this provincial intervention continues to be a contentious issue today. In the other three provinces and in Ontario and Quebec we find denominational education, whether Protestant or Catholic, alongside the generally non-denominational public-school system.

Within the Protestant and Catholic educational systems the school boards are granted control over the religious aspects of the curriculum and are entitled to implement policies that safeguard the denominational nature of the system. They are entitled to implement discriminatory hiring practices and are generally permitted to limit access to their schools to members of their particular religion. Because this denominational right is constitutionally protected it is specifically safeguarded from Charter challenge by virtue of section 29 of that document.

By far the largest number of denominational schools in Canada are Catholic schools, and in the provinces of Newfoundland, Ontario, Saskatchewan, and Alberta between 20 and 25 per cent of all students are educated in Catholic schools. The percentage is far higher in Quebec, where about 83 per cent of all students are enrolled in Catholic schools. There are approximately 4700 Catholic schools in Canada employing about 95 000 educators and educating over 1.7 million students. Most denominational schools are found in the towns and cities, since it is there that sufficiently large concentrations of population are present to make it feasible for denomination members to exercise their constitutional rights.

## *Indian Education*

As indicated earlier, the federal government became responsible for Native people in 1867. At this time the formal education of Natives took place largely in day and residential schools operated by the Catholic and Protestant churches. Natives, of course, had no say in the running of the schools, and this state of affairs was reinforced by an entente between the churches and the Department of Indian Affairs that had been worked out by the turn of the century.

A new era of Native schooling began in 1948 as a result of a recommendation of a parliamentary committee that "whenever and wherever possible Indian children should be educated in association with other children."[24] The Indian Act was amended accordingly in 1951 so as to authorize the minister of Indian affairs to enter into agreements with public and separate schools for the education of Native children. This process was known as integration, but its meaning remained unclear, especially with respect to such matters as languages of instruction, the cultural content of the curriculum, and Native participation in school governance. For these and other reasons, the transfer of Native children to provincial schools was criticized—and in some cases resisted—by many whites and Natives.

Native concerns about the strategy of integration came to a head in 1969, when the federal government published a white paper that recommended the repeal of the Indian Act and the abolition of Indian status. Native organizations responded with such counterproposals as *Citizens Plus* (1970), which affirmed that the federal government would have to change its policy direction "and give the Indians the chance to run their own education system."[25] This position, in which local control and parental responsibility were central themes, was reiterated in *Indian Control of Indian Education*, a document that the National Indian Brotherhood (NIB) presented to Jean Chrétien, minister of Indian affairs, in December 1972.[26] Chrétien, who along with members of his department had viewed the integration program as an unqualified success, reversed his position when confronted by a series of school strikes and sit-ins. As he put it in response to the NIB's submission in February 1973, "I agree with the paper's basic position of Indian parental responsibility and local control of education in partnership with the federal government."[27]

The department proceeded to sign agreements allowing Indian bands to administer all or part of the educational programs previously provided by non-Indian agencies. Since then, band educational authorities have assumed extensive responsibilities for these programs. Decisions concerning staffing, curriculum, learning resources, languages of instruction, and length of school year are among the matters that all but a few reserve schools are currently determining on their own. Native organizations such as the Assembly of First Nations (AFN), however, remain dissatisfied. In 1984, for example, the AFN (successor to the National Indian Brotherhood) undertook an assessment of the state of Native education more than a decade after the publication of *Indian Control of Indian Education*. The AFN's report, released in 1988, concluded that Natives had gained "very limited control over educational programs" and charged the federal government with failing "to implement the policy of *Indian Control of Indian Education*."[28] In the 1990s Native leaders see the education of their people as part of the much larger issue of the inherent right to self-government. Although this right has yet to be achieved, the Department of Indian Affairs continues to divest itself of any direct responsibility for Native education, other than to act as a funding agent for programs controlled by sectors of the Native community. While this change has largely occurred on rural reserves, the AFN expects to achieve the same levels of educational autonomy for First Nations pupils in cities such as Winnipeg and Saskatoon. This expectation stands in marked contrast to what is happening to urban school boards, which have less and less control over the content and direction of their school programs.

## *Francophone Education*

While Canada's official bilingual policy has been in place for more than twenty years, the adoption of the Charter, and the inclusion of section 23 specifically, constituted a direct intervention into the arena of provincial educational policy and set out entitlements which each province had to respect or be in contravention of the law of the land. The linguistic educational rights of the francophone or anglophone minority, depending on which province one resides in, were elevated to a stature previously accorded only the Protestant or Catholic denominations in some provinces and a larger number of denominations in Newfoundland. The exercise of these rights would be limited to those places "where numbers warrant" and so would be more restricted than denominational rights. Nevertheless, the courts have suggested a pattern of developing rights in which a community with only a handful of students and thus comparatively few rights arrives at a position where it assumes virtually complete control in the presence of sufficiently large numbers of students.

In Newfoundland no francophone governing structures have yet been established, but both Prince Edward Island and Nova Scotia have put in place a single francophone school board to ensure that the educational needs of francophones in those provinces are met. New Brunswick is Canada's only officially bilingual province and as such possesses a dual-language educational structure. The Quebec government received permission in June 1993 from the Supreme Court of Canada to proceed with a reorganization of the school system along linguistic rather than the current denominational lines. Under the new arrangement, denominational rights appear to be sufficiently protected to satisfy the constitutional requirements (four boards in

Montreal and Quebec City maintain their denominational character). Meanwhile in Ontario there is still no province-wide policy or provincial legislation which deals effectively with section 23. In January 1992 the third French-language school board began operation in the Prescott-Russell area. A number of Catholic boards in the province operate French and English sections, and in the three cases where francophone boards have been established they have started in this fashion rather than as a result of a provincial plan.

The Manitoba government has established a single francophone school division for the entire province and this division began operation in January 1994. In taking such a step, the province was responding to a Supreme Court ruling of March 1993 which stated that the province's Public Schools Act violated section 23 of the Charter. In Saskatchewan, francophone education is governed by a single provincial umbrella board which has representation from all francophone schools in the province, while in Alberta recent changes to the School Act (1993) provide for the establishment of a number of regional authorities to run francophone schools. This change in Alberta legislation is a response to the Supreme Court ruling in the *Mahé* case which was handed down in March 1990. The ruling, noting that the anglophone (majority) community was unlikely to understand the cultural and educational needs of francophones, directed the province to provide the francophone community with some control over its children's education. Currently, there are plans in British Columbia to put a single francophone school board in place by 1995. This board would, as in Alberta, have all the powers enjoyed by existing school boards except the power to raise revenue by means of taxation. In the Yukon and the Northwest Territories there are no provisions to permit the francophone communities to exercise control over their own schools although francophone schools have operated in Whitehorse, Yellowknife, and Iqaluit for some time.

## *Conclusion*

From the beginning of public schooling in Canada, middle-class values have prevailed with respect to the nature and objectives of publicly funded elementary and secondary schooling. That grammar-type schools were the first educational institutions to receive state support not only indicates the influence of the middle class, which was based largely in urban centres, but also reveals how this class determined what resources should be allocated to public schooling. As urban centres grew in size and complexity, schools in these communities took on architectural and bureaucratic qualities that exemplified such bourgeois values as order, refinement, and respectability. The urban poor were given access to these institutions, but not for as long or in the same environments as those offered to children of the more affluent. At the same time, urban schools set standards that rural school districts found impossible to emulate. What mattered to school promoters in the nineteenth and early twentieth centuries was that the children of the urban and rural poor attend school for a while at least and in the process be taught to accept existing socio-economic conditions and the values associated with proper and regular work. For these instructional goals to have any general effect universal attendance was essential.

Yet even before the requisite levels of attendance were achieved in the early 1920s, urban-based commercial and philanthropic interests were urging provincial departments of education to expand the scope and duration of public education by consolidating educational governance in large administrative units. Rural communities wanted to improve their schools, but for the most part they were opposed to large-scale consolidations as a way of achieving this goal. Concurrently, new subjects, such as agriculture, household science, industrial education, and commercial (secretarial) training, were being added to the traditional list of high school offerings. Access to these non-university entrance programs, however, was more readily available in urban areas. This divergence between country and town served to heighten the efforts of ministries of education to consolidate rural districts and to encourage the formation of regional high schools in major centres of the newly formed school divisions.

A second strategy used to increase access to elementary and secondary schools involved a series of methodological reforms based on what was known as progressive education, which began to have a significant impact on public schooling in the United States and Canada in the 1920s. Many of these reforms were popularized by American educators, such as John Dewey, William Kilpatrick, and George Counts, who rejected teacher-dominated, subject-centred forms of learning in favour of activities that were child-centred and group-oriented. By the mid-1930s many of these progressive ideas had been endorsed by teacher-educators and by senior officials in ministries of education across Canada. In addition to their general worth they were seen as a way of dealing with instructional problems commonly found in multi-grade rural schools. That there were enough entry-level jobs for high school graduates with general and vocational diplomas was sufficiently reassuring for most clients of the system. By the late 1970s, however, concerns began to be expressed that the skill levels of these diploma holders were well below those of the students who went on to university.

In 1959 and 1960 reports by no less than five provincial royal commissions on education stressed that greater emphasis be given to reading, writing, and thinking skills at all levels of public schooling. School boards, responding to initiatives of the provincial ministries of education, acceded to this emphasis without complaint, despite the fact that the stress on basics was accompanied by a widely held expectation that every child should obtain a high school diploma. Simultaneously, school trustees, particularly in urban areas, faced burgeoning school enrolments and unprecedented staffing and facility problems. Highly regarded provincial commissions in Ontario in 1968 and Alberta in 1972, which revived many of the progressive ideas of an earlier era, provided school boards and ministries of education with some relief from the challenges they had been experiencing.

Yet the respite was short-lived. Since the late 1970s ministries have tightened up the process of public schooling by implementing external examinations, which eventually included comparative assessments at the provincial, national, and international levels, and by prescribing an extended range of core subjects which every student is expected to master. School trustees are also encountering a host of new educational priorities, such as school councils, official-language instruction, Native and multicultural education, issues related to gender equity, and the integration of children with disabilities. Yet another recent demand upon school boards has been that they raise academic standards for all students to levels equivalent to those achieved by students in Asia and Europe. The challenge presented to school trustees is largely one of managing diminishing resources at the local level while responding to increasing demands from the provincial and federal governments and from global forces relating to finances, markets, and employment.

Decisions of departments of education since the late 1970s have substantially reduced whatever autonomy had devolved to local school jurisdictions in the areas of curriculum and administration. This move to more centralized decision making has been most strongly felt by metropolitan school boards which, because of their size and location, had hitherto had the greatest influence on provincial ministries of education and correspondingly on the activities of rural school boards. There are no indications, moreover, that metropolitan districts are discovering new choices or responses to stem what would appear to be the complete erosion of what little autonomy they currently have. This situation will not necessarily lead to the demise of existing forms of local school governance, but it is likely that school boards, as they exist today, will become increasingly anachronistic and insignificant. With educational decision making growing ever more centralized, one may reasonably affirm that local control of the governance of education is nothing more than a comfortable myth.

## *Notes*

1. Organization for Economic Co-operation and Development, *Reviews of National Policies for Education: Canada* (Paris: OECD, 1976), 69–70.
2. Patricia Albjerg Graham, "What America Has Expected of Its Schools over the Past Century," *American Journal of Education*, vol. 101 (February 1993), 83–98.
3. Ibid., 84.
4. Ibid., 86.
5. Alison Prentice, *The School Promoters: Education and Social Class in Mid-Nineteenth Century Upper Canada* (Toronto: McClelland and Stewart, 1977), 18.
6. Quoted in M.R. Lupul, *The Roman Catholic Church and the North-West School Question* (Toronto: University of Toronto Press, 1974), 173.
7. Cecil Race, "Compulsory Schooling in Alberta (1888–1942)" (MED thesis, University of Alberta, 1978), vi.
8. Robert M. Stamp, *The Schools of Ontario 1876–1976* (Toronto: University of Toronto Press, 1982), 6.

9. D.A. Schmeiser, *Civil Liberties in Canada* (London: Oxford University Press), 149.
10. Canada, Ministry of Trade and Commerce, *Annual Report on Education Statistics in Canada, 1922* (Ottawa: King's Printer, 1924), 86.
11. Government of Alberta, *Annual Reports of the Department of Education,* 1935 (Edmonton: Government Printer), 104 and 111.
12. Ibid., 1935–68.
13. Thomas O. Maguire, "Is Canada a 'Nation at Risk'? What Reports on U.S. Education Signify for Us," *Canadian Society for the Study of Education News,* vol. 12, no. 6 (October 1985), 3–5; and vol. 12, no. 7 (November 1985), 3–5.
14. National Commission on Excellence in Education, *A Nation at Risk* (Washington,D.C.: U.S. Government Printing Office, 1983), 5.
15. J. Lewington and G. Orpwood, *Overdue Assignment* (Toronto: John Wiley and Sons, 1993).
16. Angus Reid Group, "A National Survey of Public Opinion and Attitudes," *Canadian Association Newsletter,* Oct.–Nov. 1993, 5.
17. Tom R. Williams and Holly Millinoff, *Canada's Schools: Report Card for the 1990's* (Toronto: Canadian Education Association, 1990), 1 and 2.
18. This table is based on enrolment data extracted from the *Canadian Education Association Handbook* (Toronto: Canadian Education Association, 1994).
19. Herve Langlois and Murray Scharf, *School Finance and Governance Review* (Regina: Saskatchewan Education, 1991), 199.
20. David Morrison and Jim Almstrom, *Strathcona County Board of Education Report on Alternate Forms of Government* (Edmonton: David C. Morrison and Associates Management Consultants, 1992).
21. See the pertinent provincial legislation to determine whether school jurisdictions are divided into wards or divisions for election purposes. The relevant legislation may be the school legislation or the legislation dealing with local/municipal elections.
22. It appears that this principle may be ignored in the case of francophone jurisdictions where only eligible parents may be permitted to vote, but they may elect any individuals which the francophone community would consider supportive of their cause.
23. Some provincial funding is available for accredited private or independent schools in five provinces. No funding is available in Newfoundland, Prince Edward Island, New Brunswick, Nova Scotia, and Ontario.

24. Canada, Department of Mines and Resources, Indian Affairs Branch, *Annual Report*, 1948–49, 72.
25. Indian Chiefs of Alberta, *Citizens Plus* (Edmonton: Indian Chiefs of Alberta, 1970), 88.
26. National Indian Brotherhood, *Indian Control of Indian Education* (Ottawa: National Indian Brotherhood, 1972).
27. J. Chrétien to G. Manuel (President of the National Indian Brotherhood), 2 February 1973 (mimeograph copy, in author's possession).
28. Assembly of First Nations, *Towards a Vision of Our Future: A Declaration of First Nations Jurisdiction Over Education*, vol. 3 (Ottawa: Assembly of First Nations, 1988), 13.

## *Selected Sources*

Allan, E.C. "Policy-Making in a County: A Case Study in School System Governance" (PhD thesis, University of Alberta, 1985).

Cremin, L.A. *American Education: The Metropolitan Experience 1876–1980* (New York: Harper and Row, 1989).

Goodenow, R.K. and D. Ravitch, eds. *Schools in the Cities: Consensus and Conflict in American Educational History* (New York: Holmes and Meier, 1983).

Grainger, R.A. "The Participation of Parents in Local Decision-Making" PHD thesis, University of Alberta, 1984).

Lam, Y.L.J., ed. *Canadian Public Education System: Issues and Prospects* (Calgary: Detselig, 1990).

Levin, B. and J. Young. *Understanding Canadian Schools* (Toronto: Harcourt Brace, 1994).

Renihan, P.J. "Control Dimensions and School Board Decision Emphases" (PhD thesis, University of Alberta, 1977).

Vitteri, J.P. *Across the River: Politics and Education in the City* (New York: Holmes and Meier, 1983).

# 11

## *Local Environmental Politics: Principles in Conflict*

Mary Louise McAllister

IN CONTEMPORARY SOCIETY'S QUEST for economic wealth and environmental health, policy makers are facing challenges that are inherently contradictory and possibly irreconcilable. At the root of the conflict is a liberal-democratic system of values which recognizes the right of individuals to possess certain freedoms, to own property, and to participate in the political process. At the same time, the political system fosters a philosophy of the collective interest, common property, and representative decision making.

The tension between these principles becomes especially apparent when one examines local politics and the concept of "sustainable development." Cities, for example, have been planned around the demands of individuals, especially their private-property rights and their automobiles. On the other hand, environmental politics is based on a philosophy of collective rights which in market systems have usually been subordinated to assertions of private and individualist rights. In such systems, democratic politicians must always strive to achieve workable compromises among major competing interests. The agendas advanced by reformers, environmental or otherwise, however, are seldom ones that lend themselves easily to compromise. The past few decades have witnessed an explosion of activity with competing pressure groups wishing to see their own agendas advanced. Governments are increasingly compelled to undertake a broad consultative process when making environmental or economic decisions.

The tension between the traditional liberal, business-dominated decision-making process and the comprehensive planning agendas of civic reformers is by no means new; it has always bubbled along the surface of civic politics as governments have struggled to define the public interest. From the 1960s on, however, the debate has intensified. Traditional areas of local responsibility that were once largely uncontentious, such as land, water, and waste management, are now subjects of heated dispute. Local governments are being forced to react to environmental problems caused by inadequate planning. At the local level, for example, it is impossible to ignore the consequences of haphazard housing development, contaminated ground water, or leaking toxic dump sites.

Yet local authorities are constrained in their ability to deal effectively with these issues because of limited financial resources and statutory authority, as well as a lack of public consensus. The public expects local authorities to make decisions that will culminate in both a prosperous economy and a healthy environment. Attempts to marry those twin concerns do not lead readily to a harmonious, integrated community of interest. Moreover, overburdened with current deficits and accumulated debts, other levels of government are "off-loading" responsibilities to municipalities just as the public is demanding more and more from local politicians. The search for a booming economy and environmental improvements is supposed to progress in the middle of this two-way squeeze.

So what is to be done? Efforts are now being made to involve the public in participatory community-development initiatives. These exercises are attempts to restore government legitimacy in the eyes of the public, to build a sense of ownership, pride, and initiative in a local community, and to develop a vision for the future. Success, however, is by no means easy to achieve. Public-consultation exercises are time-consuming and fraught with difficulty. To some, such exercises may resemble the circular "Caucus-race" in Alice-in-Wonderland where everyone is scurrying along as quickly as they can applying undefined rules in pursuit of indeterminate goals.

This chapter examines the development of the conflicting set of values which have contributed to the shaping of "green" politics and the implications of that conflict for local decision making today. The question facing local governments is a familiar one: how does one foster and achieve a broadly endorsed vision of a healthy, prosperous, and diverse community? Unfortunately, while environmental problems are more pressing than ever before, local decision makers may find it easier to master Lewis Carroll's *Lobster-Quadrille*[1] than to plan and implement policies based on principles of participatory decision making and sustainable development.

## *Civic Boosterism and Local Environmental Planning*

As cities industrialized, they were primarily seen as institutions for the promotion of economic activity and growth. For the most part, early conservation movements focussed on the vast stretches of undeveloped land rather than on the urban domain. At the turn of the twentieth century, there were two main approaches to environmental and city-land planning; one was a liberal, the other radical.

The liberal model was also known as the "City Beautiful" movement and later was transformed into the "City Planning" approach. It held that parks, boulevards, tree planting, civic centres, and good transportation routes would create a beautiful and prosperous city. Nature was to be tamed and groomed to fit neatly within the confines of new developments. Nicely appointed landscaping would enhance the commercial potential of the city as well as contribute to a general sense of well-being. Efficient, scientific planning, with the use of zoning to increase property values, would best serve the broad public interest.

This approach was very compatible with the business ethos that prevailed at a time of rapid industrialization and urban growth. Local "boosterism"— a term coined to define the attempts of local promoters to attract industry and capital to their cities—was employed with a vengeance. Rapid land development with little regard for the environmental impact was partially a result of energetic competition between municipalities in their efforts to bring revenues into their cities. Even swamplands were drained and slated for industrial development. The importance of wetlands to the natural ecosystem is a concept that is not widely appreciated even today. It certainly was not something that would give any civic booster pause in the first half of this century.

Aesthetic considerations were not ignored in the early 1900s, but such elements of city planning as the preservation of distinctive landscape features and the creation of forested park areas were designed primarily to draw people to the community; "nature" was rarely viewed as having any intrinsic worth of its own. None of this was surprising. Given the fiscal limitations of local governments, which relied (and still do) on property taxes as a major source of revenue, the economic value of land was vital. The priorities of local governments, therefore, were directed towards economic development rather than environmental conservation. Reinforcing this outlook were the interests of homeowners, whose views predominated on city councils, and of the land developers, city planners, and business people who served as councillors.

Nevertheless, the need for a healthy social and natural environment was recognized by some. Thomas Adams, an influential exponent of the radical planning approach in the early twentieth century, argued for a holistic model with a strong government presence to ensure the well-being of the entire community. Adams's approach to urban planning was best known as the "Garden City" concept. The ideal Garden City would include a smaller concentration of people than was the case in the larger city. Greenbelts would divide industrial areas from residential areas, an agricultural greenbelt would surround the town, and efficient transportation systems would link these communities to a central city. Within each neighbourhood there would be ample gardens, parks, town centres, libraries, and shops.[2]

The richly diverse working and living environment originally envisioned by Adams resembles contemporary concepts of "ecosystem planning" and stands in marked contrast to the antiseptic suburban development that came to prevail. Sprawling, undistinguished architecture, a development pattern that fosters social isolation, uniformity, and a heavy dependence on the automobile, characterize these suburbs. Early radical planners also recognized the need for conservation and protection of natural resources. As Lewis Mumford suggested in 1938: "We can no longer leave soils and landscapes and agricultural possibilities out of our calculations in considering the future of either industries or cities . . . There is no place left to move. We have reached the end of our journey, and in the main, we must retrace our steps, and, region by region, learn to do intelligently and co-operatively what we hitherto did in such disregard for the elementary decencies of life."[3]

Critics have long questioned municipal decision-making processes that promoted large real-estate development projects and thereby hastened the demise of inner-city neighbourhoods. Activists and citizen groups have protested the disintegration of urban neighbourhood communities, the "block-busting" techniques of various developers, and the lack of attention towards alleviating the housing and health problems of the urban working class. Most recently, concerns have broadened to include other aspects of the local environment, such as the sacrifice of natural habitats to urban sprawl, inefficient use of water resources, the declining air quality that has resulted from continued reliance on the automobile, and environmental considerations relating to the disposal of massive amounts of solid waste. Community-based or grass-roots movements have called for the decentralization of economic and political decision making in order to foster healthy, sustainable localities. Like earlier radical planners, today's community-planning critics recognize the relationship between homelessness, poverty, cultural enrichment, community participation, healthy environments, and healthy economies.

## *The Struggle to Define the Public Interest*

According to a perspective that has long been widely shared, municipalities are nothing more than an apolitical administrative level of government—a service-provider—and policies and politics rest in the domain of the federal and provincial governments. This view has led to decision-making processes that adversely affect the natural environment. From the early 1900s until well after the Second World War, the belief that municipal government should operate according to allegedly non-partisan business principles predominated, as did the interests of local businesses. What was good for local business was said to be good for the public interest. Rapid urbanization and land development left limited room on the local public agenda for concerns about the impact of growth on the urban environment.

Attitudes are now changing. In the 1990s, the interests of the community are not necessarily seen as synonymous with the interests of business. Community development is no longer perceived solely in terms of local economic development, and local planning strategies are expected to be much more inclusive, encapsulating social, health, and environmental considerations. At the same time, concerns about the scarcity of certain physical resources fuels the somewhat contradictory public demand that local governments continue to provide a high level of services at low fiscal *and* environmental cost.

Some now argue that the interests of a whole community can be accommodated under an umbrella of integrated resource planning; indeed, an ecosystem approach that includes considerations of both natural and built environments is advocated in many local planning exercises. The philosophy underpinning arguments for environmentally sustainable communities stresses the importance of public consultation and participation in the decision-making process and policy implementation. In addition to recognizing the interdependent relationship among watersheds, wetlands, soils, and forests, many land-use commissions are increasingly sensitive to the diverse and interdependent needs and interests of resource users. The Royal Commission on the Toronto Waterfront, for example, adopted an ecosystem approach in addressing the diverse natural requirements of the region. Similarly, the commission took a holistic approach to public participation, initiating an extensive system of consultation which included developers, environmentalists, traffic engineers, landscape architects, scientists, community activists, federal and provincial public servants, and city officials. In its quest to develop approaches to the "regeneration" of the city, the commission felt that this process fostered consensus, trust, and partnerships.[4]

A strong case can be made in favour of the view that sustainable development and ecosystem planning cannot be realized without a "multi-stakeholder" approach and public consultation, education, and participation. With consultation, so the argument runs, the implementation of policies is likely to go more smoothly. Today, governments have no choice but to consult. The vocal elements within the public expect a much more direct say on a wide array of issues, whether it is a question of debt financing for a large capital project or the wisdom of a proposed development in a wetland area.

That said, however, it is very difficult to achieve the goal of a commonly shared holistic vision if—as is often the case with consensus-based politics—there are too many diverse and often conflicting interests represented at the decision-making table. A land-use commission in Prince Edward Island has wisely noted that "while individual citizens like to see others regulated, they prefer freedom of choice for themselves. They will, however, accept rules for which there are good and valid reasons."[5] This comment certainly applies to environmental issues. One observer suggests that, although many members of the public are aware of the need to protect the environment, the majority tends to think of land as "private property, commodity, source of income and profit, provider of recreation, means of waste disposal, emblem of social status."[6] On the other hand, the public is increasingly viewing new development in rural and urban areas in an negative light. In urban areas, the public is becoming more vocal in resisting projects that may have an adverse impact on their local neighbourhoods; phenomena such as NIMBY (Not-In-My-Backyard) and LULU (Locally Unacceptable Land Use) reflect a backlash against continuing growth and spreading development. These competing perspectives are indicative of the public's desire to continue to protect existing property rights and land uses while at the same time guarding against the environmental impact of development activities. Middle-class Canadians wish to preserve a way of life to which they have become accustomed: that is, economic prosperity and growth supported by plentiful natural resources.

In today's society it will not be difficult to get agreement on sustainable development as a desirable goal. Rarely, however, is there a consensus about exactly what constitutes "sustainability." Some see the process of capital accumulation as antithetical to the needs of the natural environment. For these people, sustainable development is an oxymoron and thus doomed to failure. Others observe that there are few options and persevere in their attempts to discover a balance between a healthy environment and a healthy economy.

The degeneration of the environment in the late twentieth century has fuelled urgent demands for comprehensive, rational land-use planning. Public-consultation exercises have proliferated. So, too, have the numbers of diverse participants—all of them with their own agendas. The environmental movement itself is fragmented—often between the larger, national, and international groups and the locally based ones. Ironically, while environmentalism has been viewed as a grass-roots phenomenon, "green" interest groups do not always find local public participation the most effective strategy. Some see the devolution of authority to local agencies and interests as a threat to the broader environmental agenda; local groups may be more preoccupied with defending their employment opportunities than, for example, protecting their local wetlands. Alternatively, it has been argued that the local residents are the ones who have the most to lose if planning and development are not handled in an environmentally responsible way. In this view, members of the community should therefore have the most influence in the process.

Governments, themselves often fragmented (particularly at the local level), are grappling with the need to cope with new environmental, social, and economic issues in a decisive, rational manner. That imperative runs counter to those demanding inclusive public participation in a decision-making process that is also open and accountable. The inevitable compromises satisfy few.

## *Local Government and Environmental Responsibilities*

Political stumbling blocks, coupled with the dependence of local governments on property tax revenues and development, may lead one to think that very little has been done to protect the local environment. Yet, in fact, a number of forces have compelled local authorities to respond to environmental issues. The increasing salience of the environment in the local media has heightened public awareness of the possibility of environmental contamination of soil and water. Daily public pressure on city officials to clean up a particular dump site or to ensure that the landfill sites meet modern standards reinforces government awareness of the public's concerns. Well-organized pressure groups lobby to prevent the rezoning of wetlands to make way for industrial development. Local officials, themselves members of the community, will share many of the public's concerns and pass by-laws that reflect changing environmental values. And as creatures of the province, local governments must conform to, and implement, the increasingly stringent provincial environmental regulations.

Communities have responded with changes to their local official plans emphasizing the importance of sustainable development. Special-purpose bodies devoted to issues related to natural resources are becoming established in many cities. We are also witnessing a proliferation of environmentally related by-laws which include everything from the preservation of "heritage trees" to housing intensification to controlling the use of public beaches.

Local governments have had long-standing responsibilities for many areas of decision making that have now grown enormously in importance. Municipal responsibilities for garbage disposal, sewage, water services, and zoning have now been recast and placed in the much broader environmental lexicon of "waste management, the three 'R's of recycling, watershed and greenbelt protection areas, and ecosystem planning." In addition, environmental controversies and/or accidents often occur in local communities, intensifying pressures on local governments to take steps to ensure public health and safety. Toxic-waste spills, tire fires, and leaking gasoline tanks require responses from the most immediate level of government. If citizens have concerns about their water quality or nearby hazardous wastes, they look to the city to deal with the issue, not the provincial or federal governments. Three areas that have achieved a great deal of prominence on the public agenda are land-use planning, water use, and waste management.

## *Land-Use Planning*

> "Indecision is a form of land use planning but it is usually the most costly one."[7]

Municipalities have extensive responsibilities in the areas of land-use planning, zoning, and subdivision control. Local governments are responsible for drawing up regional and municipal plans consistent with the guidelines established by provincial planning legislation.

Land-use plans are designed to map out the future development of a community, provide services, and prevent incompatible uses. Land-use planning is essentially concerned with the relationship among: the pattern of private land use and development; the consequent demand for municipal services and the costs of providing them; and the "assessment base" on which the municipal exchequer is heavily dependent.[8]

At one time, land that was not seen as useful for development was referred to as wasteland or even "SLOAP" (Space Left Over After Planning).[9] So-called wastelands, however, often contain wetlands and important watersheds. An economic value is now being attributed to these resources through "full-cost accounting," which includes the environmental and social costs in the price of goods and services. Land-assessment and taxation systems may be revised in order to ensure that those systems do not discourage the protection of ecologically sensitive areas.[10]

A number of "green" planning strategies have been devised to check urban sprawl and take the pressure off open and undeveloped areas. Ecosystem planning recognizes the importance of people-oriented designs first espoused in Adams's early town-planning model. With the intensification and redevelopment of urban and inner-city areas, the dependency on the automobile can be reduced, walking and bicycle paths can be introduced, and public transit can become economically feasible. Simply put, the new orientation seeks to plan cities around people, and not their automobiles.

These proposals are advanced to lessen the problems engendered by the socially and environmentally unfriendly consequences of modern suburban living. Ecological diversity in urban areas is encouraged with the introduction or preservation of greenways, waterways, and woodlands. Such initiatives are not without economic value; many people like to work or live near greenbelts. Costs are also reduced by replacing labour-intensive mowing and pesticide spraying in open areas and roadsides with the lower-maintenance planting of wildflowers, grasses, and trees. Also, volunteer groups in conjunction with private-sector investment can contribute considerably to the natural and economic values of the land.

There are examples of such plans everywhere in Canada. One often thinks of these initiatives in terms of heavily populated regions such as the Greater Toronto Area, where various plans for greenways are under development throughout the bioregion. Yet plans to protect local ecosystems have also been developed in more northern cities such as Prince George, British Columbia, where the official community plan includes sections that emphasize the importance of protecting forested and open areas and local watersheds. In some parts of the city, the forests are shared by bears, deer, and moose, a situation that creates a unique challenge for planners who must juggle the requirements of a growing urban area with the ecosystem demands of a natural and wild habitat.

Throughout Canada, a number of royal commissions on natural resources and land use have been struck to contend with the question of sustainable development.[11] All of these investigations stress the need for compatible land-use planning, an approach that recognizes the requirements of the users, the value of cultural and heritage sites as well as the natural environment, and the importance of community participation.

As mentioned earlier, stating these general principles is one thing and implementing them is another. While philosophical changes in the way resources are viewed and used are a necessary prerequisite for "ecosystem" planning, there is an equal need to come to terms with the practical realities of the conflict between economic development and land conservation. Municipalities often do try to protect natural resources and regulate development. They are, however, "confined by narrow jurisdictional limits, [and] . . . too often lack both an ecosystem context and a coherent set of environmental goals and guidelines."[12] Andrew Sancton suggests that the successful resolution of major urban issues in the future will require a stronger provincial role because of the need for funding and because many of these issues have province-wide implications. At the same time, Sancton argues, metropolitan and regional governments will become much looser and more flexible in terms of boundaries and responsibilities in order to respond to the differing needs of various urban areas.[13]

In spite of much good will and widespread enthusiasm for reform, along with resulting attempts to adjust jurisdictional responsibilities to meet society's changing requirements, the policy process has never been rational or comprehensive. Policies, particularly those based on intensive consultation, take time and compromise. After a policy has been subjected to numerous reviews and amendments to accommodate multiple views and regulations, the final product often represents only incremental change. One observer dryly notes that "keeping the same slow incremental approach in the urban environment, while seeking a rapid change towards sustainable development, is similar to attempting to escape a head-on collision without changing trajectory."[14] Yet there are really few options: environmental agendas call for co-ordinated strategies.

## *Water: The Neglected Resource*

Canadian concern about water quality and supply is a comparatively recent phenomenon. Water, unlike private property, is commonly shared and has been traditionally viewed as abundant and virtually unlimited. Over the past twenty-five years, however, domestic and industrial water use has increased at a rate dramatically disproportionate to population growth. Accompanying this trend has been a rise in contaminants that are directly introduced into freshwater supplies or seep into aquifers. Sources of contamination include leaking septic tanks, landfill sites, road salt, pesticides, fertilizers, heavy metals and radioactive materials, and the disposal of containers of hazardous waste.

Water policy and management has, until fairly recently, been a matter of responding to crises after they happen; governments across the country react when there has been an obvious decline in the quantity or quality of water. Unfortunately, the hydrologic cycle does not readily lend itself to site-specific clean-up or remedial action, and, because pollutants may travel a long way, it is often very difficult to contain the impact of a particular contaminant. Nevertheless, the combination of yesterday's practices, today's ever-growing demands for water resources, and tomorrow's limited funds to deal with mounting environmental problems will restrict the abilities of government to react in more than a piecemeal way. This is particularly troublesome because not enough is known about the assimilative capacities of the hydrologic cycle. Concerns about water quality in specific areas such as the Great Lakes, however, are beginning to receive more concerted attention. A remedial action plan for the Toronto waterfront, for example, was demanded after it was discovered that fish and other organisms showed an accumulation of contaminants.[15]

Along with questions about the quality of surface drinking water, ground water, one of the integral components of the hydrologic cycle, is now attracting public attention. Canadians have been extracting ground water at escalating rates—over one-quarter of the Canadian population relies entirely on ground water use for domestic supply—but there is only limited knowledge about the sustainability or safe yield of many aquifers. Public concerns about the quality of ground water have been fuelled by local media stories pertaining to contaminants such as dry-cleaning fluids or gasoline seeping out of old tanks and leaking into village wells.

Because remedial action in the aftermath of water contamination offers only limited, short-term benefits, planning around community watersheds is an approach that is gaining salience in local and regional strategies for sustainable development. In British Columbia, for example, most of the province's water needs are supplied by over 280 designated community watersheds. Watershed planning has been advanced as the most effective way to ensure the continuing integrity of water quality and supply. This will not be easy to achieve. First, there are technical difficulties in ascertaining the particular impact development activities will have on a given watershed because each area has its own particular geophysical characteristics. Secondly, municipal and regional political boundaries rarely coincide with natural boundaries. New special-purpose bodies will undoubtedly be established in order to co-ordinate the overlapping areas of responsibilities. While the approach for dealing with these questions will vary, watershed planning will continue to be handled at the regional level of government. Federal and provincial departments will establish environmental standards, and local governments will continue to be responsible for the implementation of policy and regulation—in general, the management of water resources.

Local governments have always played an important role in water resources. Municipalities are responsible for monitoring water quality, water pricing, and the provision of infrastructure. Local authorities must regularly test drinking water and ensure that it meets the guidelines of the federal Department of Health and Welfare; these guidelines identify and set maximum levels of particular substances that may occur in supplies of drinking water.[16] Municipal utilities supply water to households, commercial establishments, and some industries. Some users are charged a flat fee in exchange for unlimited amounts of water. Increasingly, however, the use of metering is employed in order to encourage more efficient water use, thereby conserving the resource and ensuring that the users who benefit the most contribute more to the cost of maintaining and supplying the resource.

Canadians are prolific users of water. About 1400 cubic metres of water are consumed per person (per year).[17] This is partly a reflection of the country's economic dependence on the production of raw resources, for primary industries such as agriculture, oil extraction, and mining rely extensively on water. Nevertheless, it is argued that water consumption could be reduced by half if the resource were managed more efficiently. There are various methods for achieving this goal, including the institution of metering practices and careful and co-ordinated watershed planning.

Local decision makers must also make sure that development activities do not adversely affect water resources. Many development initiatives can have a detrimental affect on local water supply. Proposed quarries, for instance, have often been the subject of the NIMBY response as residents worry whether quarrying activities will affect their supply of well water. Efficient water management will ultimately depend on the ability, will, and resources of local governments to co-ordinate and harmonize their policies both with other governments and with other resource users. Even with their vast resources, Canadians can no longer be cavalier about their water supplies. Local planning may become as complex as the hydrologic cycle itself.

## *Waste Management: Dumps to Landfills*

Besides being avid consumers of water, Canadians are world leaders in the production of garbage. In recent years, municipalities have stepped up their efforts to divert waste from landfills into recycling and composting. Such strategies have not always been successful. In spite of government attempts to create markets for recycled goods,[18] "blue box" programs suffer economically from limited and unsecured markets as well as fluctuating prices and high transportation costs. The environmental value of these programs also must be weighed against the energy consumed both in trucking the material to markets and in the production of recycled material. Tipping fees have been introduced in many congested parts of the country in an attempt to reduce the tonnes of garbage going into landfills. Unfortunately, these fees also have the unintended effect of encouraging people to search for cheaper disposal sites or to deposit their garbage illegally wherever they can find available space. Another method of garbage disposal—incineration—has been the subject of considerable debate. The argument has been made that modern incinerators can be designed in a way that minimizes harmful discharges into the environment. It is difficult for a member of the general public to determine the merits of this particular argument without possessing the necessary engineering background. Easier to grasp is the suggestion that incineration encourages profligacy in the public's unthinking consumption of raw resources and does not encourage conservation.

So, despite the difficulties of attempting to achieve massive waste reduction through conservation and diversion in the short run, local governments are confronted with public pressure and legal requirements to deal with waste in an environmentally sensitive manner. The Greater Toronto Area perhaps faces the most immediate problems of waste disposal since it contains more than 40 per cent of Ontario's population and generates half of the solid waste created in the province.[19] The Ontario provincial government has ruled out both trucking waste outside the area and incineration. The *Waste Management Act* of 1992 limited alternatives for the disposal of garbage to the "3Rs": reduce, reuse, and recycle. The aims of the legislation are to reduce the province's waste stream by half and to ensure that there is enough "environmentally-suitable landfill capacity to dispose of the remainder for at least the next twenty years"[20] These goals are to be achieved in part through extensive public education, consultation, and participation.

Municipalities must not only deal with the present challenges posed by waste disposal, they must also contend with the landfill sites of the past. The leaking, malodorous, open dumps of yesterday do not closely resemble contemporary, newly engineered landfills which are designed to capture methane gas and prevent the seepage of leachate. Soil and water contamination from those old dumps is becoming a serious problem for local governments, which are increasingly held responsible for both identifying and cleaning up contaminated sites. Anticipating and dealing with the practices of yesterday could prove to be at once environmentally challenging and economically daunting.

In sum, with standards enforced by the senior levels of government and consistent public pressure in the areas of land, water, and waste-management, local governments do not have much room for flexibility. Municipalities need to generate revenue to meet the growing list of regulations established by the provinces in order to ensure a healthy and safe environment for citizens. Local governments have historically relied on grants from the provincial government or on property taxes to provide services. With the growing federal and provincial deficits, however, the tendency to "off-load" fiscal responsibility to local governments increases. Resorting to the property tax does not provide a ready solution: the Federation of Canadian Municipalities has argued since the early 1970s that this particular tax has neared exhaustion as a source of revenue. To complicate matters further, in an age of conservation and ecosystem planning, communities can no longer seek to improve their revenue base through rapid growth and development.

The environmental agenda coupled with economic pressures are thrusting local governments into the limelight. Cast as leading players, but unsure of their scripts, they are looking for new ways to deal with their growing responsibilities. To whose demands should they respond? Should it be the downtown business association, the local wilderness society, or the silent majority which offers little guidance and indifferent support at the polls?

## *Principles in Conflict*

A spectrum of approaches has been traditionally employed in the management of scarce resources, ranging from a liberal, market-led strategy to a collectivist model that stresses the value of planning.

Liberal strategies call for the adoption of user-pay principles, market incentives for encouraging "green" business practices, and the application and development of new technologies to deal with environmental concerns. The natural environment, however, is becoming seriously compromised by the crisis-management, unco-ordinated policies emanating from the fragmented political system.

The 1990s politics of building consensus and partnerships emphasize the importance of planning and developing collective approaches to the environment. Integrated resource strategies and political processes across the country call for public participation and co-operation and such an approach also suits the complex and interdependent requirements of a natural ecosystem. Ironically, the more governments are called on to plan and the more the public is asked to participate, the more complicated the decision-making process becomes. In addition, the need for environmental protection is great while the revenue available for planning strategies is limited.

Emerging out of this tension have been new strategies which attempt to integrate competing groups into "communities of interests." Such strategies rest on the principle that, for sustainable development to be successful, more than environmental considerations need to be taken into account. As in a natural ecology, city economies and societies must be sufficiently diverse to allow for flexibility, automatic self-correction, and cultural and economic dynamism.[21] Local governments, accordingly, cannot look to the senior levels of government for help in solving their fiscal or environmental difficulties. Sustainable communities must be based on long-range, comprehensive planning, with an underpinning of widespread community support.[22] The success of these efforts will depend on the desire of diverse participants to "buy in" to the process of compromise; ultimately, there must be a common understanding of a broader public interest. Governments, for their part, will have to adopt a new attitude towards natural resources, which, at one time, were thought to have no economic value. Local councils will have to make decisions based on much more complex agendas—agendas more in tune with the original town-planning concept, which stressed the importance of the social and physical as well as the economic well-being of a community.

The right of individuals to own and develop property as they see fit will be more constrained than ever before. In the abstract, the public accepts the need for environmentally friendly measures for the sake of the collective good. Yet individuals are less willing to accept the principle of the collective good if it comes at the cost of relinquishing control over certain private property rights. This is the heart of the difficulty local governments face. Their biggest challenge does not lie in planning effective waste-management schemes, efficient "blue box" programs, or water-conservation measures—though the magnitude of these tasks should not be underestimated. More fundamentally, governments are wrestling with the question of how to harmonize basically incompatible principles which are inherent in liberal-democratic societies: How to define and accommodate individual rights while striving for the common good? How to define the common good in the context of sustainable development? It is, indeed, a complicated quadrille that local decision makers have yet to master.

## *Notes*

1. A quadrille has been described as a complicated and very difficult ballroom dance popular during the Victorian era. Lewis Carroll's "Lobster-Quadrille" in *Alice in Wonderland* was no doubt considerably more intricate since it included somersaults and mad dashes out to the sea with strange dance partners. Lewis Carroll, *The Annotated Alice*, with an introduction and notes by Martin Gardner (New York: New American Library, 1960), 131.
2. Gerald Hodge, *Planning Canadian Communities: An Introduction to the Principles, Practice, and Participants*, 2nd. ed. (Scarborough, Ont.: Nelson Canada, 1991), 51.
3. Lewis Mumford, *The Culture of Cities* (New York: Harcourt Brace Jovanovich, 1970; originally published 1938), 205.
4. Royal Commission on the Toronto Waterfront, *Regeneration: Toronto's Waterfront and the Sustainable City: Final Report*, David Crombie, commissioner (Toronto: Minister of Supply and Services Canada, 1992), 46.
5. [Prince Edward Island], "Everything before Us," *Report of the Royal Commission on the Land*, Douglas B. Boylan, chairman, vol. 1 (Charlottetown, P.E.I., 1990), 17.

6. Nigel Richardson, *Land Use Planning and Sustainable Development in Canada* (Ottawa: Canadian Environmental Advisory Council, 1989), 39.
7. "Everything before Us," 17.
8. Richardson, *Land Use Planning*, 12.
9. Royal Commission on the Toronto Waterfront, *Regeneration*, 78.
10. National Round Table on the Environment and the Economy, "You Can't Give It Away: Tax Aspects of Ecologically Sensitive Lands," Issues Paper no. 1992-4 (1992), 22–5.
11. A few examples of the numerous commissions that have been recently established include British Columbia's Commission on Resources and the Environment, Ontario's Commission on Planning and Development Reform, and New Brunswick's Commission on Land Use and the Rural Environment. There are also regionally oriented commissions, such as the Royal Commission on the Toronto Waterfront.
12. Richardson, *Land Use Planning*, 42.
13. Andrew Sancton, "Canada As a Highly Urbanized Nation: New Implications for Government," *Canadian Public Administration*, vol. 35, no.3 (autumn 1992), 281–98.
14. Gérard Divay, "Cities and Sustainable Development: Can Cities Be Remodelled?" in *The Future of Cities in Britain and Canada*, Ian Jackson, ed. (Ottawa: Institute for Research on Public Policy, 1991), 103.
15. Royal Commission on the Toronto Waterfront, *Regeneration*, 25.
16. Government of Canada, *Canada's Green Plan* (Ottawa: Minister of Supply and Services, 1990), 33.
17. According to Environment Canada, "Worldwide water withdrawals from water bodies have risen from 250 cubic metres per person (per year) in 1900 to over 700 cubic metres today. In Canada, that number is much higher—about double that amount." Environment Canada, *A Primer on Water* (Ottawa: 1990), 14.
18. In Toronto, for example, all newspapers sold in sidewalk vending machines must be composed of some recycled newsprint, a regulation designed to stimulate the market for recycled materials. Virginia W. MacLaren, "Waste Management: Current Crisis and Future Management," in *Resource Management and Development*, Bruce Mitchell, ed. (Toronto: Oxford University Press, 1991), 42.
19. The Greater Toronto Area alone produces 4.5 million tonnes of garbage annually. Royal Commission on the Toronto Waterfront, *Regeneration*, 28.

20. Interim Waste Authority Limited, "Fast Facts on Landfill" (Toronto).
21. Jane Jacobs, *Cities and the Wealth of Nations: Principles of Economic Life* (New York: First Vintage Books, 1985), 224. See also Ray Spaxman, "City Planning," in *The Future of Cities in Britain and Canada*, Ian Jackson ed., 101.
22. Christopher R. Bryant, "Sustainable Community Development: Partnerships and Winning Proposals," in "The Good Idea Series in Sustainable Community Development," no. 1 (1991), 21, Rural and Small Towns Research and Studies Programme, Mount Allison University (Sackville, N.B.).

## Selected Sources

Bryant, Christopher R. "Sustainable Community Development: Partnerships and Winning Proposals," in "The Good Idea Series in Sustainable Community Development," no. 1 (1991), Rural and Small Towns Research and Studies Programme, Mount Allison University (Sackville, N.B.).

Divay, Gérard. "Cities and Sustainable Development: Can Cities Be Remodelled?" in *The Future of Cities in Britain and Canada*, Ian Jackson, ed. (Ottawa: Institute for Research on Public Policy, 1991), 97–105.

Government of Canada, *Canada's Green Plan* (Ottawa: Minister of Supply and Services, 1990).

Hodge, Gerald. *Planning Canadian Communities: An Introduction to the Principles, Practice, and Participants*, 2nd. ed. (Scarborough, Ont.: Nelson Canada, 1991).

MacLaren, Virginia W. "Waste Management: Current Crisis and Future Management," in *Resource Management and Development*, Bruce Mitchell, ed. (Toronto: Oxford University Press, 1991).

Mumford, Lewis. *The Culture of Cities* (New York: Harcourt Brace Jovanovich, 1970; originally published 1938).

Royal Commission on the Toronto Waterfront, *Regeneration: Toronto's Waterfront and the Sustainable City: Final Report*, David Crombie, commissioner (Toronto: Minister of Supply and Services Canada, 1992).

Spaxman, Ray. "City Planning," in *The Future of Cities in Britain and Canada*, Ian Jackson, ed. (Ottawa: Institute for Research on Public Policy, 1991), 88–96.

# 12

## *Surviving City Politics*

James Lightbody

AT THE BEGINNING of the fantasy novel *The Hitchhiker's Guide to the Galaxy*, Arthur Dent awakens to the sudden realization that his town council is to flatten his house and build a bypass. Politicized, Dent lies down in front of the bulldozer despite the inevitability of the outcome. Later he learns that planet earth is also to be flattened, standing as it does in the path of an hyperspatial express route. Complaints are useless, the plans having been filed on Alpha Centauri for fifty earth-years. As Prostetnic Vogon Jeltz of the Galactic Hyperspace Planning Council puts it: "For heaven's sake, mankind, it's only four light-years away, you know. I'm sorry, but if you can't be bothered to take an interest in local affairs that's your own lookout."[1] Hence the destruction of planet earth, the result of a galactic municipal planning decision.

This last chapter's theme is that if city electors are to survive city politics certain lessons must be learned and specific steps taken. Canadians, as city citizens, seem reconciled to living with, not prospering under, the punishments dished out by local politics. At their least worrisome, Canadian big city councillors sometimes seem to make rather intellectually challenged decisions. Each of us may revel, with coffee and tabloid in the morning, over the most recent civic trivialities; it is the curse of comparative study to learn that our local guardians of the public interest are usually not exceptional even in this regard. While one alderman in Edmonton may wish to locate signs on the city's highest bridge requesting potential suicides not to jump, another down the road may be asking for a city administration report on the potential for birth control for urban gophers, while councillors in Red Deer curiously select some steroid-enhanced rodent as city mascot. These things have happened and citizens might be tempted to view property taxes as a form of general entertainment charge if there were not such important consequences.

So this anthology ends by returning to its opening argument: city politics are significant for Canada, and for Canadians. In the foregoing chapters, the writers have approached particular policy areas from the vantage-point of their own specialized university disciplines. Running through the entire book, however, are several important questions: Is there to be a new type of metro politician for the 1990s? If so, will the new politicians be followed by different patterns of elector participation, and will these patterns imply rejuvenated government forms? Will innovative public policy result? What new ethical considerations are to underpin the selection and judgment of those who will make the choices? Finally, of course, we must always ask: What difference will it make?

As Christopher Leo accurately observes, city politics are really a bit player in an intergovernmental context. The most general rule at hand to understand better the prospects for the institutions and processes of Canadian metropolitics is that Canadian cities in the metropolis are defined within a web of uncertainty and dependence. For instance, in even the uncomplicated province of Alberta, local institutions were among the first targets of restructuring on the fiscal austerity agenda; municipalities lost their grants, school boards their autonomy. Responding to school trustees' concerns, Premier Ralph Klein said bluntly, "I don't want to sound pushy or like a bully, but school boards are there at the pleasure of the legislature, they are creatures of [the] government."[2] Underlying anything ever written about Canadian metropolitics is that our cities, as defined by section 92.8 of the constitution, are absolutely and precisely no more and no less than the statutory creations of their respective provinces. As Engin Isin has accurately stated, the act of incorporation is *not* a "contract" between equal actors, the provincial legislature and the municipal corporation. Consequently, there has always been an inherent tension in metropolitics over the proper division of provincial and local responsibilities, the appropriate scale of the municipal operation wherein community identity and direct participation are inverse functions of size (but "cost-effective" service delivery seems to be a direct function), and the appropriate degree of functional delegation of specific responsibilities to single-purpose authories outside the direct realm of political control.

The perennial problem for citizens in city politics is responsibly to know, when confronted by policy problems, where to affix ultimate accountability for any crisis of the imagination.

## *New Politicians?*

Nearly a quarter of Canadian city councillors in 1993 were women, and women are more fairly represented at city hall than in any other level of government. And although new leaders within the multicultural community remain largely beneath an electoral glass curtain, constituting no more than significant opposition voices, they too are now best represented at city hall. All this is encouraging, as is the fact that activist councillors inherited from the 1970s have been successful primarily because they worried about neighbourhood protection issues. But the new city politics of the 1990s require that all councillors develop new attitudes. James Lorimer once wrote of the earlier reformers: "The usual recourse of people who think that there is 'something wrong' with city government is to argue that what is needed is 'better people' elected to office. Instead of roofing contractors, insurance agents, and dumb lawyers, what is needed is architects, engineers, and smart lawyers."[3] He was correct in claiming that new people would not be enough, that the newcomers would be locked, perhaps more smoothly, into the same old thing.

The politics of cities outside Quebec are largely non-partisan. The absence of political parties, legitimized by turn-of-the-century reform movements, now serves as a barrier to coherent policy development in Canadian metropolitics. Canadian city politics appear almost as early national politics did, as a competition over spoils among cartels of co-dependent interests. The politics between these unwieldy coalitions of mutually shared self-interest, between friends, neighbours, business associates, country clubists, and Rotarians and a competing alliance of friends, neighbours, co-workers, bike-path cyclists, and eco-groupies have been especially bitter at times, particularly when reduced to a specific issue rather than focussed on matters of general civic direction. What this has meant is that councillors tend to have short-term goals and are directly gains-oriented. The policy program is to be elected. In representing the politics of appearance with its twin emphases on style and symbolism, they have come to evince the worst aspects of cadre-style party behaviour without the thin substance of the form. The political-economy perspective, as Leo observes, adds only that the domination of local government by a special set of co-interests has implicit longer-term objectives.

This behaviour might be contrasted with a new politics of substance, however, one that offers incremental change if not bold innovation. Tim Thomas argues that the constraints of power associated with political parties, the "logic of electoral competition," has made it very difficult to institutionalize more participatory grass-roots reforms even when sympathetic social democratic leaders have been in office. He notes that, within a handful of years in Montreal, the MCM had taken on the appearance of a cadre party with caucus discipline and hierarchical control of policy. To Thomas, this means that an almost teflon law of oligarchy prevails in metropolitics. If this is so across the board is it necessarily to be deplored?

Mutually exclusive city elites, as alliances of the municipal stakeholders, have long had a continuing interest in mobilizing citizens when such is to their particular advantage, and in encouraging public apathy when one elite is absent or in disarray or when silence could be taken to signify assent. Then city politics resemble a gentle tossing of the tea cosies at four. But public-service agendas do march on; only the time-line, not the objective, is flexible. Elected representatives seem not to have professionalized as quickly as their administrative counterparts in metropolitics. The latter, after all, have always been reasonably full-time. For example, when, in his grandiloquent account of policy making in the early years of Metro Toronto, Harold Kaplan writes euphorically about "cabinet" decision makers, he is describing department heads not councillors![4]

Since councillors have become "null politicians" whose role is primarily representational and reactive (that is, not creative), and since power and influence are much more, as Leo points out, than just the conduct and results of local elections, then councils need a sense of coherence and direction comparable to that of their bureaucrats if they are to work well. Without it, there is no hope of future provincial support and only the prospect of severe fiscal restraint. Councils must learn to generate their own political world view, somewhat akin to a throne speech in parliament, to forestall benign, bureaucratic hijackings of their mandate. Their staffs do have the time, talent, energy, and ambition to become their own whips. This is what Patrick Smith essentially argues constitutes the 1990s themes of leadership, accountability, and governability in the Metro Toronto area.

Surviving city politics, then, means revitalizing knowledge of the political arts. Mary Louise McAllister employs Lewis Carroll's image of the lobster quadrille, which she submits may possibly be easier to master than the overloading of traditional decision frameworks by balancing representative structures, participatory decision making, and sustainable development. Yet the issues that drove the participatory radicalism of the 1970s are essentially resolved, and Thomas concludes that only the most dedicated, perverse, or stubborn individuals remain from those struggles. So we are back to square one, the politics of personality. These politics of limited commitment from the interested gladiators (active locally only at election times) seem clearly to need adaptation to new circumstances. In a short, powerful phrase, Linda Trimble sums up the early history of women seeking city election first: "They ran for office because it mattered." Finding people to run council well must now matter more than simply electing "winners."

## *New Patterns of Participation?*

Like Arthur Dent, any one of us may be politicized if we awaken to discover city survey stakes in the front yard. But city politics did not begin as a participatory exercise. In the 1840s municipal government was conceived as an instrument of the property class; it was never intended as an exercise in democracy. There were few town meetings in the British North American colonies owing to the widespread fear that such meetings had fomented alien concepts of popular democracy south of the border. As Engin Isin notes, local self-government after the Canadian rebellion was premised on Durham's finding that a lack of local government meant a concentration of power which was not only inefficient and but also gave rise to its polar opposite—resistance and rebellion. Even so, the Baldwin Act of 1849 predates the reformed English municipal system by nearly a half-century. Out west, Caroline Andrew adds that probable ratepayers were later reluctant to accept Baldwin-style institutions because they correctly saw local government as a scheme to raise taxes. In the 1960s city suburbs across Canada viewed two-tier metro government in a similar vein. So popular participation, even as measured by the extension of the franchise itself, developed slowly in Canada.

Today, city elections—the public's opportunity to pass judgment on the actions of benign governing cliques once every three or so years—often convey the impression of an ill-informed electorate. But, given the limited circumstances of this participation, even an electorate of half a million of the finest classical Greek citizens could not behave more intelligently. At this moment, inequities in the municipal franchise distort even the direct elections to regional governments; appeals under the Charter of Rights seem probable (and desirable).[5] For instance, in Ontario, the Regional Municipality of Lambton includes Sarnia, which in 1989 had 58 per cent of the region's population but only 41 per cent of the council seats; in 1990 Mississauga had 63 per cent of the population but only 10 of 21 seats on the regional council of Peel. For Edmonton, in its 1981 annexation debate, similar two-tier arrangements were agreed to be unworkable simply because of the size of the core city, which had 72 per cent of the regional population. Modest reforms must lie ahead.

The process of elections did permit new movements, at least in the 1960s. For instance, in Vancouver under the administration of the Electors Action Movement (TEAM), the new professionals on council had few business ties; TEAM was a middle-class revolt of the reasonably well-off. As Thomas shows, however, the TEAM experience of organizing and sustaining opposition to the developers and permanent bureaucracy proved impossible to maintain. Both the latter groups had sufficient institutional coherence over time to out-wait their electoral challengers. The Urban Reform Group of Edmonton (URGE) learned a similar lesson during this same period.

It is important in city politics to observe, as Trimble does, that they are much more than elections: "The fact that city *elections* are seen as less important does not necessarily mean that city *politics* are so seen." She is right to contrast voter turnout with "real" participation in, say, neighbourhood protests. Hence the greater number of women municipal candidates is the logical outcome of their "private sphere" work in networks of volunteers and community activism; their public candidacy has been stimulated by their private lives. The useful logic of feminist analysis, with its reflections on the prevailing distinction between public and private pursuits, suggests that if women's interests are labelled "private" rather than "public" they are considered unimportant and apolitical. Thus, if many aspects of city politics are viewed as "private," they too are less important and influential than "public" issues. If they cannot be so viewed, the Canadian city will likely no longer be as depoliticized as it was earlier in the twentieth century.

In searching for legitimate avenues for citizen involvement it is proper to look beyond formal elections and structured public hearings even though citizens exploit the latter in compensation for perceived shortcomings in the former. City politics may become the last legitimate forum for strident single-issue groups in Canadian tri-level politics. One phenomenon of the 1990s has even been the growth of CAVE groupings (Citizens Against Virtually Everything). As reported by the Toronto *Globe and Mail*, CAVEists have emerged as possible logical extensions of the reactionary, protective elements of the citizens groups of the 1960s, NIMBYs for the 1990s.[6] These new social groups oppose even such seemingly progressive ideas as composting plants and wind-generation farms, with obvious consequences for those in public office. McAllister argues that there can be no sustainable land-use plan in the 1990s without a "multi-stakeholder" consultative process, but, say CAVEists, regulate only the others! It may be that, despite the ambitious Winnipeg Unicity reforms of 1971, there is little left of the formally organized citizen reform movement in Canada.[7] Thomas, for example, concludes that district advisory committees in Montreal under the MCM seem to have had little sustained success in the 1980s. Political arrangements in the age of Generation X appear to be less permanent, though the voters themselves are more informed and cynical than their counterparts in the 1960s.

What this may mean is that, to survive, citizens had best learn to exploit the new professional bureaucratic classes. To Patrick Smith, "governance" as measured by solutions will mean sensitivity to increasing complexity in the provision of urban services. In this respect, McAllister notes that the policy process has never really been rational (it is a fictional abstraction that it may be made such) or comprehensive, and it takes time and compromise. So P.J. Smith looks for new policy-making options and finds people: "Where planners were once defined as experts on future urban forms, today it is just as important that they bring the skills of mediators, facilitators and *animateurs* to the community planning process." It is in this arena that the knowledgeable citizen of the 1990s, perhaps weary of the cave, will choose to work.

## *New Government Forms?*

All the authors in this book have raised questions related to changes in government structure, both those already accomplished and those anticipated. McAllister implicitly argues that electors must challenge the "administrative" perception of local government's role—a perception that, Thomas notes, underlies the subordinate status of cities because it treats municipalities merely as administrative tools of other levels of government. Hence, the application of unadorned "common sense" underpins municipal non-partisanship, for, if cities are nothing more than administrative tools, they do not need ideology. Feminist theorists, Trimble reminds us, see political action very much as activities that reach far beyond the formal mechanisms of decision making—that is, community activism is legitimate. And, of course, the political-economy approach exemplified by Leo recognizes the role of "politics" in suburban development. But the problem to confront is hinted at by Isin, for even modern Canadian municipal corporations are a product of nineteenth-century thought. They are historically entwined with the administration of justice and policing: this authoritarian tendency has seemed persistently to sabotage more politicized perceptions.

In terms of public policy, the last major internal institutional shake-up by citizens' movements originating in the 1960s was the abolition of Edmonton's four-member Board of Commissioners in 1984 and its replacement by an executive committee of four councillors plus the mayor (and a single city manager). Sadly, the executive committee had no focussed mission beyond the immediate settling of citizens' scores after eighty years of highly centralized bureaucratic direction. Very quickly, particularly as measured by its record in the coherent development of strategic policy, the new institutional framework proved unable to withstand the limited personal abilities of a weak mayor and a weak city manager. Still, whether one has a council-CAO structure, or council-committee, or whatever has little real meaning for ordinary citizens. Structural change determines only where in the structure, and by whom, key decisions are to be made. It has virtually nothing to do with the basic quality of those decisions.

The key changes to be made will be external to cities themselves and regional in terms. While Andrew correctly observes that the Metro Toronto model was transplanted across the country in the 1950s (just as the Baldwin Act had been accepted as the norm of provincial-municipal operations in 1867), Patrick Smith concludes that no such model metro charter would ever be appropriate for all two dozen CMAs in Canada. In any event, while the period of metropolitan reorganization in Canada may have ended with the resolution of the Edmonton annexation of 1979, there had been a widespread view during the two preceding decades that "a new level of government was needed because the centre was uninterested and the local was incapable."[8] As is noted below, what is most needed now is new imagination in the development of regional forms that actually work to resolve regional issues, regardless of how neat the formal structure is.

Finally, Isin notes that since the 1840s Canadians have always sought a balance between local autonomy and centralized authority, a point buttressed by the Ontario Committee on Taxation, the precursor to regional government in that province, in 1967. It may be that city governments are necessary not because they constitute some formidable cornerstone of democracy but rather because provinces can never decentralize policy delivery with sufficient sensitivity. Still, the relentless centralizing tendencies of provincial ministries of education, by bureaucrats not ministers, since the late 1970s (and especially with respect to metropolitan areas where particularist policy demands are most evident) have led Robert Carney and Frank Peters to question whether in future metro school boards will "become increasingly anachronistic and insignificant." In 1994, for example, the province of Alberta "led" the way in Canada by consolidating school and hospital districts, greatly enhancing central powers of appointment and revenue determination in the process.

To survive as more or less autonomous representatives in such an evolving era of top-driven direction, in a process that may blatantly manipulate any form of independent citizen action to make it conform with broader provincial agendas, metro politicians will require new "stuff." If they continue to play by the strict, watertight rules of section 92.8 as one might undertake a formal game of chess, which is the model of federal-provincial relations, they will invariably lose. To challenge provincial omnicompetence effectively during the reinventing government mood of the 1990s, these actors will need to learn and to employ the brasher tactics of poker—especially the bluff.

## *New Sorts of Public Policy?*

To survive city politics means understanding that new policies of fiscal austerity are still about the allocation of scarce resources, goods, and services to meet perceived needs (including such important matters as personal privacy and safety). There is very little that is apolitical about that process at city hall. It is also prudent to understand that, for many people, any discussion of outcomes in city politics is less important than identifying the individuals and groups involved in policy deliberations. Indeed, process itself has become policy.

In their essay, Carney and Peters have noted some of the new priorities in education: school councils, charter schools, gender equity, multicultural sensitivity, access for students with disabilities. It is sometimes forgotten how recent some of these developments have been: the desirability of fully integrating aboriginals into "mainstream" education, for instance, was not debated until early this last generation. In the same context, "environmental racism" is an American phrase which, according to some activists, describes a purported tendency to place waste dumps, incinerators, and other potential polluters in minority and low-income areas, that is, among those persons not usually accorded seats at the policy-making table. In Virginia, poor counties with sizeable minority populations were selected in 1993 as sites for huge commercial landfills that would accept out-of-state waste.[9]

In short, as Leo observes, "The suburbs and the cities we have today are the product of a complex mix of corporate initiative, popular preference, and state action." Two-tier metro governments to manage urban growth achieved certain kinds of service-provision and were once seen as formal recognition of the complexities of post-war urbanization. Americans in particular were intrigued by the miracle of Metro Toronto, but it was essentially a "brick and mortar" kind of government that was not accomplished in addressing genuine social problems. Experience suggests that we should not turn to upper tiers if these are our policy concerns.

Of necessity, the provinces have become urban-policy makers at the expense of two-tier regions. To counter such provincial intrusion, Andrew Sancton argues that "existing metro and regional governments need to be transformed into much looser, more flexible, organisations."[10] Canadians may well have to learn to live with institutions that are much messier in formal organizational terms. Perhaps the model could be something along the lines of the Greater Vancouver Regional District, which, in practice, has actually been several districts with municipal membership expanding and contracting as the agenda dictates. That is, there are more members in the water district than there would be in a discussion of hospital planning. In future, there may well be systems in which fewer municipal members are consulted about subway design than about the environmental impact of a watershed's development. Only serious constipation of the imagination limits the possible.

In many matters Canadians may stand at constitutional impasse, but we are still lumbered with lawyers and, more important, fiscal transfers. Who basically is accountable for making the equation between raising money through taxes and, then, its expenditure? In national accounts terms, Statistics Canada has calculated that in 1993 the federal government collected 47 per cent of all tax revenues and *directly* spent 41 per cent (on current expenditures); the provinces collected 41 per cent and spent 42 per cent, while municipalities had the luxury of spending 17 per cent and collecting only 11 per cent of total revenues generated. The federal share of revenues has dipped from 62 per cent in 1960 while the provincial has doubled. The municipal proportion of revenues declined somewhat. But these are only measures of comparative capability over a short time. The main question remains *who* will make such future allocative decisions. The new issue will be matching expenditure to taxation responsibility and cities will plainly be the most revenue anxious.

Environmental issues will also top any list of new policy considerations. McAllister stipulates that land-use decisions must now take into account relationships "with watersheds, wetlands, soils and forests," the entire ecosystem. Traditional local government activities (water, waste, and sewers) still lie at the heart of environmentally sensitive planning for the 1990s. It is also the case that citizens usually turn first to the city to act, not awaiting more remote federal and provincial authorities. The importance of the new environmental agenda is shown in Montreal where, in the November 1994 election, Mayor Jean Doré and the MCM were defeated by Vision Montreal—a party led by the city's former botanist, Pierre Bourque. As primarily a focussed-issue, eco-party candidate, Bourque "promised to establish volunteer associations in each of the city's 51 districts to clean up neighbourhoods [with] tree-planting, garden grooming, graffiti eradication, litter-picking and recycling . . . 50 per cent of the city's waste within four years."[11]

But even good policies that are not based on prior public consultation may have bad consequences. And there will be consequences. For example, the introduction of a dedicated bicycle lane along College Street in Toronto in 1993 eliminated street parking, drop-off and loading zones, and taxi stands, and, as an unintended consequence, led to a direct decline in business (and jobs) for adjacent establishments. The more single-minded bikers displayed an environmentalist zeal in defence of the policy: "Do you want better people or do you want more parking spaces?" cyclist Jerry Lee Miller asked. "I vote for people."[12] The problem of process was familiar: the relevant city council committee sought citizen comment following business complaints but two months *after* the lane was in place.

So, while it may be possible for governments to plan generally for certain things, who is to separate the important from the urgent? Peter Smith has implicitly argued that, if we are to civilize our cities for the future, we must abandon the traditional perception of urban planning as only a statutory way of regulating land use, and, in its place, substitute a more holistic process. At the heart of any good planning legislation lies protection for individuals and communities from arbitrary acts of other persons, and governments. New sorts of planning policy would seem to require that planners evolve past technical competence, which most possess in spades, to assume greater responsibility for the power already implied by that expertise. This may actually mean that planners will have more to do even though there are fewer new plats to plan. Engin Isin has, for instance, elsewhere written that nearly two-thirds of Canadian communities are now wrestling with plans for city-core housing intensification.

Inventing new terms will no longer be enough to disguise real intent, regardless of whether those terms are coined by bureaucrats, their consultants, or academic colleagues.[13] On the *Starship Enterprise*, for instance, Commander Data's inexperience with idiom caused him to use the phrase "untamed ornithoid pursuit" to describe a simple wild goose chase. If new policy-making processes formally emerge, conducted in plain language and inclusive of the groups the decisions affect, this may actually produce better policy and finally pen some of the wild geese in metropolitics.

## *New Ethical Considerations?*

In the popular comic strip "Wizard of Id," one sequence has the king's man Rodney stating, "I'm interviewing a speech writer for your campaign." The king queries, "Is he familiar with my views?" And the reply is, "Yes, but he says he can work around them."[14] This petty intellectual fraud is old stuff for survivors of city politics, even in the recent past. Thomas notes, for example, that in Montreal the MCM abandoned its social democratic vision as power came into view. In developing a more laissez-faire, business-acceptable posture, the MCM almost became more enthusiastic free-enterprisers than the Chamber of Commerce.

The point is that such conventional ethical preoccupations have become less important than other matters in the 1990s. Still in need of attention, however, are certain kinds of immediate conflicts of interest: Carney and Peters, for instance, point out that teachers usually cannot stand for election as trustees in their own districts (or, in British Columbia, in any district). Even this question has not as yet been uniformly resolved at city hall; where employee election is permitted, such councillors must at least abstain from voting on matters directly affecting their own employment. Of course, councillors should not vote on matters from which they may derive a direct benefit, but how far among family members should this rule apply? I have noted the extent of this problem elsewhere: "The individuals most intensely involved in major city politics may find themselves leading one of many possible triple lives of lawyer, development lobbyist and fund-raiser; small businessman, councillor and civic booster; or city planner, homemaker and careerist. Any one of these packages has in it the possibility for serious conflicts of interest."[15] Outside the press gallery, there are few absolutely disinterested monks in contemporary society.

Three general matters for action should be considered. First, the traditional rules governing conduct and conflicts of interest must be refined to limit those councillors who are such enthusiastic city boosters that they equate their politics with direct personal aggrandizement. Some have made impressive personal escapes from poverty. Others have transformed political and bureaucratic turns in office into résumé padding for the development industry. In his chapter, Leo makes the point that, from a political-economy perspective, all three levels of the state interact to respond to private interests and to mobilize state resources for urban development. When there are such huge sums at work, it is inevitable that some of the bees in authority will be drawn into the honey. Formal disclosure and prohibitions on certain kinds of behaviour (not only in obvious voting on council but also in too helpful guidance through the official process) must be the minimum. The problem remains that a large part of the civic agenda will always lie in the fertility ritual of growing assessment.

Peter Smith suggests that ethics in planning may be as simple as determining whose concept of the public interest should prevail. The essential problem here is that to say that this kind of decision is merely technical is to disguise one's own vested agenda. Any formal institutionalization will represent a mobilization of some sort of bias. Possibly the best we can expect is Andrew's prescription that, as

Canadian cities experience globalizing economic pressures and winners and losers are selected, the net benefits must accrue to a wider group in the electorate than only a few dynamic businesses.

Secondly, the various thorny issues that surround campaign finance, now largely resolved federally and provincially, must be addressed by cities. Metropolitics is expensive! In those provinces without legal guidelines (most), the absence of party caucus and extra-council formal organization means that anything goes. Individual candidates solicit the funds (forget the fiction of "arms-length" baggers), and councillors vote directly as individuals on very specific matters impinging on others' gains. At the least, full disclosure enticed by tax-deduction receipts and liable official agents must be enacted if citizens are reasonably to survive the hugely competitive 1990s.

Finally, several authors have observed the rapidly growing cultural diversity of Canada's metropolitan areas. The resulting conflicts may range from environmental matters—where, as noted by McAllister, private rights clash with collective ones—to the kind of socio-cultural issues observed by Andrew which revolve around the divergent perspectives of "ethnic" communities. Tolerance cannot be legislated. All that can be said at this point is that we must acknowledge a community that is in transition. To survive this period of change as we move towards newly agreed community standards in Canadian metropolitics will require a good deal of patience, understanding, and flexibility.

## *Re-establishing City Government*

The political unrest of the late 1960s and the 1970s inflicted two kinds of damage on the municipal governments that came afterwards. Mid-level public-sector managers who received their political socialization during the earlier period have been left with a sense of betrayal through uncertain and inconsistent political direction from city councils. At the same time, many councillors who were electoral beneficiaries of the period of unrest are themselves without coherent direction except for a deep-rooted distrust of the professionals in public service. The latter, for their part, have in no way the monolithic cohesion assumed of them.

Today, city administrators, when canvassed in confidence, concede that they are curious about the implications of possible full-time councillors. These senior managers worry about being able to exist in a more fluid political environment. It is clear in Canada's big cities that "policy administration" and "policy making" are no longer watertight compartments, if indeed they ever were. On the one hand, it is well-nigh impossible to anticipate in advance what administrative decisions may have policy consequences. On the other, much that becomes policy has developed from hands-on administration, from the active inter-working of bureaucrats and the client groups for whom service is provided. City bureaucrats, it is said, are "concerned about 'interference' from the politicians in traditionally administrative territory... We have a fractured political vision among the elected officials. Therefore the political vision of the bureaucrats will have an impact."[16] The bureaucrats' admitted prime interest lies no farther than in having potentially better informed elected decision makers.

So, senior managers, faced with issues such as employment equity, now perceive a need to become more "politically sensitive" themselves. This is ironic in that at the time of the turn-of-the-century reform movement politicians were expected to become more "efficient, impartial and honest"—traits normally associated with the professional bureaucrat. City bureaucrats are essentially arguing that more professionalism needs to be injected into the city policy process; in short, the politicians should be more like themselves.

One point is clear: certain matters do not lend themselves to legislative resolution. Winnipeg Unicity revealed that citizens cannot be legislated to participate, and the various big-city ethics packages now in place demonstrate that common decency and good sense cannot easily be set forth so as to ensure compliance. Similarly, the 1984 Edmonton restructuring reminds us that executive ability may not be guaranteed through by-laws and, further, that only the many myopic eyes of the municipal press gallery view institutional realignment as an adequate substitute for a substantial change in policy direction.

Hence, the several phases of Canadian local government reform should be assessed, not by the relative neatness of the most currently fashionable organization charts, but by real tests of change in substance. This is so because people in any form of political institution develop "state agendas" over long periods. Periodically, citizen activists will campaign, and be elected upon, platforms offering genuine change. The usual bureaucratic response, often subconscious but not always so innocent, is to divert public attention by modest changes to structures so as not to disrupt drastically the programs already in place. Even if well intentioned, this is sabotage of citizens' wishes, pure and simple. It leads to the following question: How free may local governments be to implement their own agendas without any genuine effort to conform with public expectations? The matter of how the latter may be ascertained begs another question: Is local government really closest to the people? This basic concern lay at the heart of the grass-roots democracy debates of the 1960s. To many citizens, city hall may seem as distant as any national capital.

The wider implication for all governments is that "the democratic state is frequently autonomous in translating its own preferences into authoritative actions, and markedly autonomous in doing so even when they diverge from those held by the politically weightiest groups in society."[17] Eric Nordlinger has proposed that the degree of independence enjoyed by state officials in the making of policy ranges from a level where their views are generally in conformity to those who wield most influence, to one where they work to shift social views to their own agenda, and ultimately to a level at which state representatives implement public policy contrary to the wishes of society (for instance, the federal issue of capital punishment). His views may hold genuine meaning for those who see city council's decisions as varying degrees of punishment over which they may exercise little influence—parking and traffic controls as caning!

Few Canadians wrote as eloquently about political possibilities as John Porter. Nearly thirty years ago he employed the term "creative" politics: "Creative politics is politics which has the capacity to change the social structure in the direction of some major social goals or values . . . Creative politics requires a highly developed political leadership to challenge entrenched power within other institutional orders."[18] In short, electors and political resources may be mobilized to challenge both the physical environment and dysfunctional political institutions. Although Porter would abhor the Reform Party's agenda, the alliance of individual voters that cut across traditional party lines to permit the election of fifty-two Reform candidates in the 1993 federal eelection shows that a creative challenge to municipal politics may still be possible.

There does exist a creative energy that may be more easily released in the local politics of cities themselves. Trimble observes that the traditional public/private distinction between spheres was "embedded in the structure and operation of social, economic, religious and political institutions." She ably demonstrates that there is nothing natural or inevitable about the separation into these public and private spheres. What is natural about the distinction is that it preserves, and justifies very satisfactorily, the transfer of *certain* private interests into dominant positions in public office at city hall. It is in cities—where voter allegiances are historically unstable, where citizen loyalties to formal institutions are least persistent, where the mobilization of large-scale political resources are not particularly effective, and where agenda-driven constituencies most clearly betray the narrowness of their bases—that politicized individuals may still make a vital difference. Women, for example, have sought *municipal* office precisely because it has a direct impact on their private situations; there is nothing second-string about these particular political career choices. Municipal office is not a substitute for "the real thing" when the power of personal involvement may directly and immediately yield safer streets.

The national and provincial governments can establish only the broadest frameworks for growth, development, and expansion of capital. On this front, there is the perennial danger of provincial departments operating in splendid isolation: Alberta in 1994 established fifty huge regional hospital districts without apparent recognition of social-services boundaries (or emergency services for that matter). Alas, there is yet little evidence of a new politics of integrated response as city governments are refashioned to provide services in the 1990s. Further, Andrew concludes that municipalities overall will receive fewer provincial transfers of resources in the probable future; Quebec and Alberta have already moved dramatically to put funding of local services such as roads and transit back onto municipalities.

All of this is occurring at a time when globalization pressures are forcing the choice of city winners for tacit support. Inevitably, choices will be made and there will also be certain losers before the century's end.

## *Conclusion*

The decline of Canada's urban core has been well documented. Downtowns, in about 90 per cent of North American cities, are just not as important as they once were; business, retailing (there remain few shops that cannot be found in your basic malls), and even cultural centres have deserted the black hole at the core for the bright lights in the suburban ring of the city doughnut. As commerical and cultural activity is diffused over a wider area, transit ridership to the core also declines. Leo writes of an inner city vacant of housing and dangerous at night; from 1971 to 1986, for instance, 260 000 people moved from Montreal to surrounding suburbs. He documents how the costs of suburbs have been high not only in servicing their own low-density development but also as measured in higher taxes and in the decline of transit, policing, and other services for those who do remain in the city core. By the 1990s this crisis downtown provoked strident Canadian Federation of Municipalities (CFM) demands for a $15-billion infrastructure program and the federal Liberals responded in the 1993 federal campaign.

While advanced technologies may permit decentralization of many types of corporate activities, in reality interpersonal contact has remained essential. Urban Canadians have learned that private and public lives are no longer so easily distinct as they once may have been. So the role of the suburb, which was once considered a safe haven for the "private" activities of women while men commuted to the "public" world of the downtown commercial core, has also been re-evaluated. In short, to equate the concept of city with just the CBD (central business district) core is misleading these days; social images must adjust to the growth in personal experiences over time.

The ultimate citizen's survival strategy may lie in realizing that, overall, traditional politics have not mattered all that much. In their analysis of the growth in government spending of each provincial government for the years from 1960 to 1986, Sohrab Abizadeh and John Grey have come to this dramatic but simple conclusion: "We find that the provincial political party in power, whether left, right, or centre, has had no statistically significant impact on the level of growth of provincial spending in any of the ten Canadian provinces, in spite of some dramatic political changes in government and quite marked differences in political philosophies among parties."[19] If their analysis could be applied to the policy choices of Canada's city councils, as I believe it could, it would mean that the traditional Chamber of Commerce perception that labour-left representatives are witless spendthrifts is as much nonsense as the old reformist saw that the city politics practised by the business elite are necessarily more "efficient" and hence economical.

The caution for daily living is that the city hall press gallery, upon which most citizens rely for their clinical data about council's policy peregrinations, has been historically hoodwinked by the rhetoric foaming from chamber luncheon speakers; away from the election campaign trail, when a benign neutrality must be seen at play, the chambers' free lunches have seemed to work. Few of us have either the objectivity or the perspective to evaluate particular claims of the moment. I am reminded that, in his discussion of social images and reality thirty years ago, John Porter made this essential point on his very first page: "When a society's writers, journalists, editors and other image-creators are a relatively small and closely linked group, and have more or less the same social background, the images they produce can, because they are consistent, appear to be much more true to life than if their group were larger, less cohesive, and more heterogeneous in composition."[20] In political life, perception is reality, and truth is relative to what one believes appears true, or not. Or, as Porter succinctly put it about somewhat broader issues, "Social images are one thing and social realities another."

Abizadeh and Gray do concede the obvious: "It may be that parties of the left spend more on visible social programs and public works which attract press attention, while those of the right spend money instead on grants to industry and on contracting out of services."[21] So the question becomes one of expenditure *style*, which may have substantive and redistributive impacts indeed. But, on the whole, the central point is that overall expenditures have grown pretty much at the same rate regardless of who is in power.

Surviving city politics means treating them as the art of the probable. For instance, successful promoters will likely always know that it is easier to beg forgiveness than to ask permission. It is also likely that there are many competing agendas at play within the "neutral" policy walls of the public service. Citizens should know these things. As well, we have reached a point where Canadian metropolitics must evolve beyond the thirty-second thought-zone of electronic newsclips and also beyond a style in which principals transcend principles.

Could a more creative political style at city hall really matter?

Yes, I still believe it could.

## *Notes*

1. Douglas Adams (New York: Harmony Books, 1979), 31.
2. *Edmonton Journal*, 21 May 1994.
3. James Lorimer, *The Real World of City Politics* (Toronto: James, Lewis and Samuel, 1970), 156.
4. Harold Kaplan, *Reform, Planning, and City Politics* (Toronto: University of Toronto Press, 1982), 69ff.
5. Andrew Sancton, "Canada As a Highly Urbanized Nation: New Implications for Government," *Canadian Public Administration*, vol. 35, no. 3 (fall, 1992), 287.
6. 21 April 1993.
7. Donald J.H. Higgins, *Local and Urban Politics in Canada* (Toronto: Gage, 1986), 269–74.
8. Sancton, "Canada As a Highly Urbanized Nation," 297.
9. In Edmonton in the late spring of 1994, waste managers, frustrated with locating a dump within the confines of Canada's second-largest city territorially, entertained private proposals to move annually, by rail, 200 000 tonnes of garbage and 100 000 tonnes of sewage sludge through the Paul Band Indian Reserve to a site near the Keephills coal-generation electrical facility.
10. Sancton, "Canada As a Highly Urbanized Nation," 297.
11. *Globe and Mail*, 26 April 1994.
12. John Barber, "Cyclists Ride Roughshod over Merchants," *Globe and Mail*, 16 December 1993.
13. A quick glance at any good American city politics text will reveal this annoying tendency. On my desk, for example, is Robert J. Waste, *The Ecology of City Policymaking* (New York: Oxford University Press, 1989).

14. Brant Parker and Johnny Hart, "Wizard of Id," 14 October 1992 (Creators Syndicate Inc.).
15. James Lightbody, "Cities: Dilemmas on our Doorsteps," in *Corruption, Character and Conduct*, Allan Tupper and John Langford, eds. (Toronto: Oxford University Press, 1993), 206.
16. Alex Lowy and Becky Taylor, "Executive Development in Canadian Municipalities: Current and Future Perspectives," *Canadian Public Administration*, vol. 33, no. 3 (fall, 1990), 310, 313.
17. Eric Nordlinger, *On the Autonomy of the Democratic State* (Cambridge, Mass.: Harvard University Press, 1981), 203.
18. *The Vertical Mosaic: An Analysis of Social Class and Power in Canada* (Toronto: University of Toronto Press, 1965), 369.
19. Sohrab Abizadeh and John A. Gray, "Politics and Provincial Government Spending in Canada," *Canadian Public Administration*, vol. 35, no. 4 (winter, 1992), 520.
20. Porter, *The Vertical Mosaic*, 3.
21. Abizadeh and Gray, "Politics and Provincial Government Spending," 520.

## *Selected Sources*

Frisken, Frances, ed. *The Changing Canadian Metropolis: A Public Policy Perspective*, 2 vols. (Berkeley, Calif.: Institute of Governmental Studies, University of California Press, 1994).

Higgins, D.J.H. *Local and Urban Politics in Canada* (Toronto: Gage, 1986).

Jackson, Ian, ed. *The Future of Cities in Britain and Canada* (Ottawa: Institute for Research on Public Policy, 1991).

Lightbody, James. "Cities: Dilemmas on our Doorsteps," in *Corruption, Character and Conduct: Essays on Canadian Government Ethics*, Allan Tupper and John Langford, eds. (Toronto: Oxford University Press, 1993), 197–216.

Lightbody, James. "The Strategic Planning Component in the Policymaking Process for Municipalities in Canada," *Policy Studies Journal*, vol. 21, no. 1 (spring, 1993), 94–103.

Lorimer, James. *A Citizen's Guide to City Politics* (Toronto: James, Lewis and Samuel, 1972).

Magnusson, Warren and Andrew Sancton, eds. *City Politics in Canada* (Toronto: University of Toronto Press, 1983).

Sancton, Andrew. "Canada As a Highly Urbanized Nation: New Implications for Government," *Canadian Public Administration*, vol. 35, no. 3 (fall, 1992), 306–21.

———. *Governing Canada's City-Regions: Adapting Form to Function* (Montreal: Institute for Research on Public Policy, 1994).

Tindal, C.R. and S. Nobes Tindal. *Local Government in Canada*, 3rd. ed. (Toronto: McGraw-Hill, Ryerson, 1990).

# *Contributors*

CAROLINE ANDREW is a professor of political science at the University of Ottawa. She is currently chair of that department. Her areas of research are local politics, and women and politics.

ROBERT CARNEY is professor emeritus in the department of educational foundations, University of Alberta. He was previously chief superintendent of schools in the Northwest Territories and deputy minister of Recreation, Parks and Wildlife, Government of Alberta.

ENGIN F. ISIN is assistant professor in the social science division at York University. He is the author of *Cities Without Citizens*, and is currently writing two books: *Canadian Federalism and Cities* and *Who is the New Citizen? Culture, Territory, Identity.*

CHRISTOPHER LEO teaches political science at the University of Winnipeg where his research interests are urban politics, the political economy of the city, and the particular roles assigned to downtown development corporations.

JAMES LIGHTBODY teaches political science at the University of Alberta, focussing on city politics. He has written about metropolitan reorganization, urban public policy issues, city political campaigns, and ethical behaviour in political life.

MARY LOUISE MCALLISTER is an assistant professor of political science, University of Northern British Columbia. She has been the associate director, research, Centre for Resource Studies (Queen's University) and is co-author of *Rising to the Surface: Groundwater Policy in Canada.*

FRANK PETERS is associate professor in the department of educational policy studies, University of Alberta. His research interests lie mainly in the realm of educational governance, and education and law. He has been a school teacher and administrator in northern Alberta.

TREVOR PRICE has taught politics at the University of Windsor since 1968. He specialises in urban politics, public administration, and environmental policy. He is co-editor of *Urban Policy Issues: A Canadian Perspective.*

PATRICK J. SMITH is a past chair of political science at Simon Fraser. Municipal government, global cities, and intergovernmental relations are among his many interests. He is co-author of *The Vision and the Game: Making the Canadian Constitution* and *The (1995) Almanac of Canadian Politics.*

P.J. SMITH is professor of geography at the University of Alberta, where he specialises in political-urban geography and urban planning. He has served as president of the Canadian Association of Geographers and editor of *The Canadian Geographer.*

TIM THOMAS has worked as a policy analyst for the Treasury Board of Canada and currently teaches political science at McGill and Concordia universities. He has written about Canadian and Quebec issues, political representation, and local and urban politics.

LINDA TRIMBLE is associate professor of political science at the University of Alberta. She has published articles about women and politics in Alberta, the CRTC and sex-role stereotyping, women and Canadian politics, and federalism and constitutional issues.

# Index